Paul Kesterson

THE ENVIRONMENT OF EARLY
CHRISTIANITY

STUDIES IN THEOLOGY

THE ENVIRONMENT OF EARLY CHRISTIANITY

BY

S. ANGUS, M.A., Ph.D.

PROFESSOR OF NEW TESTAMENT AND HISTORICAL THEOLOGY
ST. ANDREW'S COLLEGE, UNIVERSITY OF SYDNEY

NEW YORK
CHARLES SCRIBNER'S SONS
1951

τοιοῦδε μόχθου τέρμα μή τι προσδόκα,
πρὶν ἂν θεῶν τις διάδοχος τῶν σῶν πόνων
φανῇ, θελήσῃ τ' εἰς ἀναύγητον μολεῖν
Ἅιδην, κνεφαῖά τ' ἀμφὶ Ταρτάρου βάθη.—AESCHYLUS.

τὸ γὰρ παράδειγμα δεῖ ὑπερέχειν.—ARISTOTLE.

Printed in the United States of America

VXORI DILECTAE

HVNC LIBELLVLVM

D D D

AVCTOR

PREFACE

THE size of this volume has been determined by the series to which it belongs. Scholars familiar with the period under review will appreciate the constant difficulty attending the selection and compression of the material. It was impossible without unduly increasing the footnotes to make sufficient acknowledgment of indebtedness to modern authorities, or insert a tithe of the mass of citations and references from ancient writers accumulated during the preparation of the work. The author hopes in a later volume to discuss more adequately several themes here treated very succinctly, together with other phases of this most interesting epoch. A fairly comprehensive Bibliography has been added, which, it is hoped, may enhance the value of the volume for students. Some excellent authorities may be omitted, the list being restricted to a selection of the books consulted.

The author is greatly indebted to Professor H. A. A. Kennedy, D.D., D.Sc., of New College, Edinburgh, for valuable assistance in revising the proofs. Thanks for helpful criticism are due to Professor Alexander Souter, D.Litt., of Aberdeen University. Grateful mention should also be made of the late Professor James Orr, D.D., of Glasgow, at whose suggestion the work was undertaken.

S. ANGUS.

EDINBURGH, 8*th June* 1914.

CONTENTS

THE ENVIRONMENT OF EARLY CHRISTIANITY

CHAPTER I

INTRODUCTORY

οὗτοι ἀπ' ἀρχῆς πάντα θεοὶ θνητοῖσ' ὑπέδειξαν
ἀλλὰ χρόνῳ ζητοῦντες ἐφευρίσκουσιν ἄμεινον.

XENOPHANES.[1]

'He (Messiah) is the end rather than the product of prior history; does not so much get meaning from it as give meaning to it.' —FAIRBAIRN, *Christ in Modern Theology*, p. 373.

THE purpose of this book is not to inquire into the nature and success of Christianity, but to survey the ancient world in which Christianity was first planted, reviewing the conditions which would favour or retard the spread of the Gospel, and to present a brief account of the genius and achievements of the three great peoples to whom the Gospel was first offered. We shall be convinced both of the need and the preparedness of this old world for the Evangel ; we shall see that, as God makes no mistakes in history, Christianity came indeed 'in the fulness of the time,' and that the Graeco-Roman world was socially, politically, linguistically, morally and religiously in a wonderful state of preparation for the Kingdom.

We cannot estimate aright the history of Christianity if we are ignorant of its antecedents, nor can we appreciate its success if we overlook the difficulties it had to encounter.

[1] Frag. 16 (Mullach, i. p. 103).

A

Two extreme views about the condition of the ancient world are prevalent. First, some—e.g., B. Bauer [1] and J. A. Farrer—represent the ancient world as producing Christianity automatically. Christianity is merely a result of evolution and human progress. It is simply the juxtaposition of elements already to hand without supernatural intervention. The founders of the new faith were astute enough to put some good old things together to make a brand new article. The united ideals of Jew, Greek, and Roman gave to the world Christianity. This distorted view contains a partial truth which deserves attention. The same God who planned the Gospel prepared the soil. Men were His servants and instruments then as now, whether conscious of it or not. The Gospel could not come without antecedents, and could not succeed if men's hearts were not ready to receive it.

Others—and these the majority—would have it that Christianity is wholly new and in absolute antithesis to the world in which it appeared. The ancient world laboured and brought forth nothing : the only contribution it made to the Gospel was entirely negative— dire need. Everything excellent came only with the Christian era, God having given the ancient peoples over to their own carnal hearts. These scholars see only the vices and immoralities of the worst classes of pre-Christian society—such classes as still survive in our Christian civilisation. This picture of the ancient world is painted exclusively in the dark colours of the plays of Plautus, the satires of Juvenal, the unworthy verses of Ovid and Martial, the inanities of Petronius, the bitterness of Tacitus, and the mystic sensuality of Apuleius. The worst side of antiquity is deliberately compared with the best side of Christianity. Moral monstrosities like a Caligula or a Nero are placed beside a John or a Paul. The fact is over-

---

[1] *Christus u. d. Cäsaren*, p. 149 f.   Bauer attributes more of Christianity to Seneca than to Jesus.

looked that the same God was working in human history before, as after, the Christian era, revealing Himself as men felt their need of Him and were able to comprehend Him. The best method of magnifying Christianity is not the belittling of Heathenism. To secure the right perspective Christianity must be viewed not only in *contrast* but also in *contact* with its environment.

To appreciate Christianity or Paganism we must approach them with an open mind, if not with sympathy. We should contrast the ideals of Paganism with those of Christianity. We may admit that God is the God of the heathen as of the Christians without admitting that Christianity is only on a par with all its predecessors. We must remember, too, how easy it is, on the one hand, to over-estimate past epochs by reading ideas of our own period and religion into the records of the past; as also, on the other hand, to fail to do justice to old Gospels by unfamiliarity with their language. Thus—out of scores of examples—Seneca's thought that gifts given 'in succour to infirmity, poverty, or shame, should be given silently, with no other witness than the giver and the recipient,' is more familiar to us as 'let not thy left hand know what thy right hand doeth.' Or 'many are called but few chosen,' is better known than 'many are the wand-bearers but few the mystae.' It was at least as difficult for the pre-Christian world, as it is for us, to put away the gods which their fathers worshipped on the other side of the flood. Likewise the mere use of old expressions does not necessarily imply that those using them had not outgrown them. Many pagan institutions are to us strange, but they once represented the grasping of certain ideas by which society found a means of cohesion. Many old formulae seem empty, yet they were once the repositories of new thoughts and truths crystallized into expression so as not to be lost.

In our day we cannot dislocate history as was possible

a generation ago. The idea of evolution and progress has
too firmly laid hold of our minds. The unity of mankind
and the unity of history are articles of faith. History is
now viewed as an organism. The student cannot with
impunity dissever Christianity from the fabric of its age.
To do so is to read history with a bias, and to disregard
God's patience in the task of educating humanity and
drawing it to Himself. The Gospel of Jesus does not
disdain the many evangels which gladdened men and
brought joy, consolation, and spiritual support to thousands of the human race before the rise of our faith in
history. God has in all ages been listening to the still
sad music of humanity ; He has been walking with and
among men in their toil, error, and waywardness,[1] stretching out His hand in succour as men have in all ages
stretched forth hands to God for help.

> '. . . Feeble hands and helpless
> Groping blindly in the darkness,
> Touch God's right hand in that darkness
> And are lifted up and helped.'

The human soul has always been the ' lyre for the plectrum
of the Paraclete.' We, the heirs of all the ages, have
entered upon the rich inheritance of the toils and tears,
the victories and defeats, the experiments and fears of our
predecessors.

> 'Our fathers watered with their tears
> The sea of time whereon we sail ;
> Their voices were in all men's ears
> Who passed within their puissant hail . . .
> The suff'rers died—they left their pain :
> The pangs which tortured them remain.'

We must therefore raise our hearts in gratitude to those
who were hewers of wood and drawers of water for a

[1] 'For they peradventure err, seeking God and desirous to find him.'
—*Wisd. of Sol.* xiii. 6.

period of enlightenment that they never saw and perhaps never dreamed of—to those who desired to see our day but whose eyes God closed. The history of man's religion comes in 'many portions and in many manners.' The efforts of many generations—not unaided by God—prepared the way of the Lord.

The study of comparative religions has given rise to a degree of tolerance, and enabled us to appreciate God's gradual unfolding of His purpose and His self-revelation to different ways of thinking. There is no violent caesura in history. All portions of mankind do not move forward with equal pace : the history of a period may reveal a retrograde movement. Evolution does not always connote progress. We must make allowance for the proneness to degeneration in human nature.[1] But because we believe in God we believe His world has been, and is, progressing toward the

> 'one far-off divine event,
> To which the whole creation moves.'

---

[1] Cf. Ramsay, *Cities of St. Paul*, pp. 10-78. On p. 17 he says, 'wherever evidence exists, with the rarest exceptions, the history of religion among men is a history of degeneration.'

CHAPTER II

THE NEW ERA BEGINNING WITH ALEXANDER THE GREAT: GENERAL CHARACTERISTICS (300 B.C.-300 A.D.)

ἀλλὰ κοινὸς θεόθεν ἁρμοστὴς καὶ διαλλακτὴς τῶν ὅλων νομίζων, οὓς τῷ λόγῳ μὴ συνῆγε τοῖς ὅπλοις βιαζόμενος, εἰς τὸ αὐτὸ συνενεγκὼν τὰ πανταχόθεν, ὥσπερ ἐν κρατῆρι φιλοτησίῳ, μίξας τοὺς βίους καὶ τὰ ἤθη, καὶ τοὺς γάμους καὶ διαιτίας, πατρίδα μὲν τὴν οἰκουμένην προσέταξεν ἡγεῖσθαι πάντας . . . συγγενεῖς δὲ τοὺς ἀγαθούς, ἀλλοφύλους δὲ τοὺς πονηρούς. τὸ δὲ Ἑλληνικὸν καὶ βαρβαρικὸν μὴ χλαμύδι μηδὲ πέλτῃ μηδὲ ἀκινάκῃ μηδὲ κάνδυι διορίζειν, ἀλλὰ τὸ μὲν Ἑλληνικὸν ἀρετῇ τὸ δὲ βαρβαρικὸν κακίᾳ τεκμαίρεσθαι.
PLUTARCH (?), De Fort. Alex., i. 6 (329 a.D.).

Gerade die reichere und freiere Ausgestaltung der Lebensformen und Kulturbedingungen, die Fülle geistiger Interessen, neben einander gehender oder wechselnder Strömungen, die komplizierte Undurchsichtigkeit des Gefühlslebens unterscheiden ihn von der früheren Zeit und nähern ihn der modernen an. 'Die hellenistische Zeit ist ganz und gar anders kompliziert im Aussen- und Innenleben. Ihre Seele ist überaus sensitiv, gleich empfänglich für die weichste Sentimentalität und den harten Egoismus, für romantische Schwärmerei und das Trotzgefühl einer neuen Welt. Sie ist mit einem Worte modern.' 'In dem geistigen Antlitz des Hellenismus sind zwei Hauptzüge, die mit einander unvereinbar scheinen. Das eine ist die Freude an der Repräsentation, dem Pomp und Schmuck, der erhabenen Pose: darin liegt das, was wir an ihm barock nennen dürfen. Daneben aber steht die intimste Freude an der weltverlorenen Stille, dem Frieden des engen natürlichen Kreises, am Feinen, Kleinen. . . . In Wahrheit wurzelt beides in der befreiten Individualität, die sich je nach den Lebenszielen sehr verschieden äussert.' (Wendland and Wilamowits, in Wendland, Hellenist-röm. Kultur, pp. 23-4.)

THERE are no violent breaks in history; yet it naturally falls into eras. Each epoch is not disconnected with the preceding; it exhibits new phenomena, or old phenomena in new prominence. As the mass of men do not think for themselves, history revolves largely round outstanding personalities. Never again have father and son [1] appeared in two such great men as Philip and Alexander.

Philip by adroitly taking advantage of Greek quarrels and lack of foresight, by flattery and bribery, first secured his power at home and then entered Greece as arbiter of Greek wranglings and champion of the Delphian god. On the field of Chaeroneia (338 B.C.) Athens and Thebes lost what Athens and Plataea had won at Marathon. But Philip had much sympathy with Greece—especially with Athens—and desired to be regarded as a Greek himself. To compensate the Greeks for the loss of their autonomy and to make them oblivious of their humiliation, he proposed an expedition against a common foe—Persia. For this object he secured his appointment as generalissimo at the convention of Corinth, 338 B.C. In the same year his assassination thwarted the design.

Alexander—than whom no one has better merited the title ' Great ' [2]—became heir to Philip's preparations and ambitions. In 336 B.C. he was chosen generalissimo at another conference of Corinth. After some successful northern campaigns and the ruthless razing of Thebes in 335, he set out in the spring of 334 with an army of Greeks and Macedonians against Persia. With astonishing rapidity he fought the battles of the Granicus, Issus, and Arbela, and conquered Asia Minor, Phoenicia, and Egypt, penetrating into Bactria, Sogdiana, and Northern India. Only the exhaustion of his troops and their refusal to advance farther arrested his course by the river Hyphasis. Death overtook the great conqueror at Babylon, 323 B.C., before he had time to consolidate his dominions. But his work could not be entirely undone in the strife of the Diadochi and the conquests of the Roman Republic.

What did Alexander accomplish for humanity and

---

[1] The nearest parallel is that of Frederick William I. and Frederick the Great of Prussia.
[2] One who equally merited the title has not been awarded it—Caesar.

for Christianity ?   Conquest, usually the synonym for
Alexander, forms the least of his achievements.   Briefly
we may say that Alexander

(a) Shook the ancient world to its very foundations, and
did for it something like what Napoleon did for his and our
age.   Men like Alexander, Julius Caesar, and Napoleon
render it impossible for mankind to loiter in the old ruts ;
they compel them to re-examine their dogmas, test their
traditions, and ask whether society can still be held
together by the accepted methods of cohesion.   All great
events, like the conquests of Alexander, the rise of the
Roman Empire, the discovery of America, have given a
new impetus to the spirit.   Alexander compelled the old
world to think afresh.

(b) He also, like the Greeks before him and the Romans
later, arrested the Oriental danger which threatened to
swamp Western civilization.   Greece was exhausted, and
Rome had not yet grown to her might, so that, but for
Alexander, Persia might have overwhelmed Greece and
all that Greece stood for.   Then the struggle between
Roman and Carthaginian would have been too late, and
Zama might have had a different issue [1] (v. p. 173).

(c) Alexander not only arrested the ' Yellow peril '
and the Northern Barbarian peril of his day and protected
Greek civilization, but he greatly extended Greek culture,
opened an unbounded future for it, and inspired it with
new life.   He did not destroy the Orient, but made it
easier for it to deliver its message, while he greatly
facilitated the growth of the Western spirit.   We who have
sat at the feet of Hellas can better appreciate Alexander's
services to the Hellenes than they themselves.

(d) Alexander commenced the task of reconciliation
among the nations, and brought East and West into those
relations of interaction which have never since been

[1] He also stayed the irruptions of northern barbarians into the Balkan
peninsula.

broken, and which have benefited both. **The Greeks** regarded Alexander's victories as an opportunity of wiping out old scores : they viewed the Orient as their spoil or as a field for their exploitation. Even Aristotle advised Alexander to behave toward the Greeks as a leader but toward the non-Greeks as a tyrant. But Alexander had larger thoughts than either Greek or Macedonian could appreciate : his object was not to avenge or to destroy. He introduced a novel feature into war in treating the conquered not as slaves without rights but as men. He offended his countrymen and the Greeks by blotting out the distinction between conquered and conquerors.[1] As a means of amalgamation he tried the expedient of intermarriages, himself marrying Persian princesses ; at Susa, in 325 B.C., 100 of his officers and 10,000 soldiers married Asiatic wives. He paved the way for a larger humanity, and made it easier for men to believe in the unity of mankind. The brotherhood of man could now begin to be realised. National barriers were thrown down : racial distinctions were disregarded.

(e) He inaugurated that comprehensive cosmopolitanism which reached its apogee in the Roman Empire (v. p. 203).

GENERAL CHARACTERISTICS OF THE NEW ERA
(300 B.C.-300 A.D.)

Change and Upheaval

This was an era of change and upheaval. The unexpected repeatedly happened. Events outstripped theory. Old things had passed away and all things had become new ; old systems were gone ; old prejudices swept away. It is difficult for us looking back through the long vista to estimate aright the perplexity

---

[1] Mahaffy notices 'the studied equality of the three great races, Persian, Greek, Macedonian' on the Sidonian sarcophagus (*Survey*, p. 237).

of thoughtful men who lived in the empire of Alexander,
who witnessed the rise and fall of the Greek kingdoms,
the spread of Greek culture, the rise of imperial Rome,
the collapse of the ancient faiths.   Men were driven from
their old moorings and had not yet become accustomed
to the new order.   They were cut loose from the city-
state and from Oriental despotism and thrown into an
empire which was too large for the individual.   New
world-centres arose.   The average man was perplexed
by the rapid march of history.   In the social confusion
and the fall of long-established systems there was much
calculated to unsettle the firmest faith.   Such transition
periods are always fraught with difficulty and danger.

Striking Contrasts

The Graeco-Roman world presents the greatest contrasts
and extremes.   Every age may be so characterised, but
this holds true in a special manner of these centuries.
Monotony had dropped out of life.   The homogeneousness
of nations was disturbed.   The systems which had held
men together on a certain equality were broken down,
and the gorgon of undisciplined individualism had appeared
on the scene.   The old and the new were consorting.
Some were gazing at the setting sun ; others expectantly
toward the rising sun.   This age presents none of the
monotony of the lethargic Orient nor the homogeneity
of mediaevalism.   Hence so many contrary and even
contradictory statements have been made about it and
supported by the citation of abundant authorities.   There
appears a juxtaposition of several worlds : the world of
sensualism and luxury among the upper classes, as described
by Juvenal, Tacitus, Petronius ; that of despair and void,
but not without a ray of hope, as in the pages of Cicero,
Seneca, and Persius ; that of wholesome literary friendship
exemplified by the Plinies, Cicero, and Plutarch ; that of

the fervent religious brotherhoods of which we get glimpses
in ancient authors and inscriptions; that of the street-
preacher and moral lecturer as seen in the better class of
Cynics, in Dio Chrysostom, Musonius Rufus, Maximus
of Tyre; that of superstition reflected in the remains of
books of magic, in tablets and inscriptions, and many
references in Suetonius, Plutarch, Aristides, Lucian, and
Philostratus; that of the Nihilism of Lucretius; that of
quiet resignation to the will of God, as in Epictetus and
Marcus Aurelius; that of the great masses whose cares
and joys have been brought to light in the papyri.[1]

A Popularising Age

This age was essentially superficial. It was noted for
breadth rather than for depth:[2] it was not original,
creative, or imaginative, but imitative and encyclopaedic.
Religion, philosophy, art, letters, were all popularised.
The veneer of culture was widely spread but not always
accompanied by its essence. The art of the age is not
unworthy, but it does not exhibit the exquisite Peri-
clean perfection, and it betrays a more plebeian taste.
There was a widespread demand for objects of art, with
a proportionate lowering of the standard. It was an age
of art-collectors rather than of artists. The half-cultured
Roman carried off things which he understood to be of value
partly because they were prized by those whom he conquered. The conduct of Mummius was typically Roman
and characteristic of the age, when, having consigned
Corinth to the flames, he stipulated with the shippers of
its precious treasures that if these were lost or damaged
on the way to Rome they should be replaced by others
'equally good.' Even the literature is not original. The

---

[1] Cf. Deissmann, *Light from the Ancient East*, chap. iv. *et passim.*
[2] Froude, in his essay on *Julius Caesar*, says: 'The age was saturated
with cant.'

glorious days of Greek literature lay behind ; the Roman literature, not excepting the Ciceronian and Augustan periods, was a re-working of Greek materials and repro- duction (of a high order) of Greek models. ' The rich literary amateur, who should have been a Maecenas, became an author himself.' [1] In politics the masses had asserted themselves. They constituted a perpetual pro- blem and menace to statesmen of the Republic, and were a large factor in setting up the Empire under which they were fed, petted, and amused. Philosophy was popularised as far as possible. Much of the highest thought of Plato had filtered down among the masses, and a smattering of philosophy was an essential part of an ordinary liberal education. The post-Aristotelian philosophies tended to become religious and to take their share in meeting the general demand for moral guidance. But religion above all else assumed a popular form. Philosophy was the only religion of the educated, and the masses were no longer interested in any state cult. Popular preachers and lecturers were in demand—an ancient Salvation Army. The people had recourse to the new gods brought in from the Orient. The Roman state was constantly compelled in religious matters to make concessions to popular demands in introducing more emotional and individual methods (e.g. *supplicationes*, *lectisternia*, *ludi*), and in gradually recognising foreign cults to which the people were devoted. Even the strong hand of Rome governed by astutely yielding to the populace.

Its Modernness

This Graeco-Roman age must strike the student as very modern. In reading its records we often forget we are separated from these ancients by so many centuries. As evidence of this modernness we feel ourselves more at home

[1] Dill, *Rom. Society*, p. 95.

in the era commencing with Alexander, and can more readily sympathise with the succeeding centuries than we can with mediaevalism. There is much of the philosophy of Plato and Aristotle that seems intended for another order of things, whereas the philosophies that interpreted the world to the Graeco-Roman age—though less original and less interesting—deal with more familiar topics. Their problems—philosophical, religious, economic, social and political—touch us of a later era very closely.

The social habits are very modern : to travel for business, pleasure, or education was quite usual. The *nouveaux riches* were as objectionable then as now. The international exchange of wares, manners, thought, and religion was, more especially in the Roman Empire, as active as at the present day. Facilities of communication were more abundant than at any time prior to the invention of steam and the era of railway construction. From the second Punic war women became as prominent almost as in our suffragette age. Their virtues and weaknesses were much the same. They loved display and fine dresses ; they were susceptible to flattery. Ovid tells how they came to be seen rather than to see : ' spectatum veniunt : veniunt spectentur ut ipsae.' The excavations at Pompeii show how ladies attempted to escape with their jewels and valuables, and have unearthed sad memorials of mother love. Programmes of amusements, especially of the amphitheatre, were in regular use. Gossip and slander formed part of society's daily food. There was the same reverence then as now, even among roués like Ovid, for the innocence of girlhood. *Mariages de convenance* were in vogue with similar results. Cultivated men were alarmed at a degraded popular taste as among ourselves, when an ephemeral musical comedy will draw a packed house for a whole season while an excellent cast of Shakespeare is little appreciated. So with the later Greeks and Romans mimes and farces and even coarser amusements ousted drama possessing any moral

purpose. There were 'star' actors like Aesopus and
Roscius, and, in Pompeii, Actius. Fashions also came
and went. Shrews were not unknown, like Cicero's wife
Terentia, or his brother Quintus's wife Pomponia. Complaints come to us of the intractableness of the gentler
sex.[1] The habits of sweethearts present no novelty : they
scribbled on walls, used endearing epithets, prized keep-
sakes, became maddened with jealousy. Many were
cruel as the Lesbia of Catullus. Social life (apart from
political) was at least equally absorbing in the late
Republic and in the Empire. The dinner hour was
pushed later and later into the evening.

Comforts were generally more accessible in the Graeco-
Roman age than until the past half-century. There were
more accommodations for out-of-door life, and abundant
lounging places. Public baths with an amazing equip-
ment (sometimes with a library) are found in every town,
however small. In Timgad one finds several public baths
in a remarkable state of preservation. The public con-
veniences of Timgad are superior to those in some modern
European cities. 'Taking the cure' at celebrated bathing-
places and natural springs was an ordinary occurrence ;
we have still ample evidence from places like Hammam
R'Ihra near the desert, Wiesbaden and Bath. As we read
in the train, travellers could read and write on their
journeys : the case of the Ethiopian eunuch is familiar.
In the better houses there was a bathroom, and sometimes
several. The hot-air system, re-discovered in America,
was known to the Romans in the first century B.C.
Dentistry was practised : Cicero tells us incidentally of
gold-filled teeth. 'Every highly educated man at this

---

[1] Metellus Macedonicus said in a public speech: 'If we could do without
wives we should be rid of that nuisance ; but since nature has decreed
that we can neither live comfortably with them, nor live at all without
them, we must e'en look rather to our permanent interests than to a passing
pleasure' (Aul. Gel., *A. N.*, i. 6). Plutarch has preserved the famous saying
of the elder Cato : ' All men rule over women ; we Romans rule over all men,
and our wives rule over us.'

(Cicero's) time owned a library and wished to have the
latest book.' Men went to their friends' libraries to consult
books, as Cicero to that of Lucullus at Tusculum. It was
also an era of public libraries. On the way from the modern
museum in Timgad to the forum there stands on the left
hand the Timgad 'Carnegie' library, with a large slab
inscribed with the name of the donor and the cost. In
large cities like Alexandria there were university libraries.
Banking business was highly developed : one could deposit
at interest ; there were also current accounts with something like our cheque system. Letters of credit and bills
of exchange were negotiated, so that a traveller was not
obliged to carry much money on his person.[1]

The vices of the age wear a modern garb : luxury,
extravagance, selfishness, gambling, the mad rush to
acquire wealth. Divorce was frightfully common in the
upper classes. Idleness was the favourite occupation of
the two extremes of society. There was a disinclination
on the part of society men and women towards marriage,
and race-suicide reached such proportions as to become
a grave concern to statesmen. The restlessness and fever
of our modern life invaded their lives, but they could plead
more extenuating circumstances than we.

In many other details the records astonish us. Many of
the papyri documents, if dates and names were changed,
would read as if of yesterday. There were comic artists
who anticipated *Punch*, and cartoonists. One has represented Nero as a butterfly driving the fiery steeds of the
chariot of state. Men bet on their favourite horses. The

---

[1] 'In such matters as transit, public health, police, water supply, engineer-
ing, building and so forth, Rome of the second century left off pretty much
where the reign of Queen Victoria was to resume. The modern city of Rome
is obtaining its drinking water out of about three of the nine great aqueducts
which ministered to the imperial city. The hot-air system which warms the
hotels of modern Europe and America was in general use in every comfortable
villa of the first century A.D. Education was more general and more accessible to the poor in A.D. 200 than in A.D. 1850. The siege artillery employed
by Trajan was as effective, probably, as the cannon of Vauban' (Stobart).

Romans seem to have anticipated Pitman in shorthand. There was an imperial post, and there seem to have been abundant private postal systems, so that news travelled with astonishing rapidity. Among the Romans we find the precursor of our daily newspaper without the editorials, the *acta diurna*, giving the latest news and gossip.

Not only in external and accidental things but in sentiment it hardly seems possible that we can be separated by so many centuries. These ancients experienced wants similar to ours, were disturbed by similar yearnings, and moved by similar joys and sorrows. The Hellenistic literature, but chiefly the Roman, often betrays a quite modern sentiment. The opening of Cicero's *De Legibus II*. reveals a love of native place with its familiar seats and charming walks. The love of landscape and of nature was as pronounced among the Romans as among ourselves. No ancients took the same delight in flowers. The Roman could not rest in his *domus aeterna* if no kindly hand strewed violets or roses in spring. And in their small houses, as in Timgad, it is pathetic to see with what care they surrounded themselves with flowers. The enjoyment of nature, which became prominent in the Alexandrine poetry, is still more pronounced in Roman poetry, as in Virgil, Lucretius, Horace, and Catullus. 'The passion of love . . . became a very powerful influence in actual life during the last years of the Republic and the early years of the Empire. It is in Latin literature that we are brought most near to the power of this passion in the ancient world.' [1] The appetite for friendship and companionship was keen.

It is in their sorrow that these ancients are most modern. The tombstones in the Ceramicus tell the same tales as those in our churchyards. We find in the heart of Asia Minor the rustic stonemason burning with warm human tears memorial letters into the cold stone. On not a few tombs the broken-hearted parents yearn for the patter of

[1] Sellar, *Rom. Poets of the Repub.*, pp. 19, 376.

little feet, the widow longs for reunion, the dead plead for the sympathy and remembrance of the living. It is not the sorrow which is modern but the way in which it expresses itself. Men were no longer willing to seek the anodyne of their own grief in the common grief or welfare of the community. A more atomistic and personal way of looking at things had arisen : the individual heart clamoured for what the individual heart had lost.

Education

Education was general ; more so than in some Continental countries at the present day. There were facilities for popular education in the Roman Empire to an extent unknown in our land till the Victorian era. The papyri show us how common writing was even among ordinary folk. Greek tutors, professors, and private chaplains were in extraordinary demand. The basis of Graeco-Roman education was Greek culture. The Romans sent their sons to the University of Athens to finish their education. The young Cicero studied there, and received from his father some of the letters which we read to-day. Horace was also a student at Athens. Philo knew the city. There philosophers of every school discussed their *Weltanschauungen*. Philo says that Athens was to Greece what the pupil is to the eye or reason to the soul. It was the mother of universities in Alexandria, Antioch, Tarsus, and elsewhere. The Jews were alive to the necessity of Jewish education amid the power and fascination of Hellenism. In every city alongside the synagogue they had their schools and libraries.

Teaching was a recognised, honourable, and—in contrast to our time—a lucrative profession. It is quite common in the inscriptions of Asia Minor to read of teachers who, having amassed fortunes, bestow princely gifts on their native towns. Academic titles like *philosopher, doctor, sophist,* analogous to our M.A. or D.D., were in vogue and often inscribed on tombstones. Alexandria was the centre of learning in the Roman Empire : it was not so much a teaching university as a seat of research. The museum and library of some 700,000 volumes attracted scholars from all countries. Though libraries were known from the days of Ashurbanipal (seventh century B.C.), it was only in the Roman period that they were established in every city of importance. After the destruction of the Alexandrian library in the siege under Caesar, the library of the Serapeum came to have the foremost place there. The library of Pergamum, founded by Attalus I. and enlarged by Eumenes II., of 200,000 rolls, was carried to Alexandria by Antony. Pergamum and Alexandria created a demand for reading facilities ; we may infer from Polybius that in the second century B.C. libraries were fairly common. Asinius Pollio and Augustus inaugurated the public library system in Rome. We have already mentioned the library of Timgad. Besides, private collections were quite usual, such as those of Cicero, Aemilius Paullus, and Lucullus. In Herculaneum an Epicurean collection has been discovered. Books were numerous and cheap because of the use of convenient writing material and the facilities of production by slave copyists. The two favourite materials were papyrus and parchment or vellum, as distinguished from leather. Parchment, according to Varro, owes its origin to the rivalry between the Egyptian and Attalid kings as regards their respective libraries. It was first manufactured under Eumenes II., after Ptolemy had prohibited the export of papyrus. Ostraca (potsherds) were used by the poorer folk in Egypt. Wax notebooks were carried for ordinary use. But the increasing numbers of literary slaves was the chief reason of the enormous spread of books. One slave read and others wrote to his dictation. The demand for books gave rise to book-selling as a separate trade. 'Atticus, the first person who is known to have undertaken the multiplication and sale of books on a large scale, had numerous rivals. Under Augustus at the latest, the book-trade in Rome was a business by itself, and soon after in the provinces.' [1]

Universalism

A very striking feature of this age was its ever-increasing universalism, beginning under Alexander and culminating in the Roman Empire. Various causes contributed toward cosmopolitanism.

(1) There was what we might call the moral necessity of a reaction. This arose partly from the disgust engendered by the long tyrannical rule of exclusivism. Men had missed the *via media* between a true nationalism and an indifference to national interests. Exclusivism had worked havoc in the Greek world ; a more excellent way was now sought. In the Oriental world despotism, like Russian absolutism, rendered men insensible to patriotism. There is another side to this moral necessity : God has so endowed the nations that each is the complement of the other, and only in co-operation can they truly forward the work of humanity. The ancient nations were left for a time each in its exclusive school to develop its particular aptitudes. Each worked, as it were, behind closed doors ; then the doors of the workshops were thrown open and inspection invited. Nations began to compare notes, to teach their lessons, and to inquire into what others professed to teach. Life is many sided, and, for a rounded life, attention must be drawn to all its phases.

(2) The relative superiority of the peoples blended in the Graeco-Roman world. There were four competing civilisations—Orientalism, Judaism, Hellenism, Romanism, none of which could by itself claim an absolute empire over man, none combining completely the elements necessary

[1] Friedländer, *Rom. Life and Manners*, Eng. trans., iii. 36.

for all.   Had there been only one superior people among
inferior peoples there would have resulted a universalism
of uniformity ; but these four types of mind being in
competition, a universalism to which each contributed its
best was inevitable.[1]

(3) The conquests of Alexander and his liberal policy of
reconciliation, inherited by the Diadochi and consummated
by the Romans and by Christianity.

(4) Greek thought, especially post-Aristotelian (v. ch. vi.).

(5) The spread of the Greek language.   Out of a babel
of dialects arose a *Koiné* or *lingua franca*, which became
the medium of intercourse for all races (v. ch. viii.).

(6) Another—less potent—factor was the enormous
bodies of Greek mercenaries taking service in foreign
armies.   They acted as a solvent of Greek nationalism,
and as quasi-intermediaries between East and West.   They
learned tolerance in the ranks, and after their term of
service many settled among alien populations.

(7) Commerce is one of the strongest international bonds,
and in the post-Alexandrian world the facilities for commerce
were multiplied.   Colossal sums hoarded up by Oriental
despots were released as productive wealth or as means
of luxury which calls forth trading.   Larger fields were
opened for speculation.   As nations come to know each
other they wish to procure the comforts and luxuries of
their neighbours.   Soon luxuries become necessities.   Before
Japan was entered by the West she was indifferent to
international trade : Western merchants have persuaded
China and Japan that they need many things which they
were once able to do without.   Trade drove Jewish, Greek,
Roman and Syrian merchants to settle among alien popula-

---

[1] An illustration may be given from the British Empire.   When the British
rule among a people like the aborigines of New Zealand, the latter, without
literature or culture, produce no effect on the British settlers.   Anglo-Saxon
civilisation spreads uniformly as at home.   But when peoples like the British,
Brahmins, and Parsees live together, they learn from and teach each other, and
there results a new type which is neither British nor Indian but Eurasian.

tions. 'These merchants occupied themselves with the affairs of heaven as well as of earth.' The spread of the Greek tongue, the ever larger political unities into which men were being fused, the 'majesty of the Roman peace,' Roman roads and bridges, the gradual extension of the *jus gentium*, gave an impetus to trade. Moreover, the trading peoples lived on the shores of the Mediterranean, which when cleared of pirates and ruled by one power became a safer highway of commerce than it has been up to the fourth decade of last century.

(8) Slaves and freedmen were among the most potent missionaries of cosmopolitanism and human brotherhood (See ch. iii., p. 54.)

(9) Religious brotherhoods and guilds. (See ch. iv., p. 9.)

(10) Cosmopolitanism reached its acme in the conquests of the Roman Republic and the administration of the Empire. The foundation of the Empire was a protest against the exclusivism and the all-Roman policy of the oligarchy. The whole world united into a brotherhood and under the rule of a single individual was the dream of Julius Caesar. The Roman Empire bestowed peace on a war-weary world, and energetically commenced the task of consolidation.

Intermixture of Races

Partly as a cause and partly as a consequence of universalism, there was an astonishing intermixture of populations, especially in the Empire. A homogeneous people was hardly to be found except in secluded regions. All races were daily touching shoulders. War, forcible deportations, the slave trade, commerce, the liberal policy of rulers contributed to this intermixture. Alexander inaugurated the scheme of establishing centres of amalgamation. As such his new foundations composed of Greeks, Macedonians, and Persians must be regarded, as truly as

military colonies.   Alexandria was the first of these centres
for the nations and for East and West.   Such an experiment
was as difficult then as now, if we are to judge from the
bloody street riots in Alexandria and Antioch.   Corinth,
after its foundation by Caesar 44 B.C., speedily fulfilled
the same function.   There were the veterans of Caesar,
Hellenic elements from the surrounding districts, besides
the ever-present Greek adventurers.   The New Testament and inscriptions testify to an influential Jewish
element ; and the Oriental element was not small, judging
from the vogue of Oriental worships.[1]   This intermixture
was not confined to capital cities, trading and banking
centres, commercial seaports, university towns ; it extended to the provinces and the islands of the Aegean.
Delos rose in prominence as Athens declined.   In the
second century B.C., before ships plied direct between the
East and Italy, it was the stopping-place and distributing
centre for wholesale merchants ; it was also famous for its
slave market where as many as 10,000 slaves were sold
by auction daily.   Deprived of its freedom after the
Macedonian war and deserted by the Greek population,
it was re-colonised by the Athenians and Romans who
have left a wealth of inscriptions.   Josephus cites a decree
of the Delians exempting the Jews from military service,
and such favours were never conferred on Jews unless
under strong necessity.   In the Mithridatic war Delos
and the neighbouring islands were ravaged and 20,000
Italians slain.   In 141 B.C., the Jews of Gortyna (in Crete)
were numerous enough to secure from the consul Lucius
the promise of protection (1 Macc. xv. 23).   Cyprus was
another blending-place, populated by Phoenicians, Greeks,
Persians, Egyptians, Romans and Jews.   In the insurrection under Trajan the Jews are said to have massacred
240,000 Gentiles.   In Cyrene, Josephus says, one-fourth of

[1] The Acropolis was crowned with a temple of Aphrodite (Astarte), in
whose service were one thousand female slaves.

the population was Jewish. Many other examples of the blending of different races could be adduced. Under Mithridates 80,000 Roman residents in Asia are said to have been massacred. One of the Ptolemies deported 100,000 Jews to Libya. In the insurrection in Britain under Boadicea 70,000 Roman colonists perished.

Syncretism

As corollaries to cosmopolitanism we find syncretism—the bringing together of elements once thought irreconcilable—and eclecticism—the selection by the individual from every quarter of whatever he required for the practical needs of his own life. These two forces invaded every department—art, politics, culture, but chiefly philosophy, morality, and religion. Such conditions were inevitable after the collapse of exclusive systems, in the mixture of populations (such as may be found in the United States), through lively intercourse, and the demands of a practical and popularising age, and as the result of the competing *Weltanschauungen* of one people eminent for religion, another for culture, and a third for power. The proconsul Gellius who invited the rival philosophers of Athens to come to terms, offering himself as arbiter, was typical of the age. Morality and religion were peculiarly syncretistic. ' In the sphere of religion a sort of assimilative or encyclopaedic frenzy was abroad.' The conservative Jews did not escape ; they were Greeks in almost everything but religion. There were frequent conversions from Heathenism to Judaism, and not a few from Judaism to Heathenism.[1] The Judaeo-Greek literature of Alexandria blended East and West, acting as

---

[1] Schürer, iii. 135, and οἱ ποτὲ 'Ιουδαῖοι of *C. I. G.*, 3148. The Hellenising zeal of Jason and Menelaus in Jerusalem found much sympathy. Nothing was more syncretistic than magic, in which the Jews excelled, especially in exorcism. Cf. Schürer, iii. 409 ff. The letter of Hadrian(?) shows to what a dangerous extreme syncretism was carried : ' Nemo illic archisynagogus Iudaeorum, nemo Samarites, nemo Christianorum presbyter non mathematicus, non haruspex, non aliptes.' Cf. Deissmann, *Light from the Ancient East*, pp. 250 ff., 303 ff.

a solvent for both. Egypt has been termed by Kennedy 'the religious clearing-house of the Hellenistic world.'[1] In the Diaspora the expansive tendency of Judaism gained the upper hand over the exclusive, until the destruction of Jerusalem and the rivalry of Christianity compelled Judaism to retreat within itself. The 'God-fearing' heathen were half heathen and half Jews, and mediated between both. The Greeks, though maintaining their intellectual and cultural supremacy, were influenced by their Roman conquerors, while they assimilated the religious thought of the East. The Romans were the greatest borrowers and adapters, their genius being of a mosaic order. Their religion was like Joseph's coat. Oriental religions were pre-eminently syncretistic. Good fellowship was maintained among the gods of various nations, the gods keeping pace with every *rapprochement* among their worshippers.[2] Alexander attempted neither to exterminate Oriental deities nor to compel his new subjects to acknowledge Greek deities. The conquered and the conquerors in the Greek kingdoms and the Roman Empire proceeded to identify their gods on the principle that their functions are the same, the names alone being different in different languages. The strong movement toward monotheism gave an impetus to this practice. The list of the names of the deities so assimilated or identified is a long one. Eclecticism, which was prevalent in every system of philosophy and in practically every writer, made its standard what is common to all men—the immediate consciousness.[3] After Aristotle no original system was forthcoming, so that men fell back on those available to cull from them what they considered appropriate, and to form new schools with *membra undique collata*.[4] Syncretism

[1] *St. Paul*, p. 104.   [2] Cf. Usener, *Götternamen*, p. 340.
[3] Zeller, *Eclectics*, p. 17.
[4] Christianity appearing in this syncretistic world could not escape the contagion, but it would require a separate volume to trace to what extent *historic* Christianity is syncretistic.

reached its apogee at the close of the second century A.D., and during the third.

Individualism

The last feature for which space permits mention is perhaps the most striking—individualism ; on the one hand the self-assertion of the individual in opposition to the corporate body, and on the other the reflection of the individual upon his own inner life. Individualism arose from the ruins of nationalism and of the city-state. Ancient patriotism was too tyrannical : it was an exaggerated form of the modern Teutonic theory that the state is the end and the individual the means for its aggrandisement, as opposed to that of English-speaking nations that the individual is the end and the state the means for his self-realisation. The result was a universal strike against collectivism. Again, there was at that time no *via media* between the exclusiveness of the *polis* and atomistic individualism. Two important factors were lacking—a true nationalism, and that domain which we term ' society ' (in which we are influenced by our fellows, and in turn put our impress upon them). Finally, there was the emergence of a strong sense of individuality and personality : the inward problem had been presented and the demands of selfhood grew clamant. We of a later age need regret neither the apparent tyranny of the city-state nor the individualism which wrecked it : both were attempts of men as thoughtful as we are toward self-realisation.

Individualism, being the reverse side of universalism, invaded Oriental, Jewish, Greek and Roman life. The Orientals, whose chief bond of cohesion was the despotism destroyed by Alexander, when the central restraining power was removed went each his own way. There is a solitariness in Oriental life foreign to Western society. The Orientals sought satisfaction in religions liberated from national prejudices, into the fellowship of which members were admitted irrespective of race.

Individualism is most unexpected among the Jews, with whom Jahweh dealt as an aggregate and not as individuals. But the advance of religious experience raised the question : Can Jahweh leave a righteous Israelite unrewarded when the nation forgets Him ? Can He permit a wicked Israelite to escape because he belongs to a chosen nation ? Is suffering always penal ? Must innocent children suffer for the sins of the fathers ? The germs of the later individualisation of religion are found in the great pre-exilic prophets like Hosea and Amos, who shifted the emphasis from ceremonial to ethics, anticipating the truth that religion is communion with God. The excuse of the exiles was an arraignment of an apparently undiscriminating Providence—' the fathers have eaten sour grapes and the children's teeth are set on edge.' Individualism properly so called came in with the Exile through the necessary re-examination of the basis of religion and morality, and the influence of Persia. In the crisis Jeremiah discovered and rescued the individual. He perceived that the proverb ' the fathers have eaten sour grapes and the children's teeth are set on edge' destroyed moral responsibility : he proclaimed personal responsibility, ' every one shall die for his own iniquity.' Religion as the communion of the soul with God cannot be harmed by any national calamity. Henceforth the individual is constituted the religious unit in place of the nation which had hitherto been so regarded. ' Thus through Jeremiah the foundation of a true individualism was laid, and the law of individual retribution proclaimed.' [1] Ezekiel carried this revolutionary truth to the extreme. He proclaims, ' all souls are mine,' and asserts man's moral freedom irrespective of his own past and the wickedness of his family or nation : a man's will shapes his destiny ; retribution is strictly individual, and

[1] Charles, *Eschatology*, p. 61.

every soul receives its deserts here before the eyes of men.[1]
Ecclesiastes refuted the idea of Providence as discriminating
against the wicked. Job dissevered the idea of punishment from suffering, and expressed the yearning for individual immortality. Jewish history proved that the
individual does suffer for the sins of the fathers. In the
Psalms there is much individualism: at one time the
individual retribution of Ezekiel, at another those out-
pourings of the heart so personal and universal that all
generations can use their language. The fifty-first Psalm
shows how the individual and the collective are inter-
twined. In the Apocrypha and the Apocalyptic literature
there is a still larger growth of individualism, but also
the reconciliation of the individual with the corporate
spiritual life. The aspirations of Job have developed into
a resurrection for the individual righteous as well as for
the righteous nation: then came a resurrection of the
wicked individual for judgment. The synagogue fostered
the individualisation of religion as personal piety. Individualism as such never commended itself to the Jew:
he could not accept an individualistic immortality like the
Greek. The hopes of the individual and of the nation
were united in the faith in a resurrection and a Messianic
kingdom. Israel alone attained a true individualism—
at least in religion.

Greece and Rome suffered most from individualism. In
the fifth century B.C. Greece was overtaken by such an acute
attack of individualism as has never been equalled except in
the closing Roman Republic and in the age of Rousseau.[2]
Individualism was the projection of the Greek idea of

---

[1] 'Whilst Ezekiel's undying merit in this respect was his assertion of the
independent worth of the individual, his defects lay in two misstatements:
(a) the individual does not suffer for the sins of his fathers, but only for
his own; (b) the individual is at present judged in perfect keeping with his
deserts. In other words, sin and suffering, righteousness and well-being,
are always connected: the outward lot of the individual is God's judgment
in concrete form.'—Charles, p. 67.

[2] Individualism was pronounced in Nominalism and in mediaeval art.

freedom in an inward direction, and was nursed by democracy.   Greek constitutions were wrecked by the passions
of individuals.   Sophistic reduced society to atoms,
annihilating the authority of the state, and making man,
the individual, the measure of all things.   Socrates perceived the danger of this teaching : while he attempted to
save the state he further emphasised the worth of the
individual, and his teaching was more individualistic than
he was aware.   Plato made a heroic effort to buttress
the tottering *polis*, subordinating the individual to the
universal.   Aristotle, too, wished to preserve the state,
but saw the necessity of saving the individual from the
universal of Plato.   The post-Aristotelian schools took
up the strictly individualistic standpoint.

The Romans were infected with individualism in the
second Punic war and amid the distribution of the spoils
of conquest.   The Roman civil wars were the result of
individualism ; the rise of the Empire was merely the
survival of the fittest in the struggle of individuals.   As
Roman conquests spread, the happiness of the world was
dependent more and more on individuals.   Men sought
office for personal aggrandisement ; the state was simply
to be exploited for personal advantage.   In art the particular and realistic made its appearance ; portrait-busts
were made.   In society, selfishness was prevalent.
Individuals exercised an influence quite new.[1]   As Roman
literature was in its infancy when individualism swept
over East and West we find more individualism in it than in
any ancient literature.   The genius of Roman writers is
personal and self-conscious compared with the more

---

[1] 'The tendency to individualism was also the natural result of enlarged
experience and expanding intelligence among the upper classes.   The second
century B.C. shows us many prominent men of strong individual character
who assert themselves in ways to which we have been unaccustomed in
Roman history . . . and among lesser and less honourable men we see the
tendency in the passionate desire for personal distinction in the way of
military commands, triumphs, and the giving of expensive games.'—Fowler,
Relig. Exper., p. 340.

impersonal Greek genius. Love assumed a more acute form, like our modern sentiment. Sellar says, ' Roman poetry is interesting as the revelation of personal experience and character,' and ' in no other branch of ancient literature is so much prominence given to the enjoyment of nature, the passion of love, and the joys, sorrows, tastes and pursuits of the individual.'[1] Biography was popularised in Greek by Plutarch ; autobiography is a native form of Roman literature.[2] In the records of the sorrow of the age we see that men were no longer willing to find solace for their private grief in the grief or welfare of the corporate body. The statuesque patriotic sorrow of Pericles' *Funeral Oration* was now an anachronism. The desire for reunion was asserting itself that the heart might find what the individual heart had lost. In religion individualism was most pronounced. Satisfaction for personal needs was sought in universal religions divorced from the state and offering their message to man as man : men perfunctorily performed the rites of the state cult which had no message for the destitute individual. The interest had shifted from the outer to the inner world. Space forbids to dwell upon the results, good and evil, of ubiquitous individualism. It was the portal to the study of an infinite personality; it was of immense importance for Christianity, making men conscious of needs that only Christianity could meet.

[1] *Rom. Poets of the Repub.*, pp. 16-17.
[2] A. F. West, *Rom. Autobiography*, p. 1.

CHAPTER III

SOCIAL AND MORAL CONDITIONS OF THE GRAECO-ROMAN WORLD

Lorsqu'on veut trouver la conscience d'un peuple, ce n'est pas toujours dans ses mœurs actuelles qu'il faut la chercher: elle est souvent tout entière dans ses vœux et dans ses regrets.—DENIS, vol. ii. p. 130.

IT is impossible to understand the moral and religious conditions of the ancient world without taking into account the social conditions partly determined by and partly determining the moral and religious. Many factors must be considered which space permits us merely to summarise.

A. SOCIAL CONDITIONS

Fall of Polis

From the beginning of the fourth century B.C., society had been in a state of constant flux. The weakening and subsequent fall of the city-state involved a fearful crisis. The ancient principle was one of the strict subordination of the individual to the body politic. But the passions of individuals overthrew this long-established system. This had unfortunately been done before men were clear as to what should take its place. Having rejected a cramping authority they were in no haste to acknowledge another. Individualism became regnant. The West, which gave birth to the idea of equal liberty

regulated by self-made law, paid dearly for the boon in
the way of terrible social revolutions while the *polis* yet
stood, and, when it began to totter, by bloody conflicts
as to who should wield authority in the next régime.
From the Peloponnesian war onwards the decline of freedom and the alarming growth of mercenaries and outlaws
is ' one of the most injurious phenomena of this age,' and
indicative of approaching military despotism. The Greeks
tried monarchy, tyranny, oligarchy, democracy, and
decided for democracy. Roman history presents a
curious and instructive development. Democracy steadily
advanced as in Greece, but with the extension of Roman
conquests, when great affairs of state and foreign policy
required professional and specialised knowledge, the senate
so manipulated popular government as to establish the
most tyrannical oligarchy the world has ever seen, and all
under the farce of popular and representative government
—just as in our own Napoleonic wars the peasant and
middle classes, who gave their lives by thousands, were
sacrificed for the benefit of a scanty nobility. The Orient
was not liable to frequent and violent revolutions like
the West : it remained more sphinx-like.

Unintermittent Wars

For 400 years B.C. the nations had been engaged in unin-
termittent wars. After the struggle of Greece against Persia
began the internecine strife of the Greek states which ended
in the exhaustion of all ; then on the field of Chaeroneia
Greece came under the heel of Macedonia. Alexander's
world-conquests were followed by the struggles of the
Diadochi until the Romans made a universal conquest.
The Romans had carried on a long warfare to extend their
rule over Italy : they had also fought the Carthaginian
à outrance to convert the Mediterranean into a Roman
sea. Finally, the Roman civil wars deluged the whole

world in blood. Ancient historians have left us records of the disastrous social and moral consequences of most of these wars. Thucydides' recital of the results of the Peloponnesian war is well known. The second Punic war —though against a foreign foe—was the first serious disintegrating force in Roman morals.[1] It hastened the advent of a commercial era in a society hitherto agricultural and military.

Economic Results

The many wars of this period told on society. The material resources of many cities and individuals were exhausted and comforts diminished, a fact which partly explains the spirit of revolution and rebellion, social disturbances being notoriously conditioned by economic considerations. When a large section of society have nothing to lose they are ready to promote any revolution as likely to benefit them, and certain not to render their circumstances worse. Citizens were kept under arms for ever longer periods, and were obliged to remain years abroad where the ties of home gradually relaxed and domestic charities declined. They returned home unaccustomed to the useful monotony of daily work which only brought a bare living. Having been in the pay of the state, they looked to the state still to provide for them. They also looked for some substitute for excitement and blood-shedding. As their conquests had enriched their country, why should the country not pamper them as they deserved ? Again, many of these veterans had left home before a marriageable age and returned indifferent to the softening influences of domestic life : this naturally affected the birth-rate. Of those who went out from their homes tens of thousands never returned. Thus not only was a vacuum created at home, but many widows were emanci-

[1] Cf. Lecky, *Hist. of European Morals*, ii. 302 ff.

pated from marital control, a condition which furthered the prominence of women in the Roman Empire. Militarism, never the nurse of social virtues, became increasingly influential. The most hopeless feature was that in the Roman Republic which ruled the world the civil power lost control over the military : this deluged Rome and many of her provinces in bloodshed.

But the long wars gave rise to serious economic and industrial questions. The lands which furnished the battle-ground were exhausted. Colossal armies had been billeted upon the helpless populations. Bread-earners had been pressed into service. Crops over large areas were destroyed lest they should feed an enemy, or carried off for the needs of the devastating army ; the very means of their agriculture were removed—horses and all draught animals and farming implements. Conquered lands were compelled to pay large contributions in money or in kind, which plunged them into debt to unprincipled speculators. Their country was also opened to the exploitation of foreign capitalists. Many cities fell into bankruptcy. Thousands of the former free population had been killed, or sold as slaves, or drafted as auxiliaries into the Roman armies. There was not, in the economic depression, employment enough for those left, which necessitated migration of populations.

One of the first consequences of Alexander's conquests was to bring into circulation enormous sums of gold and silver and to scatter treasures of precious stones—the hordes of centuries of Oriental despotism. This circulation stimulated greed for a share of the spoils. It gave rise to the desire of wealth for self-gratification, created a demand for luxuries, and raised the prices so that living became more difficult for the poor.

The same thing happened later, and to a still larger extent, in Rome. The social trouble of the time of the Gracchi arose from the division of the spoils. The members

C

of the oligarchy secured most of the public lands for themselves, the state being only nominally landlord. When
the land-bills of Tiberius Gracchus proposed a redistribu-
tion, the proprietors whom the landlords had settled on
the lands were threatened with starvation, and to save
themselves cast in their lot with the popular party who had
lost everything, or had nothing to lose. With every step
in Roman history we find the class struggles accompanied
with greater acrimony. As in our developing industrial and
imperial life from the last quarter of the eighteenth century
until the era of recent social reforms, the rich grew richer and
the poor poorer. 'Trusts' were formed, small proprietors
became fewer as the oligarchy encroached. Matters grew
worse as Rome entered upon the conquest of the rich East.
Immense sums poured into the treasury to be disgorged into
private pockets; the domains of the East were exploited
by the Roman speculator. Joint-stock companies were
floated to collect with enormous profits the revenues.
Large sums were needed by the exhausted lands to carry
out public works and to repair the damage of war. In a
thousand ways the speculator was able to make large returns,
having no scruples of conscience to hamper him. A taste
for luxuries spread from the East, and the demand created
a supply. The cost of living rose, and was met by a
decreasing marriage and birth rate. The stupid extravagance of the late Republic and the early Empire has rarely
been equalled. The tough Roman character soon deterio-
rated amid self-indulgence. The unnatural and sudden
fashion in which Rome came to her wealth led to her ruin.
She had not the culture and education necessary to handle
it aright. There was more wealth than could in that age
be put to productive use. There was a field for investment
(chiefly in land and slaves) but not large enough, or rather
the banking system was not sufficiently developed. The
result was what we might anticipate if the many British
capitalists could not find all over the world a rich field for

their surplus capital, and were to withdraw it for self-indulgence at home. Luxury among the plutocrats and paternalism on the part of the administration put a premium upon idleness in which no morality can thrive.

Increasing Number of Slaves

One of the evil results of war was the augmentation of the numbers of slaves. A cringing slave made an insolent master. Experience has proved that slavery exerts a deteriorating effect upon the character of the owners. It affected also the free labouring population : forced labour, considered cheaper than free, entered into competition with it. But, strange to say, we hear of no complaints of the free against the slave, nor any problem of unemployment. The few freemen anxious to work apparently found work, and the others preferred to be on the roll of state-fed.

Work for wages and the winning of daily bread was distasteful, especially to the Greek and to the later Roman. The Greek ideal was a life of leisure freed from toil and care. The plunder of conquests inoculated the Roman with an aversion to hard work : he loved *otium*, but it was no longer the well-earned rest. The Jew alone gave to toil an honourable place. Unfortunately the Roman administration did not encourage healthful labour, but rendered the situation worse by doling out corn and oil to idle men.

Destruction of the Middle Classes

Perhaps the most deplorable feature of this period was the destruction of the middle classes who form the backbone of every nation. This set in first in the Greek world, where the civil wars of the Greek states and the wars between the Greek kingdoms after Alexander had exhausted the free civic armies. In the East Rome completed the disastrous work. In Italy Hannibal had traversed the country exterminating the yeomanry. What Hannibal spared Rome's own wars in Italy destroyed. The disappearance of the middle class created serious moral and social difficulties. This class generally keeps any country from rushing headlong to ruin ; they are the last stronghold of a people's virtue ; they mediate between the extremes of society. The absence of the middle class deepened and widened the terrible social cleft in the ancient world. An important reconciling factor had dropped out.

Drift to City Life

There was a constant drift to the cities, partly because of the decline of agriculture and small proprietorship, partly from ampler opportunities of making a fortune when commerce became brisk, partly for the sake of adventure, and other causes. The cities afforded ample means of amusement and excitement, as much sought then as now. In the first, and still more in the second century of the Empire, the world was studded with more beautiful cities than at the present day. The burdens fell on the rich more than in our time. The stone records abound in examples of private generosity for public purposes.

B. MORAL CONDITIONS

In appraising the morality of the Graeco-Roman world we must keep in view the many causes producing moral disorder—centuries of political confusion, devastating conquests, the depopulation of fair regions, the diminution of the free classes, the extermination of the middle classes, the enormous increase of slavery whereby hundreds of thousands of human beings were cut loose from the moral restraints of their civilisations, culture, and religion, and, soured by their misfortunes, became the panders and propagators of vice ; the social upheavals arising from the fall of the city-state, the march of triumphant democracy, the mental void due to the fall of the national faiths, the sudden irruption of unearned wealth, the rise of capitalism and the growth of *latifundia*, the successful revolt of individualism, the world-shaking civil wars of Rome, the grinding taxation and the noxious fiscal system of Rome. The pagan world was morally depressed by the sense of a continuous deterioration, as we are inspired by that of an ' increasing purpose ' in history. Also the Romans formed the aristocracy, the ' society,' among peoples more cultured than themselves, and thus prompted to what was often imitation of the inferior. It would be a remarkable world that such causes would not shake to the very foundations. Yet in face of all this, in the old world life, as ever, was rising from death.

It is much easier to depict the moral condition of one class of ancient society than to form a balanced judgment of its general morality. Hence exaggerations are current in most books dealing with this period.

(a) Dark Side

It is an unpleasant task to draw aside the veil which covers the vice and sin of the ancient world ; this is neces- sary, however, in order that our sketch may not be one- sided. There is a dark and lurid aspect. Paul, who knew the Hellenistic age better than any modern writer, out- lines an awful picture in his letter to the Romans i. 21 ff., though Paul knew another aspect also which he does not here mention.

Slavery

Ancient society rested upon the foundation of slavery, which could not then be abolished without precipitating society into chaos. It was the wisdom and policy of early Christianity not to seek to exterminate slavery with one blow, but first regulate it while establishing the principles which were sure to end it. Slavery was itself an advanced stage of humanity in comparison with the time when all prisoners were put to the sword. The Greek and the Roman saw no more wrong in having slaves than we see in having domestic servants. The most fruitful source of slavery was war; next to that were piracy, kidnapping, brigandage, slave-breeding and debt.[1] The total number of slaves in the Graeco-Roman world at any period is variously estimated, as also their relative proportion to the free. Le Maistre reckons 60,000,000 in the Empire. In Pergamum there was one slave to every two freemen. In the city of Rome the proportion was undoubtedly much greater : Beloch reckons 280,000 slaves to 500,000 free, Gibbon reckons as many slaves as free in the time of Claudius, Blair guesses the number of slaves and of free to be about equal up to the destruction of Carthage, and after that the proportion to be 3 to 1, giving a population of over 20,000,000 slaves in Italy. Zumpt reckons over 650,000 slaves in Rome in 5 B.C.

---

[1] A few examples will show the numbers of slaves. Alexander sold 30,000 Thebans. In a census of Athens in the time of Demetrius Phalereus there were 400,000 slaves to 20,000 freemen. In Corinth 460,000 were found. Under the closing Roman Republic and the early Empire slavery reached its acme. Aemilius Paullus at the close of the war with Perseus sold 150,000 freemen of Epirus. After the victories of Marius 60,000 Cimbri and 90,000 Teutons are said to have been sold. Before the second Punic war, when Rome annexed Sardinia and Corsica, so many captives were sold that there arose a proverb, *Sardi venales,* 'as cheap as Sardinians.' In the slave wars of Sicily Eunus had 200,000 armed slaves. In the insurrection of Spartacus the numbers vary from 40,000 to 100,000, of whom 10,000 were executed by Crassus. Caesar sold 63,000 Gauls on a single occasion. Augustus tells on the *Monumentum Ancyranum* that he delivered to their masters for execution 30,000. Trajan caused 10,000 slaves to engage in mutual slaughter to amuse the Roman people for four months. In the second century B.C. as many as 10,000 were sold in the Delos market in one day. Private Roman establishments possessed enormous numbers, amounting in some cases to 20,000. Crassus had over 500 carpenters and architects alone. Scaurus owned over 4000 urban slaves and as many country ones. A freedman under Augustus left 4116. When Pedanius was murdered 400 slaves were executed. Augustus forbad the liberation by testament of more than one-fifth, or a maximum of 100, of one's slaves. The poorer freemen could not afford to keep slaves, but the parsimonious Cato Uticensis kept twelve in the distress of the civil wars, and ten does not seem an exorbitant number from the point of view of a poor poet like Horace.

In Greece, except at Athens, the condition of the slave was wretched. In the Roman Republic it was on the whole not so bad as in Greece, though not so favourable as in Athens. The slave was a *res* not a *persona*, had no rights, and enjoyed no protection from the brutality of his master. There was no asylum as at Athens. The master could inflict any punishment he pleased, could torture and maim, could break up servile family connections, could crucify. The worst slaves worked in the country in chains and slept in the *ergastulum*. Runaway slaves met with frightful punishment when caught. A slave's evidence could only be given under torture. We read of masters crucifying their slaves after previously cutting out their tongues ; for a paltry offence cutting off their hands or throwing them as food to the lampreys, or compelling them to fight in the amphitheatre. If a master was murdered the whole *familia* was executed. Even in the imperial period which witnessed humaner treatment to slaves, we still find terrible acts of caprice. Augustus is said to have crucified Eros, his steward, for eating a quail. Roman ladies tore their attendants' faces or drove pins into their flesh if a curl was out of place. It is no wonder slaves sometimes took vengeance, and there arose the saying, ' So many slaves so many enemies.'

The increase in slaves produced important economic and moral effects. Those from the West were employed chiefly in farming the estates of the rich, and so contributed to the revival of Italian agriculture in the first century B.C. But slave labour being thought cheaper than free diminished the demand for free work and lowered the wages : this in turn sent the rural populations into the vices and idleness of the cities. The slaves from the East were more skilful and cultured than their masters : these supplied the demands of specialised and skilled labour, for after the second Punic war labour, like politics, was professionalised. But these slaves were mostly employed on unproductive toil. The enormous demand for skilled labour caused by the expansion of Rome once met, the Romans knew not how to put all their slaves to productive work.

The moral aspect of slavery is the most serious. Slavery proved in the end one of the causes of the downfall of Rome. After the cessation of Roman conquests, slavery fostered the cruel spirit bred by war and indifference to human suffering. It furnished most of the material for the most brutalising of all amusements—the gladiatorial combats. Slavery inoculated society with a moral poison from which it never recovered. Men of culture superior to their masters, brought up once in freedom, enslaved by capricious fortune and unjust aggression, cut loose from the tempering traditions of home and the religion of their fathers and made the menials of a people whom they despised, were a dangerous element in society. Their revenge was to corrupt their overlords. They pandered to their vices, and sought new and exciting debaucheries for jaded masters. It was forbidden them to exercise moral discretion : *nec turpe est quod dominus iubet*. The plays of Menander, Plautus, and Terence show us how slaves helped their masters, young and old, in immorality. It was no unusual thing for a master to have a sort of harem among his younger female slaves, for the slave-girl had no protection against his lust. Even Roman matrons were known to stoop to shame with their slaves. The most baneful influence was in the training of youth. Children were brought up in an unhealthy atmosphere in which they saw the reckless conduct of their parents, and were committed to slave tutors whom they could not respect, and who were indifferent to the morals and character of their pupils. Among the younger slaves the sons of the house found half-brothers.

The Stage

The amusements of this period were not elevating. The stage proved a degrading factor. Drama had its origin in Greece in religion, and Greek tragedy is still an unspent moral force. None were found to take up the mantle of an Aeschylus, a Sophocles, or a Euripides. The old political Comedy culminated in Aristophanes. Upon the extinction of political life followed the Middle Comedy, and finally the New Comedy, or Comedy of manners, represented by Philemon and Menander, of which Mahaffy says, ' a more *mesquin* and frivolous society has never been brought upon the stage than Attic New Comedy.' Before Rome lost her earnestness, tragedy appealed to her by giving satisfaction to her ethical sympathies, and by its didactic and oratorical qualities. The taste for comedy came in about the time of the second Punic war. The comedies of Plautus and Terence, *fabulae palliatae*, were translations or adaptations of the frivolous Attic New Comedy. Here we are not concerned with the literary value, but with the moral effects of these plays. Plautus in the ease and security which succeeded the great war appealed to the craving for unrestrained enjoyment of pleasure. He liked new ways, manners and luxury. He does not inculcate nor encourage immorality, but at the best he is morally indifferent. ' It is rather in the absence of any virtuous ideal than in positive incitements to vice, that the Plautine comedy may be called immoral.' [1] Terence in his urbane style set before his audience a refined, good-mannered, and cultivated society, in which the motto is ' to step aside is human.' Hence a kindly indulgence to weakness, a light-hearted tolerance of vice, a pervading sentimentality. In the *fabulae palliatae* gods and men are alike degraded for amusement : scheming vice is applauded ; the virtuous girl ensnared by the clever lover.

[1] Sellar. *Rom. Poets of the Repub.*, p. 194.

The stock characters are the *meretrix blanda*, the *leno*, the parasite, the sensual old man, the unprincipled father and son enamoured of the same courtesan, the cheating slave, the braggadocio. After Terence a further decline in drama was caused by the exhaustion of the Greek materials, by concession to the growing passion for coarseness, by the loss of mutual sympathy between poet and people, by the decay of healthy public life. The result was the rise of the *fabula togata* in which the scene was transferred from Athens to Rome, with a lowered moral tone and more prominence given to women. A further degradation was the displacement of comedy by the revival, in literary form, in the time of Sulla, of the Atellan farce which abounded in coarse jokes and obscene gesticulation Even this gave place in the closing Republic and early Empire to worse—the *Mimus*—which came in as an after-play, but in the Empire was put upon the stage by itself. It gratified the basest propensities of the populace ; ' its plots were in general of an obscene character, especially seduction, scenes of adultery, cheating of husbands or fathers or persons easily imposed upon.' [1] The *mimae* (female performers) were almost nude. The *Mimus* received literary treatment from Laberius and Publilius Syrus ; the latter's *sententiae* are celebrated. This rapid decline of the stage corresponded with a general moral decline.

Amphitheatre

This debased stage was not sufficiently immoral and realistic for the Romans. Their crass nature found an outlet in the spectacles of the amphitheatre—the most shocking form in which any race has ever found amusement. While Rome has everywhere left witnesses of the blessings she conferred upon the world, ruins of amphitheatres in dead cities rise up in judgment against her. By a terrible

[1] Teuffel, *Hist. of Rom. Lit.*, i. 9.

irony her greatest material monument extant is the Colosseum. Rome lost her moral balance in successful campaigns : bloodshed was congenial, and when it ceased abroad she sought it in bloody civil wars. The Romans were unfitted to settle down again to the tranquil affairs of life ; they sought excitement and recreation by witnessing in cold blood the agonies of men and animals. Gladiatorial games were introduced in 264 B.C. under the pretext of religion : they were defended as a means of sustaining the military spirit, like duels in Germany. Gladiatorial shows were given at the public games and at the banquets of the rich. The combatants were slaves, criminals or captives ; later even freemen entered the arena, so great was the glory of successful combat. Exhibitors vied with each other in the numbers exposed to slaughter. Caesar put 320 pairs up at once ; Agrippa caused 700 pairs to fight in one day in Berytus ; under Augustus 10,000 fought ; Titus, ' the darling of the human race,' put up 3000 ; Trajan amused Rome for 123 days by exhibiting 10,000 captives in mutual slaughter. Rome's holiest, the vestals, had seats of honour in the arena. Claudius liked to witness the contortions of dying gladiators. The fallen gladiator was dragged by a hook through *Death's Gate*, there stripped, and, if yet alive, despatched. So keen was the thirst for these shows that Augustus and Tiberius were obliged to restrict the numbers exposed. The *lanistae* who kept gladiatorial schools drove a thriving trade. To witness the murder of men in cold blood grew monotonous, and the Romans always loved novelty in their pleasures. Pompey introduced combats of men with wild beasts : it gave more excitement to witness an unarmed man, after his strength was exhausted, torn to pieces by a lion or tiger. Every excess of cruelty and novelty was tried. Sometimes animals were chained together to fight, or a criminal dressed in a wild beast's skin was thrown to a maddened bull. Under Titus 5000 animals perished in a day in the Colosseum. Domitian discovered another novelty in compelling an army of dwarfs to fight. Even female gladiators, especially under Nero and Domitian, appeared on the arena. Blindfolded men fought to the amusement of the crowd.

The passion spread in the provinces, especially Spain, Africa, the East and Gaul : gladiatorial shows were never so popular in Greece, except in Corinth—a Roman colony. Augustine testifies to their fatal fascination for Christian converts. That the gladiatorial games 'continued for centuries, with scarcely a protest, is one of the most startling facts in moral history.'[1] The evil influence contaminated all existence. It unfitted men for the pursuits of peaceful life, encouraged cruel passions, created a demand for excitement, destroyed the idealistic by fostering extreme realism, exterminated all sense of disgust, rendered society callous to the misery and discomforts of their fellows, and so hindered the embryonic sense of brotherhood and humanity.

Position of Women

In domestic life and the relations of the sexes we find shocking irregularity. In Greece woman never occupied the high place she was assigned among the Jews and the Romans. Although the Greek believed in monogamy he never held his wife in high honour. 'We have,' says Demosthenes, '*hetairai* for our pleasure, concubines for the ordinary requirements of the body, wives for the procreation of lawful issue and as confidential domestic guardians.' The Greek was not attracted to home life : he preferred the company of men out of doors and that of *hetairai*. These *hetairai*, unlike the modest and ignorant Greek wife, were women of culture and refinement who could talk intelligently on art and politics, could sing and

[1] Lecky, i. 271.

make pretty jokes. No shame attached to any connection between married or single men and these courtesans. Pericles was not ashamed of his Aspasia. Some of the noblest creations of art, including statues of goddesses, were copies of courtesan models. It is remembered against Socrates how he visited Theodota in the company of his disciples. Men would appear in the law-courts to contest the possession of a *hetaira*, and we read of a disputed *hetaira* being assigned to both claimants for a day each. One orator obtained a favourable verdict by exhibiting the nude charms of Phryne. Public opinion regarded these alliances as a thing morally indifferent. Statesmen were not ashamed to appear at the table of the noted Phryne. The state was more hallowed to the Greeks than the sanctities of love. The life of the Greek wife was one of seclusion, free from temptations, and protected by public opinion, while abundant provision was made for the irregular passions of husbands. Thucydides considers that wife best who is least spoken about either for her virtues or her vices by men. Fidelity and obedience, with indulgence to men's infidelity, are their chief virtues. The courtesan was sought on account of her physical beauty, her easy manners, and as a companion to take the place the Greek denied to his wife.[1]

In Rome the position of women was better. The Roman wife was as much in her husband's power as in Greece. But she was also his companion and could preside at his table. The Romans threw around marriage all the sanctities of religion. Woman gradually arose to a position of equality with her husband. The old form of marriage, ' in hand,' gave place to the free marriage of the later Republic and Empire, whereby the wife became independent of her husband. After the restraints of ages

---

[1] Mahaffy attributes the Greek lack of moral sense chiefly to three causes: (1) low condition of women, and absence of their moral influence ; (2) exposition of children ; (3) slavery.—*Survey of Greek Civilisation*, 217 ff.

there supervened a gross laxity of morals. Divorce became very common. Men could put away their wives for the slightest cause, and women could as easily divorce their husbands. Seneca tells us of women who marked their chronology by the names of their husbands rather than by the consuls. Marriage lost its sanctity : it was lightly entered upon because easily annulled.[1]

Children

The estimation in which children are held is a fair index of the moral standard of a community. Among the Greeks and Romans children never were so precious as among the Jews. They regarded children from the utilitarian standpoint. While the *polis* stood children were essential to keep up the population and to supply soldiers. Children were a state rather than a private concern. The ancients, especially the Greeks, paid great attention to their education with a view to the service of the state : physical training was particularly emphasised. So much care is devoted in the systems of Plato and Aristotle to education that one might easily get the impression of the worth of children, but they are not esteemed for their own sake but for the future of the state. With the decay of political life and the rise of individualism, childlessness increased. Greeks and Romans discovered that while large families may be advantageous to the state, they are burdensome to parents : the duties of parenthood were neglected. The love of children for their own sake was not yet common. Economic considerations suggested a restriction of the population. The cost of living rose, and was partly met

[1] Cato gave his wife to his friend Hortensius, and married her again after his friend's death. Cicero divorced Terentia partly to get another dower, and divorced his next wife because she was not sufficiently sorry for the death of Tullia. Augustus took Livia from her husband when she was three months pregnant. Divorce entailed no disadvantages. There are examples of men lending their wives to friends, or borrowing their friend's wife for a period.

then, as now, by a reduction in the family. The taste for
luxury could not be gratified with a large family to support.
The increasing childlessness and disinclination to marriage
seriously disconcerted statesmen. Augustus in vain offered
considerable advantages to a father of three children, showing that this number in a family was rare. When domestic
ties were relaxed, especially in Rome, to have progeny
proved inconvenient to loose amours, to the support and
gratification of mistresses, or to frequent change of wives.
Several social considerations encouraged childlessness. An
unencumbered man could maintain higher social rank,
could bestow richer gifts, could walk the streets accompanied by a larger host of clients, and attract the parasites
who gave their services in order to be named in his will.
It is difficult to say how far *paiderastia* contributed to
childlessness.

Abortion

It was not till the coming of Christianity that the foetus
was regarded as a creature with rights. Abortion was
widespread in all classes among the Greeks and Romans.
Among the Jews child-murder and voluntary abortion
were forbidden on pain of death. With the Greeks and
Romans it was a matter of discretion. Means of abortion,
apparently harmless to the mother, were in everyday use.
The motives for abortion were poverty in the lower classes,
and in the higher sensuality, and the desire for indulgence
or the avoidance of pain or fear of disfigurement. 'No
law in Greece or in the Roman Republic, or during the
greater part of the Empire, condemned it.' Plato and
Aristotle recommended it. Abortion was practised even
by parents who wished children, because they could easily
secure foundlings.

Exposition of Children and Infanticide

The general low esteem of children is further proved by **the** almost general practice of infanticide and exposition of newly-born children, and by the occasional sale of them by poor parents. In Greece, where legislators aimed **at** checking the growth of the population as at Rome they aimed at increasing it, the killing of children, or their exposure, was quite usual. The Greeks liked small families. All weakling and deformed children were killed, or exposed to death or to the mercies of the public. Aristotle recommended this as a means, along with abortion, of restricting the birthrate, and in Plato's *Republic* the children of old or wicked parents, as also illegitimate and deformed children, are to be exposed. In Rome an ancient law required fathers to bring up all males and the first daughter, but allowed the exposure or destruction of misshapen births. But this law was more honoured in the breach than in the observance, as we find exposition common especially among the poor, the upper classes having recourse to abortion. Infanticide did not, however, grow so serious until the era of the closing Republic and the early Empire ; at least our sources of that date contain ampler reference to the practice.

It was sanctioned on the Roman stage. It has been remarked that the same man, Chremes, who in the *Heauton timoroumenos* uttered the words ' I am a man and regard nothing human as alien to me,' charged his wife to kill her child if it was a girl. It was apparently quite usual for a husband when starting on a journey and leaving a pregnant wife to leave orders for her to destroy it if a girl. The wife of Chremes was too womanly to kill, and so exposed her child—a worse fate. Apuleius tells of a father giving this too common command on his departure, which his wife secretly disobeyed. **One of the most striking** documents of antiquity is **an** autograph letter [1] from

[1] *Oxyrh. Pap.*, iv. 744 (or Witkowski, *Ep. priv.*, No. 58, or Deissmann,

Egypt addressed by Hilarion to his wife Alis, charging
her to destroy the child soon to be born if it proved to be
a girl. Seneca in *De Ira* says, 'we destroy monstrous
births ; infants also if weak or misshapen we drown. It
is not anger but reason to separate the useless from the
healthy.' Tertullian says, 'how many among you, even
in the magistracy, destroy your children : you drown them,
or expose them to die of cold or hunger, or to be eaten of
dogs.' Suetonius tells that upon the death of Germanicus
mothers exposed their infants as a sign of grief.

Infanticide was in every way more merciful than exposition by putting an end to the little one's sufferings and
sparing it later infamy. Exposition created a numerous
class of foundlings in whom there was a large traffic. Some
made a business of collecting foundlings, some to maim
the little ones for purposes of mendicancy, some to rear
them as slaves, some to use the males for *paiderastia*
and the girls for prostitutes ; or witches picked them up
to use their brains or bones for magical purposes. Chremes,
above mentioned, reproached his wife for having exposed
instead of killing her baby-girl, thereby abandoning her
to some old witch or to become a slave or prostitute.

Vice

Vice found congenial soil in the Graeco-Roman world.
The more men were divorced from serious public concerns,
the more room there was for self-indulgence : men having
not yet found their place as individuals, abused their new
liberty as licence. Greece had a tremendous influence
on the morals of the age. The characteristic Greek virtue
was *moderation* in all things—including vice. Greek
culture and refinement was for Greek gentlemen, not for
their wives. The low estate of Greek wives and the

Light, etc., p. 155, or Milligan, *Greek Papyri*, No. 12), ἐὰν πολλὰ πολλῶν
τέκηις ἐὰν ἦν ἄρσενον ἄφες, ἐὰν ἦν θήλεα ἔκβαλε, l. 8 ff.

D

blandishments of the *hetairai* could not conduce to sexual purity. The easy philosophy of the Cyrenaics and Epicurus was used as an excuse to gloss over sensuality, for the Greeks and Romans were as skilled as some modern societies in inventing fair names for foul things. It was the proud boast of a Roman writer that for 520 years no divorce took place in Rome ; 'but here as ever *corruptio optimi pessima*. Witty ladies of loose morality were an essential of ' society.' Infidelity in married life became frightfully common and received but slight condemnation. It was hardly any disgrace to pay court to or support a mistress. The loose amours of the gods were put forward as justification of immoralities. Society was indulgent— ' to step aside is human' was its motto.

Paiderastia

The most shocking vice was *paiderastia*. Some of the best names in Greek history are mentioned as addicted to this unnatural love, *e.g.* Parmenides, Sophocles, Aristotle. Socrates, though free from it, speaks lightly about it. And when Plato speaks of *Eros* or Love he refers to the passion for boy favourites ; he even idealised this Eros in the *Symposium* and the *Phaedrus*. Some philosophers had so doubtful a reputation in this respect that parents would not send their sons to them. Male prostitution became as common in Greece as female. Formal contracts were entered into between lovers. The state derived revenue from a tax on this unnatural vice.

Paiderastia, at first unknown to the Romans, in the second century B.C. seems to have become general. The Roman poets—except the licentious Ovid—confess to such love ' with a shamelessness beyond belief.' Some of the greatest Romans were guilty, as Julius Caesar, Antoninus, Hadrian and Trajan. ' On the whole this vice exhibits a grosser aspect among the Romans than

among the Greeks; with the latter it had often a
dash of spiritualism mixed up with it; the sin, so to
speak, was crowned and veiled with the flowers of sentiment and of a devotion amounting to sacrifice. But in
the Romans it came out in its naked filth, so common
and so grossly disgusting as to defy and reject all excuse.' [1]
This awful sin encouraged celibacy and made its disastrous contribution to the depopulation of the Empire.
Its moral effects who will dare to measure ?

There are yet other sombre colours that might be added
to this gloomy picture—the frequency of suicide, the evils
of chariot-racing, gambling, stupid public and private
extravagance, the audacious indecency of the pantomime,
the licence of the Floralia with its races of nude courtesans,
the *naumachiae* (naval battles fought by gladiators and
criminals for the amusement of the public), lewd pictures
and suggestive decorations.

(b) Better Side

We turn with relief from this sickening picture to view
a better side of ancient society, and note the rise and
spread of higher and purer moral ideas. The good and
true found advocates and received expression even in
this sinful age. The Graeco-Roman world was not as
corrupt as the Roman Court, else it had been a cesspool
of iniquity. There has never been a long truce in any
period in the conflict of good and evil. We have already
noted some powerful factors conducive to moral confusion.
Without exaggeration, the period before and after the
advent of Christianity was the greatest crisis in world-
history. Old landmarks were swept away; a thousand
interests demanded allegiance from men in a state of
indecision. The purely objective phase of history was
waning and the subjective had appeared with its pain

[1] Döllinger. *The Gentile and the Jew*, ii. 289.

and questioning. The ideals by which we condemn the ancients were as yet in embryonic form. We must not overlook what a blessing it is to be born into a society with high ideals already established. Men form ideals before they endeavour to realise them : they taste the bitterness of sin before they thirst for righteousness. The history of man is largely an inconstant striving to reach ideals. Besides, if our middle and hard-working classes were as silent in literature as those of Greece and Rome, what a one-sided picture we should have of the morals of this age. It might then appear as if our divorce courts were as busy as churches, and society scandals as common as the unrecorded virtues of toiling thousands. Some old vices have almost passed away, but new vices have arrived. The Graeco-Roman age has one eternally true lesson to teach, viz. that morality cannot long thrive among any people without the sanctions and incentives of religion.

Amelioration of Slavery

There were many alleviations of slavery, and brutal masters were in the minority. At Athens abused slaves could take refuge at an asylum or an altar. If Aristotle justified slavery as necessary and natural, he recommended masters to treat their slaves like human beings. All philosophers, in fact, inculcated humanity. But Zeno and the Stoics struck at the root of slavery, declaring all men are by nature equal, virtue alone making any difference. In Xenophon's *Economics* the husband charges the young wife to treat her slaves well and care for those that are ill. Epicurus was noted for his kindness to slaves, admitting them into partnership in his studies.

In the Roman Republic protests were raised against inhumanity. Many masters lived on terms of warm personal friendship with their slaves. Cicero highly esteemed his Tiro, as his brother did Alexis. The slave was allowed to acquire a *peculium*, or private property, from which he frequently purchased his freedom. For good conduct or merit manumission was easy. A hard-working slave in the days of Cicero might expect freedom in six years. In the civil wars slaves rendered signal services to their masters, and proved faithful in hopeless disaster. Many slaves occupied high positions of trust as physicians, tutors, private secretaries, philosophic advisers. Under the Empire the position of slaves was very much improved and the caprice of masters restrained. The *lex Petronia* of Nero (or Augustus ?) forbade the selling of slaves for combat with wild beasts except on the authority of a judge. Claudius granted freedom to exposed sick slaves, and pronounced death by their masters' hands as murder. Nero appointed a praetor to hear complaints of slaves against their masters, to punish cruelty, and to see that slaves had enough food. Probably in his reign (or in that of Claudius) the emperor's statue became an asylum for abused slaves. Domitian interdicted the mutilation of slaves for immoral purposes. Hadrian put an end to the *ergastula*. The Antonines abolished the right of killing slaves, forbade their sale for the amphitheatre, appointed officers in the provinces to hear their complaints, and in other respects greatly ameliorated slavery.

A more potent factor than legislation was the extension of a humaner public opinion. Tacitus tells of the popular feeling against the wholesale execution of the slaves of Pedanius, which, though unavailing at that time, caused that to be the last of such outrages. Pages could be filled with citations from Seneca on the duty of kindness to slaves, and advice to treat them as friends and not to despise them. He tells us that cruel masters were insulted on the streets (*De Clem.*, i. 18. 3). Dio of Prusa denounced slavery as contrary to nature.

There were thus many ameliorations of slavery which made it more humane than its modern counterpart. If a

slave-marriage was not legally recognised it was sanctioned
by custom and accepted by jurisconsults. The concession
of the *peculium* and easy enfranchisement took the bitterness out of slavery. Enfranchisement had been carried
to such a pitch that Augustus restricted it by legislation.
Several distinguished authors rose from the slave class.
If slavery proved a curse it was not an unmixed evil;
in two important aspects it proved a great blessing. First,
from among its ranks were recruited the dwindling ranks
of free society—that is, freedmen gradually took the place
of the ancient middle classes and so acted as a steadying
influence in society. True, many scoundrels must have
been freed, but also a vast number of worthy men who (in
slavery) had learned habits of industry and regularity.
The freedmen thus partly filled a vacuum. Secondly, as
the free classes were recruited from among slaves, and more
had servile blood in their veins, the way was opened to
the spread of humaner ideas and to the sense of human
brotherhood. This element did much to shatter ancient
prejudices.

Protests against Gladiatorial Shows

One of the most curious facts about the amphitheatre
is the fascination it exerted upon all classes for centuries,
and then the suddenness with which, after the death of
Telemachus, the combats ceased. But men had not
remained until then altogether unconscious of the wickedness of the arena. Augustus and Tiberius tried in vain
to restrain the passion for the amphitheatre. The Cynic,
Demonax, when it was proposed to introduce gladiatorial
shows into Athens, told the people 'you must first throw
down the altar of Pity.' Cicero testifies that some regarded
the amphitheatre as cruel and inhuman, but takes up a
hesitating position himself.[1] Seneca most vehemently

[1] 'Crudele gladiatorum spectaculum et inhumanum nonnullis videri solet,
haud scio an ita sit ut nunc fit.'—*Tusc. Disp.*, ii. 17, 41.

denounces the combats. Even Petronius condemned them. Junius Mauricus, when the emperor remonstrated with him for having denied to the people of Vienne the right to celebrate the games, replied, 'Would to Heaven it were possible to abolish such spectacles even at Rome.' Aurelius offended the populace by requiring the combatants to fight with blunted swords. Plutarch went so far as to condemn combats of animals. Only Christianity was able finally to abolish gladiatorial shows.

Domestic Virtue

In spite of the corruption of the age, domestic virtue was by no means rare. Woman has never found a better advocate than Euripides. He introduced to the Greeks a love with something of modern sentiment. He asks why a man should demand a fidelity from his wife of which he is himself incapable. Socrates and the Minor Socratics contributed to the elevation of women, asserting their capability for equal virtue with men. Isocrates emphatically condemns the liberties taken by husbands. The principal progress made in both Greece and Rome was the demand for the same continence on the part of the man as the woman. The high Roman ideal of the *mater-familias* never became obsolete. And no ancient history can show so many noble women as that of Rome —women who were the companions and compeers of their husbands, their partners in their labours and cares, their support in disgrace and death. Mutual love was quite common, as we learn from literature and inscriptions. Pliny's marriage with his third wife Calpurnia was a real love-match, as is proved by their love-letters. Even Ovid writes in touching words to his absent wife, 'I address thee absent; my lips name thee alone. Never night and never day comes to me without [the thought of] thee.' The inscription containing the so-called *laudatio Turiae* (first century B.C.), is a valuable document. In it a Roman husband who had lived forty-one years with his Turia tells of her fidelity, her patience, her industry, and laments as his greatest unhappiness his surviving her. The wife of Seneca tried by suicide to depart with her husband, but her wounds were dressed by friends and her wan face ever after testified to her devotion. Best known is the story told by Pliny of Arria who braced her husband to carry out the sentence of suicide by plunging the dagger in her own breast, and handing it to him with the words, 'non dolet, Paete.' It would demand too much space to dwell upon the virtues of Roman women as recorded in literature and inscriptions. The latter source, especially, is convincing testimony that female virtue and chastity were never higher. It was the virtue of men that needed improvement. The moralists and philosophers of the Empire were unanimous in requiring equal virtue from men. Plutarch's high ideal of marriage is well known. The Stoics made men and women equals in virtue. Seneca protests loudly against the injustice of men rewarding woman's fidelity with infidelity: 'You know it is injustice to demand fidelity from your wife while you seduce another's wife: you know that you ought no more to have relations with a concubine than your wife with an adulterer.' Comic poets, like Plautus, point out the absurdity of divorcing a wife if she goes into town without her husband's knowledge, while the husband enjoys impunity in relations with a mistress, and asks: 'If an honourable woman is content with one husband, why should a husband not be satisfied with one wife ? If husbands were punished for maintaining mistresses as guilty wives are divorced, there would be more wifeless husbands than there are now husbandless wives.' Epictetus calls that man an adulterer who, on looking at a fair woman, cries, 'happy he who possesses her! happy her husband!' Thus the moralists condemned all indulgence outside wedlock, and called upon the man to rise to the height of womanly virtue. Musonius wrote a book on marriage in which he condemned all indulgence except for procreation. Plutarch wrote a book on the virtues of woman, and one on precepts for the married life.

Virginity was held in high esteem. In Athens the Parthenon, or Virgin temple, was the finest religious building in the city. In Rome virgins were sometimes credited with supernatural powers, and the vestals were granted unusual privileges.

Women were now given a better education to fit them to be companions to their husbands. They exercised tremendous influence for good and for evil in public affairs. We read of them accompanying their husbands on missions to the provinces, attending reviews of troops, giving advice in political matters. Many were notorious like Cleopatra, Clodia, Messalina, Agrippina, Poppaea, Quadratilla. Others are examples of true womanhood, as Turia, the Cornelias, Porcia, Seneca's mother Helvia and his wife Paulina, Marcia, the two Arrias, Plotina, Mallonia, Calpurnia.

Care of Children

That children were loved in that age is abundantly proved by inscriptions, the playthings found in their tombs, and by notices in ancient authors. That the love for children was extending seems evident from the numerous protests against abortion, exposition, and infanticide, from the greater care demanded by moralists in the matter of their education, and the importance of example. The inherent charm and worth of children were never forgotten. It was only, however, with Christianity that children came to their rights. Hippocrates in the oath to be taken by physicians makes them swear not to assist at abortion. Musonius condemns abortion and exposition: 'What more lovely sight,' says he, 'than to see a father and mother sur-

y numerous offspring. No solemn procession
of the gods, no sacred dance presents such a
ectacle as a numerous choir of little ones gam-
ith love and reverence around their parents.'
Tacitus, with a thrust at his countrymen, says the Germans
regard it as a crime to limit the population or destroy
their offspring. Epictetus observes that animals rear their
young with tender care. Seneca calls it a crime and an
injustice to expose children to the doubtful mercies of the
public, and maintains that parents are morally bound to rear
their offspring. Paulus, the jurist, regards it as assassination to kill or expose a child 'against the voice of nature
and of conscience.' Ovid employs his bitterest sarcasm
against mothers who give poison to creatures not yet
born in order to preserve their breast against premature
wrinkles. The theatre held up the horrors and dangers
of exposition.

A primary concern for moralists was the training of, and
example set to, children. Favorinus in an impassioned
passage requests mothers to suckle and train their own
children. 'What is this new kind of motherhood or
unnatural semi-motherhood which consists in committing
the fruit of one's womb to strangers to nourish ? ' The
value of a good education with competent and exemplary
teachers was not overlooked. Domestic example was,
however, regarded as the most potent factor. Seneca
requires the father to set a good example to his wife, his
sons and daughters, and all the household. Juvenal
warns fathers not to permit any obscene sight or word in
a house where a child is ; let mistresses and loose songs
be prohibited ; let the sight of your son stay you from
committing the sin you meditated—'great respect is due
to infancy.' Quintilian says 'we ourselves ruin the morals
of our children. . . . We like to hear them pronounce an
obscene word ; we approve by a smile or a kiss words
worthy of the shameful Alexandrine books : they see our

mistresses and darlings.   Every meal resounds with
obscene songs ; children see only things one would blush
to speak of.'   Tacitus and Pliny likewise demand moral
education for children.

The tenderness with which the deaths of children are
treated on the monuments is very modern.   In a classic
gem, Lucretius feels the sadness of separation when ' no
longer shall joyful home receive thee, nor peerless wife,
nor shall sweet children run to snatch the first kiss.'

Protests against Vice

Prostitution was indirectly inveighed against by ancient
moralists as a public menace and a danger to married life.
It was also included in all attacks upon slavery, for slave-
owners there found most of their victims.   In the comic
poets the trade of procurer is branded as loathsome.   One
of the reasons given against exposition was that it supplied
girls for prostitution.   To Dio Chrysostom [1] belongs the
honour of being the first to attack prostitution as an
institution legalised by law.   The passage (too long to
cite) is marked by an earnest moral tone, by a quite
modern spirit, and by a stern refusal to entertain any
reasons for the necessity of this ' devouring ulcer.'

The moral consciousness began to assert itself against
paiderastia.   Plato tried to wean men away from it by
contrasting the beauty of the ideal heavenly Eros with
the crass Eros, and in his last book, the *Laws*, he sternly
condemns male lovers.   Socrates had, at least by his
example in keeping himself pure, condemned his countrymen's worst vice.   In the *Symposium* of Xenophon (?),
paiderastia appears as a disgraceful practice.   Epicurus
denounced it, and Lucian removes the mask of sentimentality to expose its utterly sensual character.   Plutarch

[1] Or. vii. (*Euboean*, or the *Hunter*) 133, v. Denis, *Hist. des théories et des
idées morales*, ii. 149.

lauds Agesilaus for refusing to gratify a passion for a boy Megabetes—an act which Maximus of Tyre considers as worthier of praise than the heroism of Leonidas at Thermopylae. Seneca describes in terms of contempt these epicenes ; Cicero denies the presence of any ideal element in such connections, affirming them to be altogether carnal.

Lack of Moral Enthusiasm in Pagan Religion

The student of pagan morality is impressed by the failure of pagan religions to exert any potent influence upon morals. A man's religion did not elevate his conduct. The truth is, that the morality of the gods was lower than that of their worshippers. The gods were gradually improved by their worshippers, but not *vice versa*. Morality was thus heavily handicapped and obliged to advance without the moral enthusiasm and incentive derived by us from religion. A religious man was not necessarily moral in his conduct—a fact not unknown still, but so rare as to arrest attention and appear incongruous. Such incongruity would be felt in that era by the Jews but not by the Greeks or Romans, who possessed not the Jew's zeal for righteousness. Hence some of the loftiest teachers of Greece lived what would seem to us immoral lives. Yet such teachers did not appear to their contemporaries moral monstrosities or hypocrites. Caesar was chief pontiff of Rome, yet he rejected immortality, was notorious for his connections with women, and reputed guilty of *paiderastia*. Some of the most devout worshippers in the temples of Eastern cults were the frail mistresses of Roman writers. The gods of the Graeco-Roman world never offered a moral dynamic to their devotees, and even smiled indulgently on human weakness. Sensualists justified their conduct by citing the examples of immorality among the denizens of heaven.

But man's innate moral sense can never be eradicated, however lethargic it may become. The moral sense was ever asserting itself among the Greeks and Romans. The question arose, 'What about the conduct of our deities?' Foucart has remarked of the Greeks, 'They were better men than their gods : it was not the gods who improved them, but they who improved and elevated their gods.' The expanding moral sense was shown by throwing overboard the gods, or by offering apologies and excuses for their conduct, or by branding the offensive stories of mythology as lies, or by explaining them as allegories of high moral truths. Allegory was the favourite method. Plato would banish Homer and Hesiod for telling unedifying lies about the deities. What were once only naturalistic rites were explained as symbols of spiritual truth.

Man's Moral Consciousness

One of the features of this age is the expanding consciousness of man's innate moral sense as a guide to conduct that imperiously calls for recognition. Greek philosophy spread the teaching of Socrates' *daimon*, or inward monitor, who presided as a restraining (but not initiating) power in his daily life. Platonism filtered down among the masses, instructing them that the soul in a previous state had seen the things of God, and was so impressed with the love of the true and the beautiful that, though enshrouded in the muddy vesture of decay, it recognised and yearned for the highest. It was universally recognised that virtue and vice were not identical, and that each man could tell which he ought to choose and which eschew. The Greek dramatists saw that any theory of Destiny as thwarting freewill subverts moral responsibility, and the Stoics also perceived that man to be responsible must be able to assert his freewill in moral choices in spite of their doctrine of fate. Socrates had already recognised that ' for positive truth there is no process : our knowledge of it is *immediate* or *instinctive*,' coming by feeling rather than by proof. ' His final test of the highest Truth is not dialectic : it is unassailable conviction, so soon to appear as the final criterium in Stoicism.'[1] This position was never henceforth lost to Greek thought. All schools rejected the uncertainty of probability offered by the sceptics. It was scarcely possible that all the world could be deceived as to a cleavage between good and evil, but this *consensus gentium* was only the register of the sense of right and wrong implanted in man. Cicero was perhaps the first to give definite expression to this inward consciousness in the famous words ' sunt enim ingeniis nostris semina innata virtutum, quae si adolescere liceret ipsa nos ad beatam vitam natura perduceret.' The truth of natural theology was not hidden ; Paul could declare ' God is angry : because what may be known about Him is plain to their inmost consciousness ; for He Himself has made it plain to them.'

Practical Sense

Another encouraging feature of this age is its earnest practical sense. This arose chiefly from three causes: (1) the impatience with further speculation for its own sake. The pursuit of truth as an end in itself had offered different solutions of the problem of the universe which a practical age looked upon as contradictions. They asked : what is the use of all this pursuit of knowledge ? Let us apply the knowledge we have acquired. (2) The times were full of perplexity, and men demanded some practical moral guide in the new order of things. (3) The advent of the Roman who was eminently utilitarian, and had no patience with speculation except as applied to

[1] Bussell, *School of Plato*. pp. 87, 88.

life, who desired a firm hold of realities. With the decline
of the city-state, and from the days of Socrates, a new
morality was arising—an ethical instead of a political.
The centre of gravity had shifted from the state to the
citadel of the heart, from politics to conduct. All the post-
Aristotelian schools abandoned speculation to offer guides
for conduct. This practical and personal tendency was
very favourable to the growth of morality.

Oneness of humanity

We note the growing conviction of the oneness of
humanity and the brotherhood of man. The Hebrew,
in spite of his exclusiveness, looked forward to the universal
kingdom of God upon earth. The Greek, although he
could conceive no perfect social life apart from the *polis*
(and was opposed equally to federation and to empire),
proved by his culture and language one of the greatest
universalising powers; the Roman, who occupied a unique
political position, best recognised the logic of events, and
by his law and administration united and fused the races.
The Empire first made possible a philosophy of history,
and suggested the writing of *universal* history. Asiatic and
European were more reconciled by Hellenism and by Roman
rule than they have ever been since, and racial antipathy
was at least no worse than at present. The Cynics were
harbingers of world-citizenship. Diogenes, asked to what
state he belonged, replied he was a world-citizen. They
regarded banishment as no evil; they would destroy all
states that men might live together without laws. The post-
Aristotelian schools, and especially the Stoics, furthered
unity by severing morality from politics; renouncing the
rights and the duties of nationality, they proclaimed a
citizenship of the world. After the fall of the *polis* the
universal city or republic became the ideal. Plutarch

thinks a good man can be at home anywhere because he
is nowhere a stranger.   Exile is not an evil,

> 'All places where the eye of heaven rests
> Are to a wise man ports and happy havens.'

Cicero loves to dilate upon the universal city or republic
to which all men as such belong. Universal law is contrasted
with the law of convention and statute.[1]   Only the infinite
heaven is the boundary of our world : the same God
punishes transgressors according to the same universal
law.   Before the laws of nature all men are equal, and all
are alike humbled before death.   Not nationality nor
race, but virtue alone makes any difference among men.
All had shared in the misery and poverty caused by the
Roman conquests.   The large numbers of slaves and the
increasing influence of freedmen hastened the faith in
brotherhood.   The many with servile blood in their
veins, or who had memories of bad treatment themselves,
favoured humaner ideas.   The Virgilian sentiment would
find many an echo in that day, 'non ignara mali miseris
succurrere disco.'   Only under the Empire could the
oneness of humanity be fully realised, or become an article
of faith.[2]   Then practically the whole world was under
the rule of one man, and looked to one centre of government.   Thus Statius could say 'terrarum leges, foedera
mundi,' and Ovid, 'the area of the Roman *city* and *globe*
is identical.'[3]   The retreat from the civic to the inner
life of man was the discovery of common ground, as it is

---

[1] Cf. Cicero, *De Leg.*, i. 15, 43.   Nam haec nascuntur ex eo quod natura
propensi sumus ad diligendos homines, quod fundamentum iuris est.

[2]   Haec est in gremium victos quae sola recepit,
Humanumque genus communi nomine fovit,
Matris non dominae ritu ; civesque vocavit
Quos domuit, nexuque pio longinqua revinxit.
                              (CLAUDIAN, cited by MERIVALE.)

[3] That Rome had converted *orbis* into *urbs* was a favourite thought ; cf.
Rutilius (cited by Merivale).
Fecisti patriam diversis gentibus unam
Urbem fecisti quod prins *orbis* erat.

externals that most sharply divide men. Paul echoed a
Stoic sentiment when he said, ' He made of one every
nation of men.'

Humaner Ideas

The practical fruits of this faith in human brotherhood
are of great interest. The cosmopolitan spirit gave rise
in the Empire to gentler and humaner manners. Lecky [1]
attributes this chiefly to (1) the humanity of the Greeks,
who first revealed the beauty of the gentler virtues.
When Greek thought seized Rome it was the thought of
a cultured people freed from local sentiments. (2) The
breaking down of aristocratic bigotry and tyranny. The
empire took a terrible vengeance on the nobility. The
Civil Wars caused a reversal of fortune, and wealth was
passing into new quarters where old prejudices were of
no account. (3) The colonial influence, especially the concourse of strangers at Rome, the facilities for travel, the
blending of populations. Finally, the coming of provincial
emperors like the Flavians and the Antonines. (4) The
brotherhood fostered by the populous slave world. The
bigoted pan-Roman policy disappeared ; Roman citizenship was gradually extended until under Caracalla all the
free were granted citizenship. The brotherhood of man
in a universal republic was more actualised then than at
any time since. Only one bond was lacking—a universal
religion—which the imperial and the Oriental cults tried
in vain to supply. The universal religion was to come
from Galilee. The responsibilities and privileges of the
wonderful unity attained in the empire were not overlooked. A frequent thought is the equality of all in
presence of death, and by natural right. Men are by
nature akin. ' We are members of a great body. Nature
brought us forth as *relations* when she produced us from

[1] i. pp. 227 ff.

E

the same beginnings and for the same ends. She it is
that has inspired us with mutual love,' says Seneca.

Kinship with the Divine

The pagans had some sense of a greater bond—kinship
with the Divine, or the Divine sonship of all men. Aratus
and Cleanthes agreed in the sentiment approved by Paul,
'We are of His kinship.' Epictetus asks why a man
should not call himself a son of God as well as a citizen
of the world. Seneca speaks of the community of gods
and men as one. The kinship of man with deity was a
common tenet. Men were asked to be kind and tolerant
to each other, for we have all sinned. In condemning the
faults of others we should consider whether we are better
ourselves. 'Men were made for men; correct them or
support them.' We should not do to others what we
resent at their hands. We should not revenge an injury,
but 'when one is angry with you provoke him in return
with kindness. Some one has struck you, withdraw.' Men
should mutually support each other, and reach out a hand
to the perishing. Misfortune is itself a sufficient reason
for giving help. Almsgiving was quite common. For
several reasons to be mentioned in the next chapter there
arose a new sensitiveness to suffering.[1] It is impossible
to measure the moral influence of the Jew living in the
midst of the Greeks and Romans. While he drank his
cup of odium his neighbours cannot have been indifferent
to the power of a moral life. The 'God-fearers,' impressed
by the practical morality of Judaism, became examples of
morality to others.

Reviewing this period as a whole, we may discover some
general progress. If sin abounded it was not passed over

[1] 'La souffrance et les larmes avaient enfin instruit les maîtres de la vie
humaine, et les tristes leçons de l'expérience, sans abattre la fierté de
leur courage, leur inspiraient cette compassion aux misères d'autrui'
(Denis, *op. cit.*, ii. 66).

in silence. Despite many circumstances conducive to moral anarchy there was a moral awakening. The interest shifted from politics to ethics, from theory to practice. Moralists in no small number came forward to lash vice, to show it up as a disease, to hold up models of virtue to men. Morality undertook to do for ruined lives what religion does for us. Man's innate moral consciousness received clearer expression. Moralists began to teach that a morality based on external laws and traditions, and exercised from fear of the consequences of wrong-doing, was an inferior morality to the conduct of a pure heart that does right because of its love of right irrespective of hope of reward or fear of punishment. Personal responsibility became almost a dogma: the rights and the dignity of man as man were converted into motives of conduct. The attention to the personal life, to be mentioned in the next chapter, was sure to produce moral results.

CHAPTER IV

RELIGIOUS CONDITIONS OF THE GRAECO-ROMAN PERIOD

Tendebantque manus ripæ ulterioris amore.—VIRGIL.

Res ipsa, quae nunc religio Christiana nuncupatur, erat apud antiquos, nec defuit ab initio generis humani, quousque Christus veniret in carnem, unde vera religio, quae jam erat coepit appellari Christiana.
                                                                AUGUSTINE.

L'humanité cherche l'idéal ; mais elle veut que l'idéal soit une personne ; elle n'aime pas une abstraction. Un homme, incarnation de l'idéal, et dont la biographie pût servir de cadre à toutes les aspirations du temps, voilà ce que demandait l'opinion religieuse.
                                                                RENAN.

I. RELIGIOUS DESTITUTION

IN studying the religious life of the Graeco-Roman period one is first struck by its religious destitution and by the earnest strivings after a new and universal religion. The Gospel of Jesus could not have come at a better time to find men in a serious mood. Men were living in a dangerous transition stage—between collectivism and individualism, between a cramping *polis* and a universal state, between a political and a personal-ethical religion, between the religion of nature and that of revelation. More light was demanded than nature and reason could supply. A crisis in religious life occurred when the idea of a strictly local god was shattered, and with it the traditional cult and national faith. A universal deity could not be enthroned in a day. The worships of Greece and Rome left men in a helpless spiritual plight : they had no message for the individual heart, no strength to impart to the fainting spirit, no response to make to the craving for salvation.

The gods who could not keep pace with the march of their worshippers were abandoned and derided. It is perilous when men turn to scorn what they have long revered. The collapse of nationalism, the great social upheavals, the rise of individualism and therewith the emergence of an anxious personality, the intermixture of nations and races, the expansion of the human mind created new religious conditions. The value of the individual as he stood in the bewildering light of his personality suggested new needs. The god whose cult was arranged by the state for the state must give place to a God who could hold personal intercourse with human hearts. When a system that had given beauty and dignity to every phase of social life was overthrown, morality could not well thrive. The religion of the fathers being dead, man might for a time imagine it possible to live without a God, but must soon become disillusioned.

The Graeco-Roman world was heavy-laden. One recalls the epigram of Gibbon that to the politician all religions were equally useful, to the populace equally true, and to the philosophers equally false.[1] Greek Rationalism arose to explain away the gods and destroy their power. Some discovered the origin of religion in the crafty wisdom of statesmen. Euhemerism represented the ancient gods as merely deified men. Others regarded them as only names or personifications of natural processes. Scepticism asserted for each the right to do what was pleasing in his own eyes. Certainty was unattainable, and no better light than probability was offered.

Fatalism

As a result of nature-religions, blind necessity, known as Fate or Destiny, occupied a high place and survived

---

[1] Cf. the dictum of the pontifex Scaevola, 'tria genera tradita deorum: unum a poetis, alterum a philosophis, tertium a principibus civitatis' (Augustine, *De C. D.*, iv. 27).

faith in the old gods. Men stood helpless before these implacable forces. The gods were not able to overrule Destiny : they must carry out its decrees. No power was so inexorable as Fate which pursued a man's steps from cradle to grave. The gods might be placated, but Destiny had no ears. Dramatists and philosophers wrestled with the problem of moral responsibility in face of Fate until they gradually moralised the latter as the avenger only of guilt, or they cut the Gordian knot by practically identifying Destiny with God. Stoicism, a system of fatalism, so handled necessity and freewill that what was in one respect Destiny was in another Providence. The widespread astrological lore of the east was throughout fatalistic. Among the Romans no deity was so fervently adored as the capricious Fortuna.

Need of Religious Authority

The Greeks and Romans were left in dire need of an authority for the human spirit. They had lost all faith in their state religion. Of the Greek oracles some were quite silenced, others were still visited, but there was a marked diminution of inquirers. Roman augury and state divination were abandoned for more private methods. Roman ecclesiastics tried to retain the masses by introducing popular and emotional rites. But the Greeks and Romans never had gone to their priests for guidance. In the *Apology* Plato represents Socrates as making inquiries in regard to the response of the Delphic oracle from the politicians, the poets and the artisans, without mention of theologians. Dio of Prusa reckons as the sources of religious knowledge besides the *consensus gentium*, poets, legislators, sculptors, painters, and philosophers, but not priests. The priesthood of Greece and of Rome was almost entirely secular ; at any rate nothing contributed more to the religious destitution than the officials of religion. The religious teachers of Greece and Rome were laymen, somewhat on the analogy of the Hebrew prophets.

Formalism dominated in the maintenance of old religions. The educated laughed at the popular gods. They saw nothing wrong in attending religious ceremonies to gods in whom they did not believe. The masses were still pleased with the pomp of processions which relieved monotony ; but even the masses were not content with the old deities or forms : they sought additional help in foreign superstitions.

Taedium Vitae

The Graeco-Roman world came slowly to itself, through confusion and pain. Greece, in the Peloponnesian war, lost her once joyful faith and cast off the last restraints in the Alexandrian epoch. From the second Punic war Rome found herself religiously destitute. Self-indulgence following upon restraint brought its inevitable fruits, especially among the Romans. We can detect from the beginning of the first century B.C., until the end of the first A.D., a widespread disgust with life—a *taedium vitae.* A rising sense of personality brought pain. Self-indulgence was one of the many antecedents of satiety. While men were healthily occupied in public and national affairs, the cry of the individual was not heard. The misery and poverty caused by the Roman conquests and civil wars destroyed the basis of a regular social life. Idleness brought its concomitant—weariness. Amusements began to pall, and means of excitement were exhausted.[1] There was frequent *migratio* to avoid being bored, but in vain.[2]

---

[1] On a stone in the forum of Timgad one may still read—scratched upon the design of a vase of flowers over which hovers a bird—the six words of six letters each : Venari Lavari Ludere Ridere Occest (hoc est) Vivere.

[2] Cf. Hor., *Ep.* 1, ii. 27 :

Caelum non animum mutant qui trans mare currunt :
Strenua nos exercet inertia ; navibus atque
Quadrigis petimus bene vivere ;

and Seneca, *Ep.* 28.

The lords of the world who had less education and culture than the majority of their subjects were most oppressed *by* ennui.

> 'On that hard Pagan world disgust
>   And secret loathing fell :
> Deep weariness and sated lust
>   Made human life a hell.
> In his cool hall with haggard eyes
>   The Roman noble lay ;
> He drove abroad in furious guise
>   Along the Appian way ;
> He made a feast, drank fierce and fast,
>   And crowned his hair with flowers—
> No easier nor no quicker passed
>   The impracticable hours.'

Pessimism

Side by side with this taedium we find a deep-seated pessimism, from which only the Jew escaped. The gay light-hearted Greek, just because he was so sensitive to joy, was early overtaken by a melancholy which gradually deepened into unrelieved gloom and 'the weariness of living which proclaims itself in the graceful and fugitive utterances of the Anthology.' The thought frequently recurs that life is so full of trouble, so haunted by black destiny, so brief and uncertain, that death is preferable to life. 'Life and pain are akin,' says Menander. The eternal hope that ever lighted the path of the Hebrew was but a faint and flickering gleam for the Greek. Nowhere do we find despair expressed so pathetically and so sublimely as in Greek literature.

The Romans were infected by Greece with pessimism as with rationalism and scepticism. We find among Roman writers a large proportion of pessimists who are disgusted with the present, and see no hope for the future. They think that matters were never worse and cannot grow

worse. They contrast their own age with the good old
barbaric times. Historians and satirists dip their pens
in the blackest colours. Livy says ' we can neither cure
nor endure our vices.' Tacitus has no good to write of
his countrymen whom he compares with the Germans to
the disadvantage of the former. Pessimism finds expression throughout all the works of Seneca.[1] He saw his own
age weary with indulgence, without any strong moral
dynamic, feeling the *ennui* of satiety. ' Men complain
that the hours drag too slowly past,' he says. It would
demand too much space to speak of the pessimism of
Lucretius,[2] Lucan, Persius, Juvenal, Marcus Aurelius, and
other Romans.

The educated fled for refuge to philosophies that had
become religions. Some to Stoicism which sustained
countless souls and formed the loftiest characters. Some
to the lofty spiritualism of Plato, not undiluted with
elements from other schools. Some adopted Scepticism
and professed to have no convictions. Some fled to the
cold nihilism of Epicurus and Lucretius. Some turned
to the east to find a religion with a satisfying message.
The masses still perfunctorily performed the rites of a
national cult, the religious spirit of which was dead.
But they too had recourse to old private and native
superstitions that revived as the public religion died,
more especially to those of the Orient which swept as a
flood over the Roman Empire.

II. RELIGIOUS AWAKENING

On the other hand we find a religious awakening. Man's
religious nature was not dead. The practical tendencies

---

[1] Cf. **Omnis vita supplicium,** *Ad Polyb.* 9. 6., tota flebilis **vita,** *Ad Marciam* 11. 1.

[2] Deinde animi ingratam naturam pascere semper,
   Atque explere bonis rebus satiareque nunquam, . . .
   Nec tamen explemur vitai fructibus unquam.—*N. D.* 3, 1003 ff.

of the age are especially active in religious things.   Purely speculative theories were neglected because of the demand for what was of practical value for the moral and spiritual life.   The Graeco-Roman philosophies were converted into religions : ethics claimed great attention.   The age was too serious to trifle with speculation except as bearing on the spiritual questions of the day.   Faith succeeded scepticism.

Preaching

The ancient world resorted to preaching.[1]   Philosophy, which then covered the fields of morality and religion, led the way ; Porphyry demands that the aim of philosophy should be ' the salvation of the soul.'   Free speech was everywhere permitted.   Oratory, of which antiquity was more appreciative than we, followed this practical trend.   Philosophers avowed themselves to be physicians of the soul, ambassadors of God, whose functions were to cure diseased souls and produce conversions.   These missionary philosophers revived the spiritual truths of religious teachers of the past, and condensed them into a popular form to suit the age.   Some philosophers, like some theological professors nowadays, did not take the field themselves but reduced their philosophy to a practical training for those who were to carry the message farther afield.   Men went out from the lecture halls to preach self-examination and self-culture.   They brought forth things new and old.   In the burden of their preaching were many commonplaces—counsel to cultivate a good

[1] So prevalent was preaching that there was a recognised form of sermon. Norden speaks of ' des festen Bestandes eines Typenschatzes religiöser Rede, zu dessen Prägung der Orient und Hellas in gleicher Weise beigetragen haben, und den die synkretistischen Religionen der Kaiserzeit, einschliesslich das Christentum übernahm.   Das hellenisierte Judentum hat bei dieser Herübernahme von seiten des Christentums eine bedeutende Rolle gespielt ; die eigentliche Vermittlerin aber sowohl für Juden wie Christentum ist die Orientalisierte Stoa—vor allem Poseidonius—und der an sie anknüpfende Platonismus gewesen.'—*Agnostos Theos*, pp. 277-278 ; cf. pp. 129-134, also Bultmann, *Der Stil der Paulinischen Predigt.*

conscience, to act as if conscious that God sees all ; virtue
is its own reward, and is attainable by all ; sin is its own
punishment. They insisted on man's inherent dignity
and his ability to save himself by his will. They knew
no original sin. Life should be a contemplation of death,
so that men may die without fear.

This preaching was not confined to the upper circles.
One is more impressed by the enormous amount of popular preaching. By putting together notices and hints
in ancient authors we must conclude that there was a
great demand for and a corresponding supply of ' itinerant
homilists ' and mendicant monks. Preachers, like emperors, courted popularity with the masses. We read of
artisans forsaking their trade to join the ranks, as now
men join the Salvation Army.

The street-preaching and Salvation Army work was
started by the Cynics, who were exposed to as much
ridicule as any street-preachers have ever been. There
was a proportion of hypocrites among them ; men too
lazy to work donned the philosophic garb as a congenial
means of livelihood. Others offered the ignorant charms
and cures for which they took up a collection ; others
found in the profession a cloak for sensuality. These
very facts attest the popularity of Cynic preaching. The
caricatures of the Cynic were not undeserved, but the
counterfeit here as elsewhere points to the genuine. The
Cynic was mocked chiefly by cultured persons like the
witty Lucian, in whose eyes a Cynic was contemptible.
The Cynics delivered their message, wrote nothing, and
left it to their enemies to immortalise them. Again, there
is always a section of society who attribute to a cause only
the imperfections of its representatives : many can more
readily detect the hypocrisy of one preacher than appreciate
the earnestness of ninety-nine. Also some people are more
irritated by the collection necessary in a workaday world
than edified by the sermon. The Cynics and their kind

despised culture and left no volumes of sermons. We hold no brief for the Cynics, as Bernays does; but they, at any rate, observed that the masses needed a gospel and shepherds. They 'threw down the gauntlet to a materialised age.' 'This was a kind of moral ministry . . . the missionary movement of Cynicism was one of undoubted power and range.'[1] Demonax and Demetrius are the best representatives of the later Cynics. Both were noted for their courageous independence and their healthy moral influence, and they were both reverenced by their contemporaries. As Demonax walked along the streets he received tokens of affection from old and young. The Athenians honoured him with a public funeral, and for long decked with flowers a bench on which he used to sit.

Outside the Cynic school, but sharing some of their spirit, were other missionaries and lecturers, such as Plutarch, Musonius Rufus, Maximus of Tyre, Dio of Prusa (Chrysostom), and Apollonius of Tyana. Philosophy was to these men not a system of speculation but of salvation, 'medicine of the soul,' 'soul-culture.' Some of their sermons make dull reading for us, but their discourses were not trite in that epoch. The life of Apollonius by Philostratus is mainly a romance, but it is no less valuable as reflecting the ideal of a heathen preacher: 'the preaching at least of Apollonius seems to belong to the world of reality.' He is represented as in season and out of season holding up to his hearers the unattractive picture of their vices ; he settled public quarrels, and taught the people to pray as he conceived it : 'Thus I pray: Grant me, O Gods, the things due me.' He is credited with causing a religious revival in Rome in the time of Nero.

Another searching preacher was Musonius Rufus, of whom we have too few fragments. According to Epictetus he sifted would-be disciples, and 'he used to speak in such a manner that each of us who heard him supposed that

[1] Dill, p. 361.

some person had accused us to him : he so hit upon what
was done by us and placed the faults of every one before
his eyes.' His object was to produce conversions. He
inculcated forgiveness, kindness, purity, and self-
examination.

Epictetus belongs partly to the class of public preachers
and partly to that of private directors. He had a lofty
idea of his mission : ' the school of a philosopher is a
surgery. You ought not to go out of it with pleasure but
with pain, for you come there diseased.'

Brief mention should be made of the discourses of
Maximus of Tyre in which ' we have perhaps the nearest
approach in antiquity to our conception of the sermon.'
In reading him we are most impressed with a strange
blending of old and new, of spirituality and moral earnestness with a cult of the past. One of the most energetic
of ancient preachers was Dio of Prusa under Domitian and
Trajan. Converted in his exile he determined to reach
the needy masses. Every moral and spiritual idea that
he thought would elevate man above the life of the senses
he brought forward. He endeavoured to arouse men to
see their faults and to correct them, but, in Greek fashion,
he treated error as ignorance rather than rooted in the will,
hence, ' conversion must be effected, not by appeals to the
feelings, but by clarifying the mental vision.'

These, and such apostles, aimed at a moral and religious
revival ; they believed reformation of character possible,
and within the reach of all. They gave clear expression to
certain great truths. Who can say how many conversions
they produced, or who can measure their influence for
righteousness ? They claimed to be ambassadors of God,
and they executed their mission as well as they could.
But their truth was too abstract : [1] they misplaced the
seat of authority ; they failed to realise the true nature

---

[1] 'Trusting too much to the intelligibleness of the Abstract,' like
J. S. Mill's father (*Autobiography*, p. 23).

and extent of human sin.   Nevertheless, they were voices
crying in the wilderness of Paganism, preparing the way
of the Lord.

Spiritual Directors

Another phenomenon deserving attention was the custom
among the richer houses of the Roman world of retaining
philosophers as moral and spiritual directors corresponding
to our private chaplains, though apparently more practical.   This habit commenced in the second century B.C.,
when Rome came more intimately in contact with Greece,
and Roman generals carried Greek scholars with them to
their camps.   As religious interests soon began to be affairs
of the greatest moment, the practical Romans looked to
these companions for help.   The affairs of state and public
life were no longer so absorbing ; there was less scope for
personal ambition, ancient laws and institutions no longer
lent moral support ;   the uncertainty and suffering caused
by the civil wars, and then the vengeance taken by the
court upon the nobility, made men call for spiritual aid.
The post-Aristotelian philosophies had shifted the emphasis
from speculation to conduct, from politics to morality.
It is impossible to estimate the influence of these spiritual
directors to whom the anxious brought their difficulties.
In one respect it must have been powerful—in the formation of the characters of the sons of the house.   Roman
masters themselves were schooled by their private chaplains
in their duties (officia); they were given prescriptions for the
control of passions, and instructed as to the summum bonum.
They consulted the chaplains on all the crises of life, as on
the death of friends, the confiscation of their estates, or dis-
favour at court.   The directors aimed at imparting an ars
vivendi   They discussed the questions of life, death, immortality, and reunion: they supported their masters in
death, especially at executions, dwelling on the examples of
men who had lived and died bravely, expatiating on the

nature of the soul and the prospects of immortality. Many
a Roman received much consolation in life, and departed with
a better hope, strengthened by these spiritual guides. It
was as usual to have a spiritual adviser attend the closing
scene as with ourselves, so that a historian thinks it worthy of
record when a man went to death ' without a philosopher.'
Canus, a victim of Caligula, accompanied to execution by
his philosopher, addressed his friends, ' Why this sorrow
and tears ? You are wondering if the soul is immortal,
while I am going to understand.' When Thrasea's death-
warrant arrived he prepared at once to die while discussing
with Demetrius the problem of immortality. The empress
Livia sought comfort on the death of Drusus from Augustus'
director, Areus.

In addition to these humble directors retained in rich
men's service, there were men like Plutarch, Seneca, and
Epictetus, who spent much time and pains in giving
spiritual advice to inquirers. Seneca is best known to us
as a director in his *Letters to Lucilius*, which will repay
reading by any one interested in this period.

Inwardness

The ancient world had turned to take the inward look.
This was partly the natural development of thought and
partly a necessity of moral progress. Self-culture, upon
which interest centred, was impossible without self-
knowledge. After a clear self-consciousness follows its
exploration in self-examination. As the individual with-
drew, or was forcibly dissevered from civic and racial
collectivism and found himself a denizen of a universal
empire, the more the inner problem pressed for solution.
As peace was restored to society, and faith in the brotherhood of man gained ground, and men were relieved from
the public concerns that made such inroads upon their
time and energy, they became conscious of the heart's

unrest.   Under the Empire we find an increasing ' tendency
to subjective emotion, to self-analysis, a discovery of the
value and dignity of the individual, and of the separate
life which a free spirit could lead in a land of wonders,
quite apart from the turmoil of domestic or political
strife.' [1]

But though self-analysis was more commonly practised
from the first century B.C., and became more poignant with
the rise of the Christian consciousness, it was not unknown
at an earlier date.   Pythagoras is credited with having
originated the practice and recommended it to his disciples.
With Socrates self-knowledge assumed a new prominence.
The appearance of Augustine's *Confessions* at the close
of the fourth century A.D. is an answer to the demand
urged by Socrates, 'Know thyself.'   Socrates made philosophy a criticism of life with a view to moral improvement : ' A life without examination should not be lived
by man ' (Plato, *Apol.* 38 A.).   Here was return upon the
inner life,[2] and Socrates was the forerunner of the era of
subjectivity, which from about the time of Alexander dis-
placed the previous era of objectivity.   In the third century
B.C. the *Golden Verses*, attributed to Pythagoras, were
reduced to their present form to take their place among
volumes of moral precepts and to encourage reflection.
Self-analysis was fostered by the expansion of conscience
in the later Graeco-Roman period and the belief in man's
innate moral nature.   Plutarch says, ' If you like to study
the history of sin you will find plenty of material in your-
selves,' and asks men to let their neighbours' faults alone
and turn their inquisitiveness upon themselves.   The
Neo-Pythagoreans seem to have made an evening self-
examination a part of their discipline.   Horace says he
frequently took moral stock of his life.   Titus considered

---

[1] Bussell, p. 212.
[2] Cf. words of Augustine : **In te ipsum redi ; in interiore homine habitat**
veritas.

each day whether he had done any good, and if not exclaimed, 'diem perdidi.' Sextius, a teacher of Seneca, practised self-examination and taught his disciples to do the same. The *locus classicus* on this subject occurs in a passage from Seneca (*de Ira*, III. 36) : ' Every day I plead my case before myself. When the light is extinguished, and my wife, who knows my habit, keeps silence, I examine the past day, go over and weigh all my deeds and words. I hide nothing, I omit nothing : why should I hesitate to face my shortcomings when I can say " take care not to repeat them, and so I forgive you to-day?"' Epictetus is likewise constantly turning the light upon himself, and in Marcus Aurelius self-analysis and introspection have become the order for every day of a much-engaged life.

Examples demanded

To the earnestness of this period abstract teaching was not congenial. A more practical method was required. As nowadays Christians find guidance in Bible texts, so at that time men needed some simple directions all the more owing to the isolation of the individual. Personal character and conduct were now of deeper concern. Definite precepts were demanded, and demand creates supply. All the writings of the wise were ransacked by teachers to find texts and precepts for their pupils. Collections of oracles were made. Definite prescriptions were dispensed to meet individual cases. The pathology of the soul was studied with a view to know its diseases and so to discover remedies. These precepts were predominantly negative, the object being to escape evil rather than attain righteousness ; positive directions, however, are not wanting. It was discovered that precepts are better clothed in ideals. Every system had its ideal man, the picture of what a man ought to be. Such ideals were creations of the imagination, dreams of man at his best. They were too elusive for the majority. An ideal that had never been incarnated was too cold and powerless. Accordingly the Hellenistic age was emphatic in its demand for *examples* to supplement precepts and ideals: we may doubt if ever, in any age, morality and religion were more persistently taught by examples. Earnest men wished to behold beings of flesh and blood and see how they lived, and from their examples to draw inspiration. A real kind of spiritual hero-worship resulted. All history and legend was explored for incarnate examples to teach men how to live and die. Strangely enough the Greeks and Romans never thought of looking to their gods as examples; Orpheus, Pythagoras,[1] and others were held up before men's gaze. Socrates, whose personality was greater than his teaching, now came to his own as the very ideal of humanity. He became a kind of pagan Christ. He himself in his trial was strengthened by the example of Palamedes. Readers of Plutarch remember how everything he says is buttressed, if not by a text, by an example from history or mythology. His *Lives* of outstanding Greeks and Romans were written with a moral and didactic purpose: the ethical predominates over the historical interest (cf. his own words, *Timoleon*, ad init.). Epictetus constantly reinforces his teaching with historic examples, especially that of Socrates. The practical Roman thought that one of the best methods of educating his sons was by an appeal to the great men of the past. Varro wrote fifteen books of parallel *Lives* of Greeks and Romans. Valerius Maximus composed his history for educational purposes: he illustrates the gamut of virtues by examples from Roman and Greek history. Seneca, in this, as in so many other respects, reflects the need and practice of his day in the familiar direction given to Lucilius, to keep constantly before his mind the picture of some upright man, and so

[1] *Lives of Pythagoras* were written by Porphyry, Iamblichus, and Diogenes Laertius.

to live as if he were always in his presence. **Religious teachers** felt the need of an uplifting example.

III. DEMAND FOR A UNIVERSAL RELIGION

The keynote of the day was universalism : the demand was for a universal religion. The isolation of the individual revealed common human needs. The growing sense of the unity of mankind created a prejudice against any enchoric or national religion. As man was one, his religion must be one. There was a kindly tolerance in religious matters. The practically general belief in Monotheism led men more eagerly in search of the *One*. Men said, with Plutarch, that all worshipped the same god, his name merely being different in different languages. In the days of Cicero the universality of man's religious nature was as common a tenet as when the study of comparative religions began among us. That there was a demand for a catholic religion is further shown by the interesting fact that every living religion became missionary. And philosophy left speculation to play its part in supplying religious guidance on strictly human and universal lines.

Eastern and Western Modes of Salvation

Evangels were offered from East and West, and men were not satisfied as in our day to owe allegiance to one sect or form of religion : they tried all. We find a characteristic contrast between Western and Eastern methods of salvation. There were two concurrent views of man which we may term the Hebrew and the Greek : the former exalted God, the latter man. Hebrew religion was, like all true religion, theocentric ; Greek culture anthropocentric. Excluding details, we may say that God was to the Hebrew transcendent and far exalted above man, who was a creature unworthy to appear on God's footstool : the lofty thought of the eighth Psalm, 'Thou hast made him a little lower than God,' did not permeate Hebrew as it did Greek thought. To the Greek God was immanent and not far away from any one of us; He was, as it were, an exalted man, or man raised to his highest power. The sense of sin was congenial to the one temperament, as that of man's native dignity to the other: the one needed grace, the other believed in merit. To the Hebrew man's spiritual constitution was weakened by pre-natal sin and poisoned by actual guilt; he is a helpless creature before Divine justice, incapable of saving himself. The Greek knew no original sin; he was almost unconscious of the ravages of moral evil in his nature; he believed he was his own saviour by exercising, after the illumination of wisdom, his personal will-power.

Of the religions competing in the Empire, those of Greece were philosophical, appealing primarily to the reason and intellect; that of Rome was wholly political; those from the Orient were most akin to Christianity, making their appeal primarily to the heart.

The 'religion' of Greece, an anthropomorphic polytheism, exerted its spiritual power chiefly in art. The Greek religion of Beauty and Joy was such an interpretation of nature as to make the Greek feel at home in a world conceived as beautiful and peopled with fairy deities; but this religion had no message when the element of trouble entered with an enlarging spiritual experience. It never enabled the Greek to embark upon the Infinite. It was to her philosophies that Greece looked for her evangels: it was these that endeavoured to meet the universal demand for support (v. Ch. VI.).

Although Rome had, especially since the second Punic war, despaired of her own gods, she did not despair, in her political wisdom, of supplying her Empire with a religion borrowed, adapted, or created for the purpose. A revival, inaugurated by Augustus, swept over Rome about the beginning of the Christian era. He realised the moral confusion resulting from the civil strife. His revival of the old religion was partly due to religious motives, but mainly to political. He claims to have repaired eighty-two temples in Rome. Throughout Italy, and in the provinces, new temples arose with astonishing rapidity, and dilapidated temples were restored. The more religious side of the revival is represented by Virgil, whose *Aeneid* is a trumpet-call to Rome to remember that it owes its greatness to the goodwill of the deity and to the reverence of their fathers. The *pius Aeneas* was intended to be the ideal Roman.

Imperial Cult

The universal religion which Rome offered the world was a political one, the cult of the emperors.[1] It was Roman policy to draw the attention of all to the centre of power, and the imperial cult was one of the best means of giving cohesion to a vast empire. This cult was never intended to persecute or displace national or enchoric faiths, nor to impose any religious dogma. It may seem very strange to us, though with our remnants of mediaevalism and feudalism we are not so far removed from it as we imagine. Imperial apotheosis was the result of flattery, gratitude, policy, and historic precedent. Several historic causes prepared the way. The Roman worship of the *Manes*, who occupied the place of saints in Catholicism, was a point of departure. Roman writers like Cicero (*N. D.* II., 24, 62) admitted that mortals by merit could be deified. For a time quasi-divine honours were paid to men like Scipio and Metellus Pius. Contact with Greece and the East fostered this latent germ. In Egypt the Pharaohs were adored as sons of Ra, the incarnation of God upon

---

[1] In this section I am much indebted to the Abbé Beurlier, *Le culte rendu aux empéreurs romains.*

earth, though not regarded as the equals of God. The monotheism of Persia did not permit such excessive worship, but allowed prostration before despots. Egypt and Persia transmitted to Alexander and the Diadochi the adoration of kings in their lifetime. Philip associated himself with the immortals. Alexander was adored as an earthly deity by the Persians : he was proclaimed ' son of Zeus ' by the oracle of Ammon, though his countrymen reluctantly acknowledged his divinity. The Ptolemies succeeded to the divinity of the Pharaohs, whereby double allegiance was due them. The Seleucids styled themselves ' saviour and god,' and appointed one priest to honour the dead kings, and another to honour the living kings who would one day join the Celestials. The kings of Pergamum and Commagene made themselves divine. The Greeks had for long practised a hero-worship, in which men of distinguished merit were regarded as quasi-divine after death.

Julius Caesar opened the door for himself and subsequent rulers into the Roman pantheon. After Pharsalia he was acknowledged as ' semi-god,' and his statue was placed beside that of the King of the Gods. He modestly refused the position, until, seated securely in power, his scruples were mitigated : a chair and his statue were placed in the circus among the gods, and a statue placed to him in the temple of Quirinus inscribed ' to the invincible God.' Later he became Jupiter Julius : a temple was begun in honour of his *Clementia*. His assassination and the appearance of the comet secured his consecration. He was decreed *divus*, which does not mean ' god,' but ' divine,' and the senate gave authority ' to honour him as a god.' An epidemic of divinity-seeking now broke out among the Romans : ' Etre dieu, ou tout au moins fils de dieu, était une condition indispensable pour aspirer à l'empire du monde.' Sextus Pompey gave himself out as son of Neptune ; Antony became the new Dionysus, whose worst qualities he imitated.

His exploits and the battle of Actium quenched his divinity. Octavian became *Divi filius*, son of the Divine ; but after Actium flatterers and poets hailed him as a deity with the attributes of Apollo. Only a god could give the earth such repose, according to Virgil, who, with Horace, prophesied his apotheosis as son of Venus. We find him addressed on inscriptions as Zeus and son of Zeus. All this was private adulation, but connived at by Octavian : he refused the titles *Lord* and *God*, accepting that of *Augustus* in 27 B.C. In Rome he refused shrines to himself, but we find in Italy a cult addressed to him in his lifetime. In the provinces the cult spread most rapidly : temples were raised to the divinity of the emperor ; in these he insisted that the divinity of *Roma* should be associated with himself. Soon after the provincial arose the municipal cult : *Caesarea* and *Augustea* were erected in every town of importance. Of all the Caesars Augustus received the most genuine adoration, partly because of his unique position, it being the first time in human history that one man was so necessary to all, partly out of gratitude for the *pax Romana*, partly because the cult had not yet been sullied by the elevation of unworthy rulers, and the honour was not yet lessened by a crowd of similar divinities. Philo says that ' the whole world regarded Augustus as equal to the Olympians.' On his death his apotheosis was decreed by the senate. Tiberius refused divine honours in Rome, but encouraged the provincial cult. Caligula was punctilious about his divinity. Nero was the first living emperor to wear the *corona radiata* symbolic of descent from the sun-god. In the first and second centuries the best emperors were content with the name of some ancient deity, expecting full divine honours only after death ; but in the third they were styled *gods*. Domitian claimed the title *dominus et deus* in his lifetime. Finally from the East came prostration before emperors. The most extravagant forms of the imperial cult belonged to

the East, where emperors were addressed by such terms
as μέγιστος θεῶν, θειότατος, *sacratissimus*, or 'God,' 'God
manifest,' σωτήρ (Saviour), 'God the Deliverer,' 'invincible
God,' etc.

Gradually the purely political character of the cult became manifest to all.[1] Apotheosis was a civil honour—the
ratification of the acts of the dead emperor—and was in
the gift of the senate which usually discriminated wisely,
rejecting Tiberius, Caligula, Nero, Domitian, and yet admitting the infamous Commodus and Caracalla. The admission
of the emperors' families and the growing number of such
deifications lessened its glory. The claims of emperors like
Caligula or Nero completely destroyed the religious character
of the cult.

The imperial cult was Rome's endeavour to supply to her
empire a universal religion as political as was her own
religion. It was intended as a bond of union and a sign
of the greatness and ubiquity of Rome. The trend since
the days of Alexander had been politically toward monarchy
and in religion toward monotheism. This cult was one
in which all could unite and which represented a visible
unity. It strengthened Roman authority and helped to
unify the world. The living emperor was a visible god
dispensing justice. It discredited polytheism by admitting
mortals to the privileges of deity. Also ' prayers addressed
to the god Augustus were more surely answered than
those addressed to Jupiter.'[2]

Never possessed of any religious value, the imperial cult
betrays in a remarkable way the tendency of that age to
look for an incarnation of deity, and to prefer a *praesens
deus* to all the gods of polytheism. When Christ was
preached as Son of God who had tabernacled among
men, such an idea was not unfamiliar to the people of
that day, who recoiled less from it than some do now.

[1] In the first two centuries the populace had a real belief in the divinity of
the *Augusti*.—Beurlier, p. 321.   [2] Beurlier, p. 319.

There were plenty of nonconformists. **The emperors never** insisted on strict conformity : in the provinces the cult was a convenient means of detecting any disloyalty. In its palmiest days the educated classes smiled at a practice which was only an act of civil homage. Roman emperors doubted their own divinity. Seneca's *Apocolocyntosis* turns to ridicule Claudius's apotheosis. Vespasian jested on his deathbed about his becoming a god. The chief nonconformists were Republicans, **Jews,** and Christians. The first were foremost in the senate to oppose apotheosis, as did Thrasea (Tac., *Ann.*, xvi. 21) ; they even refused to swear by the genius of the emperor. The Jews were more stubborn, but too powerful to antagonise : they were excused in this as in other acts of religious nonconformity. The relations of Christianity to the imperial cult belong to church history.

Oriental Religions

It was toward the East that the Graeco-Roman world turned to find spiritual support : the conquest of the Empire by Oriental religions is one of the most striking facts of religious history. The aesthetic religion of Greece and the institutional religion of Rome lost their charm before the emotional, mystic, salvation-religions of the East. The Magna Mater was introduced from Pessinus, the Syrian goddess and Baals came from Syria, Isis and Serapis from Egypt, Mithra from Persia, Jupiter Dolichenus from Commagene. It is difficult to explain the enthralling charm of these Eastern faiths which in the beginning were gross and naturalistic, but with the progressive moral sense of man were purified into means of grace. ' In times of moral renovation, and in face of powerful spiritual rivalries, a religion may purge itself of the impurities of youth. Religious systems may also be elevated by the growing refinement of the society to which they minister.

It is only thus that we can explain the undoubted fact that the Phrygian and Egyptian worships, originally tainted with the grossness of naturalism, became vehicles of a warm religious emotion, and provided a stimulus to a higher life. The idealism of humanity, by a strange alchemy, can marvellously transform the most unpromising materials.' [1] We may attribute the success of the Oriental religions to three causes : (1) favouring circumstances, (2) their organisation and methods, (3) their intrinsic merits and ability to foster and partially meet spiritual wants.

(1) They entered the Empire at a time when national religion was discredited, when men who had lost faith in the religion of their fathers were willing to experiment with any substitute. There were hosts of Eastern slaves whose zeal for their gods seemed to grow more intense when living among masters who had lost their religion. Eastern merchants, retailers, and speculators carried their ancestral faith over the Empire, as also did the hosts of recruits from the East who served in the Roman armies. The success attending Roman arms after the introduction of the first Eastern deity, the Great Mother, gave her prestige from the beginning. She became sponsor for later invaders who sheltered themselves from persecution as her protégés. From the days of Herodotus and Plato the eyes of the West were turning toward the Morningland for enlightenment in religion ; the first religious revival experienced in Greece (in the sixth century) was due to Eastern influences. The Oriental religions were the only religions that could thrive outside the original territory of their god, and keep pace with the tendencies of the day—they fostered syncretism, maintained the unity of mankind, helped to monotheism through their henotheism ; they abounded in mysticism, advocated asceticism, and satisfied emotional and individualistic demands. (2) They invaded the West

Dill, p. 554.

encircled with the hoary authority of a venerable past,
with esoteric doctrines, established dogma, and a well
organised priesthood. From the beginning they were
missionary and proselytising faiths, like Judaism; as
such they were *religions of enthusiasm*. They believed
in themselves and in their mission. No Eastern slave or
trader ever forgot the god of his fathers. They were
universal religions, not enchoric, intended to embrace all
nations. The only religion of the West that spread east-
ward was the official imperial cult backed by the might of
Rome, but as a religion it never became a competitor with
Eastern religions; whereas the cults from the East spread
to the ends of the Empire and were as much at home at
York, on the Rhine, or on the borders of the Sahara, as
in their native territory. No national or racial distinction
was maintained. These religions were brotherhoods in
which rich and poor, slave and master, were united. A
slave found there his lost liberty; he might be president
of the local brotherhood in which his master was only a
private member or an acolyte. In these religious guilds
men found that fellowship and sympathy which were
missed in a vast empire. Many a slave and soldier after
long hours of toil must have been refreshed by the companionship of a few initiated who met together to contemplate the symbols of the deity, and to join in hymn and
ritual. It was a decidedly democratic era, and these religions
were democratic. Like Christianity, they began with the
lower classes and worked upward. Rank and birth did
not count. The populace was captivated by the impressive
pomp and ritual, by the excitement which appealed to
the senses : the eye and ear were pleased as well as the
heart. They were sacerdotal cults in the hands of a
professional priesthood which explained the meaning of
symbolic acts to the people, and claimed the authority
of a long tradition. These cults represented the 'free
churches,' into the membership of which a man did not

enter by birth, or as a matter of course. They were not state-supported. Man values his spiritual wares proportionately to the price they cost him ; so these cults were all the more valuable in that they were supported on the voluntary system. The contributions to the support of the priesthood and to the treasury of the guilds must often have called forth self-denial. Oriental creeds at first won their way because of the clamour of the populace, but from the days of the Antonines through the sympathies of emperors who found in them a doctrine akin to that of the divine right of kings. With the exception of Mithraism, women played a prominent part in all Eastern cults, which had a special attraction for their sex. (3) All these considerations would have been ineffectual had not Oriental religions met and partially satisfied religious needs. They confronted rationalism and scepticism with faith in established dogma, whereas Greece and Rome had no system of theology. They claimed to have a certain authority over the spirit : they had a message for the individual ; like Christianity they aimed at universalism through individualism. They were to a considerable extent ethical : man could not in his natural state approach a holy God. He must humble himself and purify himself from sin. Rites of purification were characteristic of them all. Asceticism and self-denial were enforced on special occasions. The soul must be cleansed from the impurities of flesh and matter to enjoy the beatific vision. This was accomplished by mortifications and penances, by lustrations and ablutions in holy water—a ' veritable spiritual disinfection.' The chief charm of these cults lay in their appeal to the emotions, which also caused grave moral aberrations. They aroused in the worshipper hope, fear, pain, joy, ecstasy. The services were warm, interesting, and enthralling as compared with the formal prosaic state-cult. The initiated could enter the little chapel with a few comrades to gaze upon the sacred symbols, to hear the priests explaining and applying the lesson to man's own life, to join in prayer and hymn and feel lifted above the earthly. There is in every true religion a large element of mysticism, and these cults encouraged mysticism. We trace this in the rites used to enable the worshipper to rise above the sensible and material, and in the confessions put into the lips of the initiated whereby they claim to have escaped from evil and attained the better. By mortifications, by fasting, by exhilarating music, by self-mutilation, by drugs and stimulants they endeavoured to rise into another state in which they were united with the Deity. To surmount the ills of dualism in union with the Deity or apotheosis was their aspiration.

The Deity was more human than those of Greece and Rome ; the Eastern gods could die and rise again, could suffer and enjoy. They understood better how to comfort. In a remarkable passage in the prosaic treatise *On Isis and Osiris* (27), Plutarch says that Isis has not grown oblivious of her own toils and sufferings, and is present in the representations of these past sufferings to console humanity in its trials—a *mater dolorosa*.[1] These cults offered strength and spiritual support by bringing men into union with sympathetic gods. The priests, unlike the busy secular priests of Greece and Rome, undertook spiritual guidance, gave directions how men were to escape from the evils of dualism, and prescriptions for quieting an uneasy conscience. The chief means of sacramental grace were the mysteries, and the chief promise was a blessed immortality.

IV. Higher Ideas of God and Man

Higher ideas of God and of man prevailed in this period. From the beginning of time the existence and necessity of the Supernatural were felt. As the moral and spiritual

---

[1] Cf. also Apul., *Met.*, xi. 25.

education of man advanced there was an expansion in the conception of God. The Greek was working for man, the Hebrew for God ; these met in the Graeco-Roman world to carry on their simultaneous mission.

Monotheism

A belief in the unity of God was one of the most marked advances. Of this the Jews were the first missionaries, who 'had a passion for monotheism in their blood.' A movement set in toward monotheism from the earliest days of Greek philosophy and in Greek tragedy. The first problem that Greek thought set itself was to discover the One amid the many, unity amid plurality. Xenophanes said ' the best can only be One.' Many paths led to monotheism. Philosophers first attacked polytheism : only confusion could reign in the universe so long as it was partitioned out among different and often hostile deities. Antisthenes said ' there are many Gods according to law, but only One according to nature,' and Xenophanes, ' there is one God, among gods and men the greatest, unlike mortals in outer shape, unlike in mind and thought.' Some rejected the popular gods, replacing them by an abstract monotheism ; some regarded them as manifestations or modes of the One ; a more usual method was to elevate one and make the others his vassals, like Zeus among the Greeks, and Jupiter among the Romans, or to choose a trinity like the Capitoline Jupiter, Juno, and Minerva. As universalism and the idea of the unity of mankind spread it was natural to suppose that all men stood in the same relation to the same God. If one man could rule the world, surely one God could rule the universe. The syncretism of the age was in no respect so active as in its blending of gods into one. Deities of different peoples exerting the same functions were identified. It was maintained, as by Plutarch, that the gods of all nations are the same, only called by different names in different languages. Expressions like ' the gods ' were used by force of habit without meaning plurality. It was only natural that the old terminology should linger. Maximus of Tyre says that the names of the gods are many but their essence one, their names being due to our ignorance, just as we speak of Ionian, Aegean, and Cretan seas, though there is only one sea. Some of the Church fathers, Justin, Clement of Alexandria, Tertullian, and Lactantius, admitted that pagans believed in the unity of God. The philosophic monotheism of Plato, in which the idea of Good and God coincided, was widely spread as Platonism became a spiritual force in the Empire. Hatch says of the latter portion of our period : ' It was an age in which men were feeling after God and not feeling in vain, and that from the domains of ethics, physics, metaphysics alike, from the depths of the moral consciousness, and from the cloud-lands of poets' dreams, the ideas of men were trooping in one vast host to proclaim with a united voice that there are not many gods but only One, one First Cause by whom all things were made, one Moral Governor whose providence was over all His works, one Supreme Being " of infinite power, wisdom, and goodness." ' [1]

Goodness and Providence of God

There was a practically universal faith in the goodness and love of God. Plato argues that God can be only the author of good. Seneca holds that as God is our father we may expect only good from Him. Celsus tells Origen that God is good and free from jealousy. A frequently recurring thought in Epictetus, Plutarch, and Maximus of Tyre is the goodness of God. As the idea spread that man is made in the image of God, there went with it the faith that God could maintain only a sympathetic

[1] *Influence of Greek Ideas and Usages*, p. 14.

attitude to His creatures. The ancient world of Judaism and of Paganism had begun dimly to conceive the Father-hood of God, which was to be so fully revealed in Christ.

The Providence of God was a common conception.[1] God was viewed as the one all-seeing and all-governing power, the Creator who watches over all His works, and in a special manner over men who are His ' relatives.' The adoption of means to ends, the dependence of cause on cause reaching back to God, was as familiar then as now. The universe was neither made nor governed at random. Anaxagoras had long ago made Mind the regulator and governor of all. Socrates appeals to the universal belief in the existence and Providence of God as proof of its truth : as the soul manages the body so Providence does the world ; the Divine sees, hears, and cares for all. Socrates reminds his judges that a good man's interests are not neglected by the Deity, nor had his trial and condemnation happened accidentally. Plato recognises a reasoning Intelligence as ruling the world. Aristotle, it is true, rejected Providence, as did also the Epicureans. In spite of these exceptions faith in God's Providence steadily grew. The Stoics used many argu-ments to establish their contention for Providence, appeal-ing to the generally accepted belief, and to the argument from God's perfection and foreknowledge. They desig-nated their universal law sometimes Nature and sometimes Providence. Their Providence was concerned primarily with the universal, and only secondarily with the individual in his relation to the whole. The Providence and goodness of God is an article of faith with Cicero, Plutarch, Seneca, Epictetus, Aurelius. So firm was this faith that prayer was regarded as unnecessary : God may be trusted to give what is needed and good for us. This Providence was not capricious—not that of a despot. Fate, Fortune, Necessity

[1] Friedländer, *Roman Life and Manners*, iii. 145. Cf. Cic., *de Legg.*, ii. 7, 16.

were identified with God, or otherwise brought under His sway, or made His ministers in the education of good men.

Moral Government

To the Graeco-Roman world the mystery of the moral government of the universe was perplexing. There was much that apparently could not be easily reconciled with faith in Providence. Only a limited number could accept the comfortless theory of the Epicureans whose gods enjoyed an immortality of repose, contemplating only their own perfection, free from all care for the sorrows of men. On thoughtful minds the question pressed : Why so much evil in the world of a beneficent Creator ? why do the wicked profit equally with the good by the gifts of Providence ? why do the wicked prosper while the righteous suffer calamity ? why do God's judgments fall upon the guiltless ? The old world stood sobered before such problems ; they realised that there are domains in which only faith can say the last word. They offered tentative answers : that a good and wise God would do all for the best, that God could not in a general providence benefit the good without conferring blessing on the evil. It was better to benefit all than allow the righteous to suffer in a general dearth : God could not make the sunshine fall only on the good, neither could He make the same wind advantageous to the good and disastrous to the bad, nor cause the showers to fall only on the fields of the righteous, as Seneca remarks. But where apparent discrimination comes in, as in the loss of children or wealth, the problem was more acute. Faith suggested that calamity tries the good man and makes him like God. Suffering may be like the pain of a surgical operation, for lasting good and health. The Stoics held that suffering is not penal. Democritus remarked that he had never seen anything more wretched than the man who had never suffered

G

calamity. Paganism believed that whom God loves **He**
chastens,[1] that virtue can only live and grow under trial.
Or God sent suffering that mankind might have examples
of strength like Socrates, or He might by showing favour
to a good man's descendants elevate such a scoundrel as
Caligula—the Roman form of the Judaic 'merits of the
fathers.' Another method of exonerating God was found
in the prevalent dualism of East and West, by presuming
that evil was the work of demons intermediary between
God and men. Evil and good were engaged in eternal
conflict, and evil is necessary to give scope and exercise
to good. Some, burdened with this thought, looked forward to an ultimate triumph of good over evil, when
Ormuzd would exterminate Ahriman, or when in the
Messianic kingdom evil would disappear

There was another short cut as familiar to the ancients
as to us—a simple denial of the existence of evil. Thus
the ancient world not only protested against what seemed
divine oppression, but it did all that the human spirit
could do to 'justify the ways of God to man,' and defend
God's moral character.

Dignity of Man

Man is elevated in proportion to his conception of God :
the holier and purer God is, the more righteous must man
be. When God's love becomes equally prominent with
His power, man is the recipient of His goodness : the
nearer the approach to God the larger becomes man's
spiritual life and outlook. We have already referred to
the two concurrent views of man, the Hebrew and the
Greek ; the former dwelling rather on the weakness and
sinfulness of man, the latter on the inherent dignity of
human nature with a proud self-reliance. The former is

---

[1] 'Hos itaque deus quos probat, quos amat, indurat, recognoscit, exercet.'—
Sen., *De Prov.*, 4, 7.

the more religious view. The dignity of man and his kinship with the Divine was a common thought in ancient Paganism : ' Through the course of Greek religious thought a single thread may be traced, in the essential unity of man and God.' [1] Paul had noticed this : ' As certain also of your own poets (plural) have said, " for we are His offspring." ' The gulf between man and his immanent God was never so wide as that between the Hebrew and his transcendent God. Some gods were only deified men raised to heaven for services to mankind. Pantheism brought God within the reach of man. Greek anthropomorphism at first conceived God as made in the image of man, as when Xenophanes asserted (attacking anthropomorphic polytheism), that the negroes depict God as black and flat-nosed, the Thracians as red-haired and with blue eyes ; and if oxen, lions, and horses could conceive of God, they would represent him as an ox, a lion, a horse. Later Greek thought conceived man as made in the image of God. Plato opened the way for that divine discontent and boundless aspiration by which man seeks to escape from the evils of dualism and from the prison and tomb of the soul, to find scope for his higher nature in the contemplation of the Divine and Abiding : our souls seek to return to God whence they came, for with God is our true home and fatherland. We are a ' heavenly plant.' In the later schools we find a growing conviction of the kinship of man with the Divine : a conviction that

' L'homme est un dieu tombé qui se souvient des cieux.'

Cicero finds this thought congenial : we are the ' relatives ' of God. According to Seneca, God is our father ; our Divine origin calls us above. ' Between good men and the gods is a friendship founded on virtue. Friendship, do I say ? nay, rather an intimacy and likeness, for a good man only differs in point of time from God whose disciple

[1] Mrs. Adam, *Greek Ideals of Righteousness*, p. 67.

and imitator he is and His offspring.' We as part of God contemplate our Parent, says Manilius. Epictetus was foremost in using this idea in a practical way to elevate the lives of men. He asks why should not a rational being call himself 'a son of God? . . . Shall kinship with Caesar, or any other great man, enable us to live secure? . . . And shall not the fact that God is our Maker, Father, Guardian, free us from all sorrow and anxiety?' 'Do you think that God would suffer His own son to be enslaved?' Simplicius in his famous prayer requested his Father and Saviour to make us mindful of the noble origin 'Thou hast deemed worthy to confer upon us.'

Worth of the Soul

Side by side with this conviction of the Divine in man, with the increasing desire for immortality and the yearning for salvation, the worth of the soul became more apparent. From the days of Socrates and Plato, Paganism was learning to ask, 'What shall it profit a man if he shall gain the whole world and lose his own soul, or what shall a man give in exchange for his soul?' The exceeding preciousness of the soul is prominent in all the great works of Plato, especially in the *Phaedo*, the noblest work ever penned by a Pagan. The whole business of a worthy life is to disengage the *Psyche* from the pollution of the flesh, maintain it in communion with the Good and Beautiful, and after death restore it to God in a condition fit for the fruition of endless felicity. There is not space here to point out the difference between the Platonic intellectualism of salvation and the Christian conception ; but never was the higher life of man more exalted above the life of sense. In the Graeco-Roman world the political conditions that in Plato's own day rendered men deaf to his lofty spirituality were removed, and his great truths spread to larger

audiences. In the moralists and preachers of the Empire
we find great emphasis upon the high origin and worth of
the soul, and the saving of it was a matter of engrossing
interest. The individualism of the age brought men
race to face with their inner life. Oriental religions
deepened the conviction of the worth of the soul and the
imperative need of its salvation. Men were willing to
practise asceticism, take lustral baths, undertake weary
and expensive pilgrimages, seek initiations in every
mystery, undergo or inflict self-mutilation, struggle with
demonic powers—all for the health of the soul. In the
regnant dualism the soul was winning, while the body was
steadily losing.

Immortality

Closely connected with a belief in God and in the worth
of man is the doctrine of immortality. When we reflect
what a veil of mystery is drawn over the grave even for
the Christian, we shall not be astonished to find that
the pagan world without a revelation was troubled by
uncertainty. As thought in Greece and Rome was free
from clerical sway, men could speculate as they pleased.
It is not so much the belief in immortality that arrests
our attention in this period, as the interest which the
subject created even in those who probed it only to
flout. The yearning for continued existence was one
symptom of the individualism of the age. As death
became more of a personal loss it was felt to be so intoler-
ably oppressive that we can still hear the repeated desire
for reunion. Men were peering wistfully into the Beyond :
'They were stretching out their hands in longing for the
farther shore,' says Virgil. 'The inextinguishable instinct
of humanity craves for a voice of revelation to solve the
mystery of life and death.'

So tenacious was the racial consciousness among the

Jews that it was only after the Exile they felt much need of immortality, and it was apparently in the trying Maccabean days that they demanded an individual immortality for the righteous, and then for the wicked. Job had long before expressed the yearning for another life (see p. 27).

The earliest Greek (Homeric) conception of the existence beyond was that of a life so thin and gloomy that it was better to serve as a hireling upon earth than to reign in Hades : moreover, it did not possess any moral worth except in the torment of a few egregious sinners. The Hesiodic Islands of the Blest are reserved for a few favourites of the gods. The earliest promise of a happier lot such as would render a continuance of life desirable is made to the initiated in the *Hymn to Demeter*. The Dionysiac and Orphic religious brotherhoods, entering Greece at the close of the seventh century, inculcated the doctrine of immortality : their teachings were taken up and spread by the Pythagoreans and Pindar, and later by Plato. In Pindar existence beyond has taken on brighter colours, and has been moralised. The next important epoch begins with Plato, to whom we shall return.

The Romans had, from the earliest times, a belief in continued existence on which later an ethical immortality could be ingrafted. The cult of the dead, in its brighter aspect, as the *Manes* who were propitious, and in its gloomier aspect, the *Lemures* who were malevolent, is typically Roman. But here, too, Roman faith was driven by its penury to Greece, whose eschatology she appropriated, and through Greece that of Orphism and Pythagoreanism.

In the Graeco-Roman age the question of immortality was much discussed. There were materialists who denied and sceptics who doubted. Among those who desired it there were various grades of faith. As Socrates was to this period a kind of pagan Christ, and Plato came to his own, it is worth while to begin with them. The Socrates

of Xenophon says nothing upon the question : the argu-
ments put into his mouth in the *Phaedo* are those of Plato.
Socrates argues that death is a boon : either it is a dream-
less sleep or a journey to where are the true judges and the
renowned dead (*Apol.* 40, A. f.). He closes his defence with
the words, ' Now it is the hour to depart, I to die, you to
live ; which of us enters into the better lot is hidden from
all save God only.' The ' divine Plato ' was one of the
chief sources of the belief to after ages. He intellectualised
the ritual and ceremonies of Orphism which brought
immortality to Greece, and imbibed from Pythagoreanism
all the satisfaction it had to offer to a mystical world-
weary spirit. After much independent reflection and
enlarged spiritual experience, he completed—especially in
the *Phaedrus, Symposium,* and *Phaedo*—the lofty structure
from which historic Christianity has borrowed so many
stones. He dwells upon the divine origin of the soul, its
spiritual nature, its pre-existence, its longing to return to
its home, its defiance of all diseases both of the body
and those which attack itself. His life beyond is distinguished by moral values, *i.e.* his immortality is ethical.
Plato's labour of love is ' the noblest single offering that
human reason has yet laid upon the altar of human hope.' [1]
Aristotle offered little hope. He defined the soul as the
entelechy of the body ; only one part of the soul is immortal,
active reason, which persists as incorporeal spirit, but in
such a fashion as to render personal immortality very doubtful, if not impossible ; for the dead are not happy being
deprived of self-consciousness. The Peripatetics rejected
immortality. The Stoics usually admitted that the soul
survived till the conflagration ; some like Panaetius denied
even this. The Epicureans were the apostles of annihila-
tion. Lucretius—another Omar Khayyam—contemplates
blank nothingness and extinction of all desire in the *leti*

[1] Geddes, *Phaedo of Plato*, p. xxvii., cited in Salmond, *Christian Doctrine
of Immortality*, p. 149.

secura quies. Sallust (*Cat.* 51-2) represents Caesar, the high-priest of Roman religion, as opposing the simple death penalty proposed for the Catilinarian conspirators, because 'death puts a period to all human ills, and beyond the grave there is no opportunity for either anxiety or joy'; in this opinion Cato Uticensis concurs. Cicero also refers to it (*In Cat.*, iv. 4, 7), without any contradiction. Thus this famous trio denied all moral nexus between this life and the next. Catullus— the Shelley of antiquity — anticipates 'one perpetual night' closing down on his love for Lesbia, and on a sadder occasion, by his brother's grave, he takes an everlasting hopeless farewell. Horace in exquisite verse commends a 'carpe diem' existence before we pass into 'eternal exile,' where *pulvis et umbra sumus.* Pliny (*H. N.*, vii. 55, 188) maintains that death is an unbroken sleep from which there is no awakening, the desire for immortality arising from human vanity. The funeral inscriptions are for the most part hopeless. They represent largely the scenes of this life and of past happiness; they are not concerned with the future. Some are frivolous and even immoral : ' I was not, I became ; I am not and I care not.' 'While I lived I drank as I pleased, you who live drink.' 'Baths, wine, indulgence, corrupt our bodies, but they constitute life.' 'Eat, drink, enjoy yourself, then join us.' 'What I have eaten and drunk, that I take with me; what I have left behind I have forfeited.' 'While I lived I lived well; now my little play is ended, soon shall yours be; good-bye and applaud.' 'Hold all a mockery, reader ; nothing is our own.' The poems of the Greek Anthology—especially the later ones —are without a ray of hope. Death brings the peace of nothingness, and takes us away from the ills of life. The burden of these pieces is ' vanity of vanities, all is vanity.' As death may snatch us away at any moment let us quaff the cup of pleasure now ; the only regret at the end is that of having lost any opportunity of enjoyment; for the rest 'all is laughter, all is dust, all is nothing.' 'All life is a stage and a game; learn to play it without seriousness or bear the consequence.'

There is another side. The question of immortality was being approached with increasing earnestness. Men were asking, 'If a man die shall he live again?' Amid the uncertainty and misery of the present, many were crying with the author of Obermann, 'Eternité, deviens mon asile.' The demand for continued existence and for remembrance asserted itself strongly. Even Lucretius realised the sadness for the human heart of parting with loved ones without hope of a reunion. Roman tombs were erected near the roadside so that the living might not grudge the time to read the epitaph. 'The wish to maintain . . . a bond of communion between the living and the departed was one of the most imperious instincts of the Latin race.'[1] The dead demand that loving hands scatter roses and violets with a prayer over the grave: they dreaded loneliness. A few learned sceptics and materialists could not stem the rising aspirations of the people. Some men of eminence would not deny this hope: others fostered it till it became a faith. The work of Orphism, Pythagoreanism, and above all Platonism, could not be in vain; their spirituality filtered down among the masses. Tacitus concludes his life of Agricola with the faint hope that such noble souls may be granted a life beyond. Sulpicius Severus consoles Cicero on the death of Tullia with a hesitating 'if the dead retain consciousness.' The demand for *Consolations*, characteristic of this period, promoted the eternal hope. It is strange that while belief in the old fables of punishment in Tartarus waned, the hope of immortality increased. The future was increasingly ethicised from the days of Orphism and especially of Plato. Plutarch is an advocate of immortality, to which he thinks

[1] Dill, p. 487.

the innate desire for a perpetuity of life points.[1] At the end of his *Consolation to his wife* he considers it harder to doubt than to believe. He also consoles her with this faith which they learned in their initiation into the mysteries. In his (?) *Consolation to Apollonius* the same hope is present, but sometimes faint. The cases of Cicero and Seneca are interesting as giving some insight into ancient religious experience. In the day of prosperity both paid little attention to the subject, but in the face of bereavement and misfortune they fell back on the eternal hope. Cicero, acknowledging Sulpicius' consolatory letter (*Fam.*, iv. 5), admits that his friend had offered all possible consolation, though the highest he could offer was a continuation of consciousness in Tullia (*si qui etiam inferis sensus est*). Writing to Torquatus (*Ib.*, vi. 4, 4), a few months later, he views death as bringing insensibility (*sine ullo sensu*). On the other hand, in the beautiful *Dream of Scipio*, published 51 B.C., a blessed immortality is promised to those who have served their country and lived virtuously, in contrast with which ' what you call life is death.' In the year of Tullia's death he addressed a *Consolatio* to himself, in the extant fragment of which he dwells upon the divine and spiritual nature of the soul. In the same or the following year he began the *Tusculan Disputations* (' a work of despair '), in the first of which he reviews the Platonic arguments for the immortality of the soul, but arrives at no certainty. Death is no evil, but it is not a blessing : we shall either ' return to our eternal home or become unconscious and free from anxiety.' Again he boasts that if the hope of immortality is a delusion it is one in which he wishes to persist. Seneca wavered. At one time he viewed immortality as a ' beautiful dream ' (*bellum somnium*), but after the bitter experiences of his life he came to depict the blessedness of heaven in terms

[1] In *De sera Num. Vind.*, 18, he says a belief in continued existence must follow from that in God's providence. Cf. also *Non posse suaviter vivi*, 26 f.

akin to the Christian. Death is not penal but a boon to
tired mortality ; this mortal life is a ' prelude to a better
and longer life.' Stoic as he was he preferred the Platonic
spiritual view of the soul. The day of death is the ' birth-
day of eternity' (*aeterni natalis*) : ' our soul will then
have cause to rejoice when, sent forth from these shades
in which it is immersed, it shall see things no longer dimly,
but with the light of perfect day, and shall have been
restored to its heaven and shall have reached the place
which is its birthplace.' Maximus of Tyre regards death
as the entrance upon a new immortal life.

Some of the most earnest souls were in doubt. This
is the attitude of Quintilian. Epictetus is very faltering
in his utterances about things beyond : though he asserted
the divine kinship of the soul and the joy of communion
with God here, he never felt the need of a personal existence
beyond. Marcus Aurelius, conscious of the inveterate
longing of man for continued existence, crushed it out
in his absolute submission to the will of God, whatever
that might be : he felt no need of another life to complement this.

Thus some of the best men were indifferent to the hope
of man ; others clung to it as a frail raft. So far as we
can gather, the masses had more faith in immortality than
their leaders, and that because of the spread of the Oriental
religions. The chief sources of faith in a continued moral
life in the Graeco-Roman age were three : Platonism, which
took up and spiritualised Orphism and Pythagoreanism ;
the Greek mysteries, and, above all, the mysteries of the
Oriental cults. Speaking of Athens, Cicero says she produced ' nothing more excellent and nothing better than
those mysteries, by which from a wild and savage life we
have been trained and raised to a higher humanity. They
are truly called *initia*, for it is through them we have
learned to know the beginnings of life. And we have
received from them not only good reason why we should

live with joy, but also why *we should die with a better hope.*'
A continued existence of some kind was almost universally
admitted : it was the mysteries that cast light upon the
gloom and promised a different position to the initiated.

The Mysteries

Although we distinguish Greek and Oriental mysteries,
the Greek mysteries were probably introduced from the East
by the cult brotherhoods after the spiritual upheavals
and religious revivals that swept over the North Semitic
world in the seventh century B.C. The mysteries were
at first private and conducted by religious guilds. They
introduced into Greece the revolutionary idea of a
religion detached from the tribe or *polis* and open to all
men: membership was free and spontaneous. In the sixth
century[1] one Greek state, Athens, took over the Eleusinian
mysteries as part of the state religion, thus partly adopting
the new principle of membership in a divine community
by initiation instead of by birthright. Side by side still
persisted many private mysteries. The introduction of
these foreign mysteries into the Greek world was epoch-
making : they lent to men a moral inspiration by making
the future life worthy of high endeavour, and by introducing
into it moral distinctions qualified by man's conduct
here. The gloomy non-moral after-existence of Homer
gave way to a hereafter of bliss for the initiated. Both
the state-acknowledged and the private mysteries offered
to men a hope through the symbolism of nature. The
Hymn to Demeter says, ' Happy is he among deathly men
who hath beheld these things. And he that is uninitiate
and hath no lot in them, hath never equal lot in death
beneath the murky gloom.' Pindar speaks to the same
purpose. Better known are the words of Sophocles,
' thrice blessed they of mortals who descend into Hades

---

[1] Cf. Jevons, *Introd. to the History of Religion* (1896), pp. 358-9.

having seen these mysteries.' Mysteries, like everything else, were abused. Plato speaks of them with disapprobation, first, because they tended to give the idea that ceremonial expiation for sin in this life was enough—an idea subversive of righteousness; and secondly, because they offered rewards, including an 'eternity of drunkenness,' for virtue, which to Plato was its own reward.

The new Oriental cults that began in the second century B.C. to invade the Empire supplied the masses with the most fascinating ritual and mysteries. The cults of the Great Mother, Isis, and Mithra, taught immortality and attached to it grave moral responsibility. Men were prepared for the life beyond by penances, fasting, abstinence, baptism and purification. In the yearly return of life in nature they recognised a symbol of the hope of man. The emotional rites of a naturalistic religion were not in the first case elevating, but with the developing moral experience of man were translated into symbols of higher truth. They saw in the alternate grief and joy of a mother of sorrows joy born of grief and life issuing from death. Life was a probation for eternity, and after death there followed another life and a great judgment.

The Taurobolium (not found in the West till the second century A.D., attaching to the Great Mother cult, and probably also to Mithraism) was the most impressive of sacraments. The worshipper knelt in a trench over which was a platform on which was slain a bull; the blood ran down upon the devotee, thus cleansing him of sin and causing him to be 'born again for eternity' (*in aeternum renatus*). The votaries of Isis had inscribed on their tombs ' be of good cheer,' or ' may Osiris give thee the refreshing water.'

V. Change in the Religious Spirit

The more one studies this era the more will he be persuaded that the Christ came in the fulness of time; that

all its activities, political, social, moral and religious
were converging toward His appearing. The natural joy of
life (*Weltfreudigkeit*) was gone : men had become serious.
The problems that agitated them most were those of
ethics and religion, above all, the problems of the individual
soul, or those universal enigmas that concern man as
man everywhere and always—the issues of life and death.
We have noticed a demand on all hands for a universal
religion. Toward the beginning of the Christian era the
religious instinct asserted itself in a surprising degree :
' men were thirsty to believe and worship,' says Denis.
The God of the city-state passed away with the city-state
which finally expired under Caesar and Augustus ; state
religions were maintained by custom not by faith. The
world had come to believe in the unity of God which
suggested one religion. If one man could rule the world,
surely one God could rule the universe. Social, political,
and legislative unity had been impressed upon the Empire
by Rome ; philosophical and, to some extent, ethical unity
had been emphasised by Greek thought ; only religious
unity was needed. As men were persuaded of the unity
of God, the unity of man and the divine kinship, no parti-
cularistic religion could satisfy. If sin abounded, it was
also an age of intense religious activity. Greek thought
made as noble an effort to supply a religion of humanity as
was possible for philosophy. The era of the subjective had
arrived which is specially favourable to devotion. Rome
offered her subjects a universal religion in the imperial
cult to impress the world with her own majesty rather
than that of God. Her subjects accepted it with good will
as a form of civil homage, while they went their own way
to find satisfaction for the life of the soul : the *praesens
deus* of the emperor might appeal to the imagination but
not to the emotions. The throne of the human heart was
declared vacant and there were abundant candidates ;
in this department Greece and Rome retired before the

religions of the East. Individualism is in no department
so pronounced as in the religious. Personal access to the
Deity was offered through the Oriental priesthoods. The
world was convinced that the two great realities in the
universe were God and the soul. The worshipper was no
longer content to remain a silent and passive observer : he
wished to take part himself in the worship. Religion was
regarded as an individual concern, and not as a province of
politics. The mysteries and the Eastern faiths supplied the
place with the ancients which the Church occupies with us.
Membership in these and state citizenship were separate :
man selected his religion, he did not any longer enter it by
birthright.

Emotionalism

We observe a rising tide of emotionalism. It is easy
to understand how this was restrained in the severe
but necessary discipline of the old régime.[1] When the
individual is detached from the collective unity there is
more play for the emotions. Religion is rooted in the
emotional.[2] Jerome says Plato placed the soul of man
in the head, Christ placed it in the heart. Emotionalism
entered the Graeco-Roman world by a twofold path, first,
in the consciousness of deep religious needs disclosed by
individualism, which reacted upon men like the discovery
of a new sense; and secondly, in the Eastern religions which
professed to meet while fostering these wants. Emotionalism betrayed itself negatively in the depreciation of the
state cults, and positively, in the efforts made by the
Roman religious authorities to make the worship more
congenial by introducing emotional and individual elements.
Fowler [3] speaks of ' the first lectisternia in 399 B.C. as

[1] Contrast the statuesque sorrow of Pericles' *Funeral Oration* with that of
Cicero over the loss of Tullia.
[2] M. Arnold's definition of religion as morality touched with emotion
contains a half truth.
[3] *Relig. Exper.*, p. 261.

the earliest authentic example of the emotional tendency
of the Roman plebs.' While this emotional element is
necessary for religion, it does not constitute religion, nor
does it necessarily conduce to it. It may issue in true
religious enthusiasm and mysticism, or sink to moral
anarchy.[1] Hence too the Oriental religions have been so
differently estimated in antiquity and now. In one sense
men find in a religion what they bring to it, and derive from
it what they most desire. Those who approached these
religions in earnest to find spiritual support discovered
in them means of grace ; others sought in them palliatives
of and even incentives to immorality. Ceremonial purity
was required rather than spiritual : the emotional mistresses of men like Catullus, Propertius, and Tibullus were
eager devotees of these cults. The sensual romance of
Apuleius is another instance. A further evidence of
emotionalism is the prominence of women in the Oriental
cults, including Judaism and Christianity. We have
already referred to the prominence of the passion of
love in the later, and especially in Roman, literature.
The very realism, characteristic of the age, is evidence
of the emotional.

Personal Religion

There was a considerable advance in the recognition
of the inwardness and personal nature of man's higher
life.[2] This was in line with the general drift toward
individualism. Man had turned from the investigation
of the problems of the external world to probe the secret of
his own nature. Although the ancient world did not arrive
at any adequate conception of personality (the depths
of which have not even yet been plumbed), there was
a developing sense of personality with its pain and responsi-

[1] Many of the greatest musicians led immoral lives.
[2] Cf. Seneca, *Ep.* 28.

bility. The city-state had presented only the external and collective side of religion ; the personal and inward aspect now overshadowed the other. Man turned aside from political life to regulate his own, and find satisfaction for Self in religion. Amid the terrible social strife and devastation in which the Empire was founded, men were compelled to think about themselves in a new way. It seemed as if God had set the emperors to keep guard in order to give men time to reflect about themselves. In the stillness of the *pax Romana*, the need for inward peace grew all the more clamant. The collective covenant with God had been broken, and as men cannot live without the supernatural, the personal bond was sought. The external sanctions and authority of morality being threatened, another sanction was discovered in the innate moral nature of man and in a God-implanted conscience which demanded obedience while states rise and fall. There was acknowledged an objective and eternal law of righteousness to which the God within bears testimony. The worthiest rewards of righteousness and the acutest penalties of sin are enacted in the theatre of the inner life. Socrates maintains that the worst consequences of our conduct are the disastrous effects upon our own spiritual nature. The famous line of Virgil represents the same truth : *quisque suos patimur Manes*, ' each of us suffers in his own spiritual being.' The call of the heathen preacher was for introspection and self-examination : this era dated from the ' Know thyself,' by which Socrates produced one of the most momentous epochs in the higher life. The later schools without exception aimed at bestowing upon man independence in his inward life. Stoicism took the lead in asking men to retire to the citadel of their own being where external things could not ruffle : the only worthy life was amid the secret triumphs and agonies of one's soul. ' Retire within yourself' was the motto of Aurelius. Peace may be found within when it is denied without. There are many pagan texts, especially in Seneca, Epictetus, and Aurelius, parallel to ' the Kingdom of God is within you.'

Character

Closely connected with this inwardness is the importance attached to character, though the old world was even fuller of inconsistencies between a man's ideals and his conduct than the modern. Ovid could say ' I see the better and approve it, but I pursue the worse.' Men had begun, in the words of Emerson, to test the passion of the moment by the verdict of the centuries. The *Apology* of Xenophon, prosaic compared with that of Plato, contains one memorable passage. Socrates, seeing Anytus leaving the court in triumph, exclaimed, ' How wretched is this fellow not to reflect that whichever of us has done that which is the best and noblest for all time, he is the victor.' A Stoic, asked if he had lost anything in the sack of his native city, replied, ' I carry all my goods with me.' More attention was paid to moral education and the formation of character ; precepts and examples were in demand. The whole mission of Stoicism was to form strong and fearless characters that could bid defiance to any calamity, and it admittedly achieved great success. All the attention that used to be paid to politics was now centred upon morality. That what a man is, is of more importance than what a man has, is a doctrine quite familiar to Seneca, Epictetus, and Aurelius. Probably the most impressive testimony of early Christianity was the upright lives of its adherents.

Demand for Authority

The ancient world was anxiously searching for an authority, especially about the time of the appearance of

Christianity. The Orient, relying less on the capacities of man, looked to God for knowledge given by revelation and embodied in the lore of priesthoods. The Greeks looked to man himself for knowledge ; they considered it no irreverence to pry into the secrets of the Almighty. As the Greeks sought salvation by wisdom, the question of a criterion to distinguish truth from falsehood was a matter of supreme importance. The question arose, What and wherein is the authority of Thought ? Socrates vindicated the validity of thought and the existence of objective and universal truth : he believed in the possibility of knowledge through concepts arrived at by dialectic. He was the first Greek to enthrone conscience as an authority above law and the state. He asserted that man's moral nature is not a lie, and that we have a conscience which must be obeyed at all costs, even at that of life itself. He believed he had an inner guide—his *daemon*. He also gave the first utterance in the Western world to the need of a revelation—a heaven-sent guide to teach us our religious duties. Plato found the authority for the moral life of man in innate ideas, in the recollection of the Good and the Lovely which our souls contemplated with God in their pre-natal condition. The Cyrenaics despaired of knowledge. Aristotle gave prominence to empiric knowledge, defending sensuous perception on the ground that the senses never deceive us. The Stoics were sheer empirics. The Epicureans theoretically accepted sensuous perception and the resulting concepts as criteria of truth, but in practice they held to the personal feeling of pleasure and pain as the basis of moral conduct. The Academics rejected both the evidence of the senses and the intellect as guides ; they also repudiated knowledge by concepts because these bore no hall-mark of veracity, and the same object generated different concepts in different minds. Man must rest in suspension of judgment, and the highest criterion for moral conduct is probability. Man grew weary of uncertainty, and as attention centred more upon the ethics of the individual, he demanded a working criterion. The Eclectics were the most practical thinkers of a practical age. They placed the standard for decision between true and false, right and wrong, in each man's self-consciousness where truth is given immediately; the ordinary self-consciousness gives the final decision in philosophic questions. 'Thus innate knowledge forms the transition to that form of philosophy which only goes back to self-consciousness, in order to receive in it the revelation of God.'[1] Eclecticism opened the way for, and went hand in hand with, the philosophy of Revelation. External Revelation is complementary to internal.[2] This is the position taken so strongly by Cicero and Seneca. The Greeks, the first to doubt, were not yet satisfied. A higher authority was needed to regulate the liberty of independence secured by individualism. The Greeks had trusted themselves to Reason, which had carried them as far as Reason can; they were now conscious that there is a domain into which the intellect by itself cannot enter, that there is in life a mysterious region where only faith can say the last word. Denis[3] observes that, 'grown old in logic, wearied of uncertainty and scepticism, they were less conscious of the need of arriving by any path at the emancipation of the spirit, than of discovering a rule to terminate their discussions and their doubts. They would view the letter of a formal and holy text rather as an alleviation than as a subjection and a restraint.' Justin Martyr says, 'It is impossible to know either by nature,

---

[1] Zeller, *Eclectics*, p. 20.

[2] 'These two currents [an urgent demand for knowledge in the practical interests of religion, and a disbelief in the truths of existing knowledge and knowledge generally] coalescing, we arrive at the thought that truth, which could not be attained in the form of intellectual knowledge, exists outside of it, and is partly to be sought in the religious traditions of the early days of Greece and the East, partly by immediate divine revelation.'—Zeller, *Stoics Epic., and Scep.*, p. 30.

[3] ii. 321.

or the sheer power of thought, things so sublime as the divine : that can only come by the gracious gift of Him who knows all.' Pilate was unconsciously voicing the demand of his age when he asked in the presence of ' the Way, the Truth, and the Life,' ' What is Truth ? ' without recognising the Revelation of Truth. From whatever causes—the discordant voices of spiritual directors, the mistrust in man's capacity for knowledge, the shattering of external restraints, the isolation of the individual soul, the weariness that overtook Greek thinking, the contact with the Revelation philosophy of the East—there spread a deep sense of the need of a Revelation,[1] which was intensified by the contact of East and West in Alexandria; in the Hermetic literature Revelation has become the source of knowledge.[2] ' The last motive in this speculation (which ended in Neo-Platonism), was the yearning after a higher revelation of truth ; its metaphysical presupposition was an opposition of God and the world . . . its practical consequence was a combination of ethics with religion.' [3] Neo-Pythagoreanism, later Platonism, and finally Neo-Platonism trusted rather to a revelation than to logic. They sought the knowledge of God in communion with Him, in rising in ecstasy from the sensuous to the supersensuous. The idea of Revelation was encouraged by the Oriental religions to which people thronged. The contact of Judaism with the West, and the tremendous influence of the world-historic Septuagint version, promulgated this faith. In addition, Messianic ideas were widely diffused (p. 136). The ecclesiastical councils were not isolated phenomena; they were the result of an agelong search for an authority for the spirit.

[1] Cf. Neander, *Ch. Hist., Eng. Tr.*, i. 43.
[2] This Revelation is granted either immediately by a God (Hermes, Thât, Asclepius) or mediately by an inspired prophet.
[3] Zeller, *Outlines*, p. 305.

Nearness of the Supernatural

A consciousness of the supernatural was keener with the ancients than with some modern Christians. They knew no religion without miracles. The supernatural was in close propinquity to them, and their whole life was filled with its influence. What to us would seem miraculous and incredible was to them of ordinary occurrence—miracles of healing, visions, apocalypses, resuscitation of the dead. There was an evil side to this belief in the supernatural : religion was debased to superstition.[1] The divine was feared lest it should hurt, not loved for its beneficence. The gods could be threatened, cajoled, bribed. All means were used to deflect their wills from evil designs. Astrology, witchcraft, necromancy, thaumaturgy were rife. Some of the most degrading practices were performed under the name of religion. We realise the force of ignorant superstition in reading the great poem of Lucretius : his whole effort is to weed the fear of the gods out of human life, for 'to so many evils could *religio* prompt men.' The ancients believed that the Deity revealed himself in trifling accidents and in preternatural fashion. Sober historians like Livy and Tacitus pause to relate miraculous events, and Suetonius revels in the miraculous. With the spread of dualism the whole world was portioned out to a hierarchy of beneficent and malefic spirits ; the life of man was the theatre of a truceless conflict for his soul between the opposing spiritual forces. Paul was not a stranger to the earnestness of this perpetual struggle.

Mysticism

A strong flood of mysticism was sweeping over the world. Mysticism has been often asserted to be alien to the leading

[1] De Jong (*Das antike Mysterienwesen*, p. 198) speaks of the mysteries as *official* magic.

peoples of the Empire. It was undoubtedly uncongenial to the Romans, to whom the material was so real. Inge [1] maintains that the 'Jewish mind and character in spite of its deeply religious bent was alien to mysticism,' but in the Psalms and the Prophets we often find a genuine religious mysticism, and another type in the Apocalyptic visions and the Cabbala. To the Greek mind in its heyday the mystic temperament was foreign.[2] Mysticism entered the Greek world in the religious revival of the sixth century B.C., in Orphism and Pythagoreanism; it was too individualistic to lay hold on a civilisation entrenched in the *polis*. It laid hold on Plato and became prominent in the subjectiveness which prevailed from the third, but particularly from the first century B.C. onwards [3]—in Neo-Pythagoreanism, Neo-Platonism, in Philo, and in Paul and John. Wherever we find religion, we find mysticism as one of the channels connecting with the Invisible. There was a demand for the experimental knowledge of God [4] and a *unio mystica*. In one respect, mysticism is the cultivation of the last element discovered in probing personality—the emotional. Socrates was as much a mystic as a true sceptic. Plato is the father of Greek and Christian mysticism. He silences his doubts by faith; he believes that in the body we are exiled from home; his whole effort is to rise from the finite to union with the Infinite. No one was ever more oppressed with the sense of the dualism of man's nature. The 'truly mystical sense of salvation—the return of the prodigal to his father's home from the far country, where this high affinity had been almost forfeited in "vagrancy among the manifold"—will appear again

---

[1] *Christian Mysticism*, p. 39.

[2] Rohde, *Relig. d. Gr.*, p. 338. 'Mystik war ein fremder Blutstropfen im griechischen Blute.'

[3] Cf. Kennedy, *St. Paul and the Mystery-Religions*, index, *Mysticism*; Lehmann, *Mystik im Heid. u. Christentum*, chaps. 5-8; Norden, *Agnostos Theos*, 97 f., 109, 222.

[4] 'γνῶσις θεοῦ wird das Lösungswort im Konkurrenzkampfe der Religionen.' Norden, *ib.* 109.

as a special type of Platonic thought . . . an overpower-
ing conception of Unity; and of some scarce compre-
hensible form of Being, to which the longing aspiration
of the awakened soul ever tends, rising through images
and figures and types of the sensible world to the perfect
vision of Beauty beyond.' [1] When religion turned inward,
and philosophy was converted into religion, the mystical
elements of ecstasy and passivity were emphasised. When
the intellect grew weary of long-sustained activity, when
knowledge seemed exhausted or men were overtaken by
despair in man's capacity for knowledge,[2] when they became
more sensitive to the pain of isolation [3] and more convinced that our moral nature is not a lie, when *il y avait
dans les âmes un vide immense*, they cried out for Revelation; ' the gulf of mysticism invites the hardy speculator
to its profound repose, and constrains and fascinates him,
until he is overcome by dizziness, and falls as if drawn
by some irresistible influence into the abyss.' The effort
was made, as in Philo and Neo-Platonism, to rise above
conscious thought into immediate union with God.
Mysticism also betrays itself in the frequent other-
worldliness, in the prevalent world-weariness, in the
asceticism which aimed at detaching the soul from the
attractions of earth, in the rebellion against formality in
religion and idle speculation in philosophy, in the increasing power of Platonic idealism, in the demand for salvation-
religions, in the fresh emotional elements in life, in the
quest after the deification of man, in the spread of indefi-
nite Messianic expectations. These elements find their
practical illustration in the spread of ascetic brotherhoods
like the Therapeutae and Essenes, and in the purifications

[1] Bussell, pp. 241-2.
[2] 'So tritt Glauben und erleuchtetes Schauen an die Stelle von Wissen und
Begreifen, ein tief innerliches Erlebnis an die Stelle der Reflexion; fromme
Hingabe an das Unfassbare ersetzt den stolzen sich selbst die Grenzen
vorschreibenden Forschersinn.'—Norden, p. 127.
[3] 'Mystik kann, ihrem Wesen nach, nicht wohl Religion einer Gemeinde
werden.'—Rohde, *ib.*, p. 336.

and the mortifications required by the **Oriental cults.**
Such principles were the tenets of Neo-Pythagoreanism,
the school of Philo, and finally of Neo-Platonism. If
the spread of dualism did not foster mysticism, it at least
caused men to take refuge in mysticism as the means of
escape. God and the world, spirit and matter, were set
over against each other in antagonism. Greek thought
wrestled for centuries to discover a reconciling principle,
a larger synthesis in which all antagonisms are harmonised ;
but Greek thought never found the synthesis. It believed
from the first in Unity, but could not discover the terms or
principle or mode. At last in despair, in Neo-Platonism,
it surrendered logic, and, seeking to rise above conscious
thought, made a leap for unity in the ecstasy of the Vision
Beatific. At length it found that ' nothing worthy proving
can be proven nor yet disproven.' Mysticism has been
defined as ' an attempt to solve, by love and emotion,
the dualism of the world ; and especially to reconcile the
constant struggles and defiance of the individual will
with universal law.' And mysticism was the last word of
Greek philosophy. Theory was abandoned for immediate
experience, just as in Christianity we appeal to the
Christian consciousness.

Intermediaries

God became more transcendent, and **intermediaries**
were needed between man and God. Several causes
contributed to this—the greater hold which dualism
gained, the rising sense of sin, the influence of the Oriental
idea of an exalted transcendent Deity, monotheism, the
consciousness of the limits of knowledge. God was
consequently removed far above the realm of sense and
placed beyond reach of the world. An impassable gulf
yawned between God and Nature : matter is inherently
evil, so that God cannot come into contact with it. The

highest principle being spirit it became difficult to account
for the Creation at all. That a pure spirit could sully
itself by finding expression in the material, and that a
good Creator could produce a universe with so much evil,
was impossible. The activity of God in the world would
invade that serenity of the only worthy activity of the
Highest — self-contemplation. Through intermediaries
God created and governs His creation. The whole universe
was peopled with demons or semi-divine beings, of whom
some were beneficent and some malevolent. The idea
of a medium between God and man is very old. In the
Timaeus Plato puts an immanent World-Soul between a
transcendent God and the world : this World-Soul is the
image of God, His steward, or even another God. 'The
maker and father of this universe is difficult to discover ;
when discovered he cannot be revealed to all men,' says
Plato. This World-Soul is therefore one of Plato's most
important links between the finite and the infinite. By
a singular coincidence, both East and West were converging
to a belief in a medium which at first was an abstraction,
but was gradually personified and finally regarded as
personal or an incarnation. In the Old Testament we
find a quasi-personification of the Word of God, sometimes of His Name, and more especially of Wisdom ;
' Hebrew thought tended to represent God's self-manifesta-
tion as mediated by an agent, more or less conceived as
personal and yet blending with the divine personality
itself.' [1] In the West the doctrine of the Logos or Word
goes back to Heraclitus of Ephesus. His doctrine has
occasioned much discussion, but an excellent authority
sums it up in three propositions : (1) ' The Logos is eternal,
both pre-existent and everlasting.' (2) ' All things
happen through the Logos. Its authority is not confined
to the sphere of human activities ; it is a cosmic principle,
" common " or " universal." ' (3) ' The duty of man is to

[1] Purves, art. 'Logos' in Hastings' *D. B.*

obey this universal Logos,' though most men refuse to see or hear it.[1] To the Stoics is due the honour of popularising this doctrine of the Word as medium. Zeno took over the Heraclitean Word, regarded it as the manifestation of God, the all-pervading principle, even identified it with Fate, with Providence, and finally with God. It was an immanent Logos. Cleanthes transformed the fire of Heraclitus and Zeno into spirit and then made the Logos spirit. The Logos became the principle of all unity. Posidonius upheld the Logos doctrine, passing it on to Roman Stoicism and perhaps to Philo and the Jewish Christians. In Alexandria, where East and West first blended, this important theological doctrine gained fresh impetus, especially from Philo. The medium is personified till it becomes almost personal. Philo became the vehicle of expression for a greater truth than he was conscious of. His theism separated the Word from the highest God. He designates his Logos as the 'image of God,' the 'eldest son,' the 'first-born,' the 'prophet' or 'interpreter,' the 'consul' or 'vicegerent' of God, the 'mediator,' the 'intercessor,' the 'paraclete,' the 'high-priest of the universe.' He is also the 'impress' of God, the instrument of creation, the 'lower God,' the 'second God,' partaking of the nature of God and man. Thus in the Word as ever assuming a more personal character, Eastern and Western anticipations converged and met : ' Hebrew thought tended to conceive of the medium of revelation as personal,'[2] and one mark of post-Aristotelian philosophy was ' its ever-increasing disposition to personify the ethical ideal '[3] Finally, ' the Word became flesh and tabernacled in our midst.'

Asceticism

As an evidence of the seriousness of the age, the growth of asceticism is noteworthy. To the Western spirit

[1] Adam, *Relig. Teachers of Gr.*, p. 219, and chap. iii. of his *Vitality of Platonism*. [2] Purves, *ibid*. [3] Adam, p. 240.

asceticism was alien, as opposed to its conception of self-expansion as contrasted with Eastern self-repression. It entered the West with the religious revival of the sixth century B.C.; it does not seem to have gained much ground until the age of the subjective schools. It was partly a result of ethical dualism. The Orphics had introduced the conception that 'the body is a tomb' and prison of the soul. Throughout his works Plato calls for self-renunciation, the subjugation and even contempt of the body in order to preserve the soul unsullied. The Stoics summoned men not to regulate but to extirpate their passions. Ascetic brotherhoods like the Neo-Pythagoreans, Essenes, and Therapeutae were formed to foster morality. As the moralists raised their voices against the vices of their age, these men advocated the renunciation of even the lawful pleasures of life. The worth of the soul and the value of character were regarded as justifying any sacrifices in the way of abstinence, penance, or self-mortification. Juvenal laughs at the devotees of Isis breaking the ice to take their ceremonial bath and crawling on their knees on the Campus Martius. The unhealthy growth of asceticism in early Christianity was fostered by the spirit of the preceding age. It was a moral protest against the self-indulgence of the times. It provided a refuge also for numerous world-weary spirits: the ennui of the age swelled the numbers of the ascetic guilds which repudiated marriage and were dependent on converts for their continuance.

Prayer

In the records of this period no subject was discussed more frequently than that of Prayer, which may be regarded as an index of its importance. Treatises were written on prayer, as by Aristotle, the author of *Alcibiades II.*, Persius (*Sat.* 2), Juvenal (*Sat.* x.), and Maximus of Tyre (*Dis.* xi.), and the subject receives attention from all moralists, as from Cicero, Seneca, Epictetus, Lucian, etc. Prayer was universal : it is the efficacy, the quality and content of prayer on which interest is focused. Pagan preachers protested loudly against all prayers for immoral objects, against asking the Deity for something which their own conduct renders impossible. Prayer for self-aggrandisement, for wealth, for ambition, for revenge is forbidden. Men should pray as if all men could hear them ; 'it is an impiety to say to the Gods what could not be uttered without shame to man.' Seneca directs Lucilius to ask for health of mind first, and then for health of body : ' so live with men as if God saw you, so converse with God as if men heard you.' In another epistle,[1] he directs Lucilius not to ask heaven for what is in his own power ; he need not gain access to the ear of the statue because ' God is nigh thee, with thee, in thee : a holy spirit dwells within us the superintendent and guardian of all our good and evil.' As now, men were not unanimous about prayer. The Epicureans viewed it as futile to address Gods that dare not be disturbed by the troubles of men. Maximus of Tyre said that God cannot be changed by prayer as it is inconsistent with Providence ; a man is worthier by not being importunate ; the wise man's prayer is not a request for something he has not, but a communion and conversation with God (Porphyry and Maximus of Tyre). Plato had said that God hears only the good and refuses to accept the gifts of the wicked. The lives of Socrates and of Pythagoras were regarded as a continuous prayer, not for gifts but as a means of strength ; they and all other wise men left to God to choose for them what was best. The wicked do not know what to ask, and the wise can trust God to give the best. There was a general conviction that God cares less for cult and sacrifices than for the worship of a sincere heart.[2] The quality of

---

[1] 41, which the Bipontine edition hails as 'O pulchram altamque epistolam.'
[2] Cf. Cic., N. D., ii. 28, ' ut eos semper pura integra incorrupta et mente et voce veneremur '; and Publilius Syrus, ' Puras Deus non plenas aspicit manus.'

prayer was elevated by the abundant protests against all unworthy praying.   Prayer entered more the spiritual life rather as a 'conversation with God.'   As spiritual wants increased and men stood in perplexity in the greatest moral crisis of history, their undefined cry was 'Teach us to pray.'   The emotional tendency of the age, the spread of Oriental worships with their regular services of prayer, the demand for spiritual support, the increasing inwardness of religion, contributed to the practice of prayer. The ubiquitous Jew, always a man of prayer, with his synagogue and its services and its influential following of 'God-fearing' heathen, was a living example of the power of prayer.   Merivale [1] suggests that the Jew taught the pagan world to pray, but the pagans were willing to learn. The frequent treatises on prayer by early Christian writers are an answer to the pagan interest in prayer, and a continuation of the Jewish practice.

It is impossible here to give any idea of the—often conflicting—opinions [2] of heathen writers on prayer, or specimens of extant prayers.[3]

---

[1] *Conversion*, p. 114.

[2] On which cf., *e.g.*, H. Schmidt, *Veteres philosophi quomodo iudicaverint de precibus* (Giessen, 1907).

[3] We may perhaps insert a fragment from Cleanthes:—

> 'Lead me, O Zeus, and lead me, Destiny,
>   What way soe'er ye have appointed me. .
>   I follow unafraid : yea, though the will
>   Turn recreant, I needs must follow still.'
>
> (G. H. RENDALL's tr.).

And two selections from his *Hymn to Zeus*:—

> 'Hail ! for 'tis meet that men should call on thee
>   Whose seed we are ; and ours the destiny
>   Alone of all that lives and moves on earth,
>   A mirror of thy deity to be. . . .
>   But skill to make the crooked straight is thine,
>   To turn disorder to a fair design ;
>   Ungracious things are gracious in thy sight,
>   For ill and good thy power doth so combine
>   That out of all appears in unity
>   Eternal reason, which the wicked flee
>   And disregard, who long for happiness,
>   Yet God's great law can neither hear nor see.'
>
> (PORTER's tr.).

Resignation

Not only in prayer did men seek support and solace, but in calm resignation to the will of God. After the rebellion of the individual and his self-seeking, this resignation is all the more remarkable. No age has surpassed this period in cheerful acceptance of the experiences of life. Oppressed by fatalism, ejected from a system that had given scope for long to their best activities, standing in isolation amid the wreck of the old and confronted by the confusion and suffering of the present, men turned to God and sought their liberty in acquiescence in His purposes. Fate was identified with God or put under His control. The Stoics were foremost in teaching resignation to what they spoke of as Fate, or Universal Law, or Providence, or the will of God. One of the most frequently recurring notes in the literature of the age is that of acquiescence. Seneca's famous expression is characteristic, 'I do not *obey* God, I *assent* with Him.' Pagans were slowly learning to say 'Thy will be done.'

Suffering, and a new sensitiveness to Suffering

Suffering was performing its perfect work among the peoples of the Empire. To the Jew in his early history suffering was penal, an evidence of divine displeasure. This explanation would not work in all cases, especially where righteous and wicked Israelites were associated in calamity. Israel in the light of her own history and the teachings of her prophets, began to view suffering and disappointment in another light. The suffering Servant of Jehovah—the incarnation of Israel—is the grandest spiritual interpretation of suffering : the suffering is undeserved, but redemptive and vicarious. Israel almost came to realise that her mission was to suffer for the world.

To the joyful spirit of Greece suffering was a dread visitation. The *Prometheus Vinctus* of Aeschylus protests against suffering which seemed divine oppression. When the element of trouble entered, the Greeks first fled to pessimism. But Greek pessimism was not the last word. Their religious teachers wrestled with the question. Socrates and Plato asserted that no real misfortune can overtake a good man, and that he is never neglected by the Deity. The Stoics denied that all suffering is penal, as Job had done for Israel. Suffering must be good for man, for the Deity knows best what to give. It is only in suffering that men come to their fullest self-consciousness, and that virtue can be put to the test to produce examples of spiritual strength. In Roman literature the subject is frequently touched upon, but Cicero and Seneca are the classical instances. Overtaken by sorrow they became stronger and better men, and learned to strengthen their brethren. The disciplinary mission of suffering was acknowledged. ' Whom God loves He tries,' says Seneca.

There was a new sensitiveness to suffering brought about through the displacement of collectivism by individualism and the scope now allowed to the emotions, and by the prominence of private over public life. Kaerst [1] says, ' the peculiar character of the religious life in the Hellenistic period is clearly expressed in the characteristic form of private associations or cult-brotherhoods (Thiasoi),' and this phenomenon is due largely to demand for sympathy. The Empire was founded in suffering.[2] Neither the conquests of Islam, nor the religious wars of the sixteenth century, nor the Napoleonic wars were fraught with such suffering as the terrible period, say, from the destruction of Carthage and Corinth, 146 B.C., or from the era of the Gracchi, 133 B.C., to the establishment of the Empire in 31 B.C. The ruth-

---

[1] *Gesch. d. hellenistischen Zeitalters*, vol. ii., i. 280.
[2] Hegel sees in the tremendous misery and universal suffering produced by the Roman spirit of power a sorrow which was to be the ' birth-throe of the religion of truth' (*Phil. of Relig.*, Eng. Tr., ii. 322, and *Phil. of Hist.*, p. 330).

lessness of Roman conquests, the savagery of her civil
wars, her proscriptions, the increase of slavery, the cruel
slave insurrections, the rise of capitalism, complete economic
disorganisation, the tyranny of the military over the civil
power, these and similar causes produced an untold amount
of suffering. The gods of Greece and Rome had no message
for men in such agony.[1] It was the opportunity for Oriental
deities who were more human and sympathetic,[2] who
alternately suffered and rejoiced, who died and rose again.
Their whole worship was instinct with human sympathy ;
they offered what men most needed. It was the opportunity also for Judaism which had so often drained a bitter
cup, but never without hope. The message of her prophets,
her undying Messianic hope, the influence of her synagogue
and her faith in prayer, made their appeal to many an
earnest heathen.

Consolation Literature

This keen sensitiveness to suffering and demand for
sympathy gave rise to a most curious literary phenomenon
—a Consolation literature in the closing Republic and
early Empire. We infer from Dio Chrysostom (*Dis.* 27)
that it was quite usual to call in a philosopher to administer
consolations in misfortune. Crantor was the father of this
literature ; he wrote a book to a bereaved father so helpful,
that Cicero speaks of it as a ' golden book, to be learned
by heart.' Crantor had catalogued and expounded all that
the wisdom of Greece could offer as solace in calamity.
Consolations being in demand, there arose a profession of
consolers. Cicero on the death of his daughter wrote a

---

[1] Except Aesculapius, who was known as 'greatest lover of men'
(φιλανθρωπότατος).

[2] Lucius in his prayer to Isis says, 'thou tendest the mischances of
miserable men *with a sweet mother's love* . . . alway by land and sea thou
guardest men, thou drivest from them the storms of life and stretchest out
to them thy saving hand, wherewith thou unbindest even the inextricable
weft of Fate' (Apul. *Met.*, 11. 25, Butler's tr.).

Consolatio addressed to himself; his *Tusculan Disputations* is really a consolation—at least, he seeks to gather comfort from every part of the compass of philosophy and experience. Plutarch wrote a book to prove that exile could be tolerable; he also wrote a *Consolation to his wife* in which he commends her courage in grief over the loss of their two-year-old daughter, and holds out a faint hope of immortality. His *Consolation to Apollonius* is less hopeful, or rather despairing. Some of Ovid's letters to his wife in the *Tristia* are consolatory, and a spurious *Consolatio ad Liviam Augustam* has been attributed to him. Seneca is the classic of extant consolers: he addressed a *Consolation to Marcia* on the death of her son, one to *Polybius* on the death of his brother, while the *Consolation to his mother Helvia* was intended to console himself rather than her on the hardships of his exile. We know the name of a lost work of his *On premature Death*, and we have fragments of his *De Remediis Fortuitorum*. Apollonius (*Ep.* 58) consoled Valerius on the death of his son. Consolatory formulae were discovered for every calamity, for exile, old age, loss of health, physical suffering, confiscation of property, and chiefly for the death of friends. Some of the ingredients are to us trite and commonplace, but when they first were offered to a sorrowing world they were apparently efficacious. It was recognised by consolers, especially by Seneca, that in order to benefit those in distress one must study the psychology of each individual case; different remedies must be applied to different cases.

Sense of Sin

One of the characteristics of Greek and Roman paganism was the absence of a sense of sin and a proud reliance on human nature. But with a growing spiritual experience this self-sufficiency of man was shattered, and a sense of sin appeared.[1] Man is more sensitive to sin in proportion to his progress in spirituality. Several causes contributed to inoculate the peoples of the Empire with something akin to the Hebrew sense of sinfulness : the contact with the East, the extension of religious dualism, the accumulated results of self-examination, the influence of the Jew with his zeal for righteousness and his abhorrence of sin, the individualising of religion, the new emphasis on *will*. Stoicism had no high idea of the general mass of mankind, who were regarded as fools ; only the wise man could be a saint. Cleanthes complains that men will not hearken to the *Logos*, preferring to live in wickedness. Numerous voices were raised against vice, hypocrisy, formality : there were more protests against sin than positive calls to righteousness. This need not surprise us ; the destructive precedes the constructive. Livy complains ' we can neither endure nor mend our faults.' The abundant protests against the corruption and sins of the age were a healthful sign. Moral directors and preachers are persuaded that men are moral invalids with sick souls in need of healing.[2] The writers who most clearly reveal a sense of the sinfulness of man are Virgil and Seneca. The mystic religious spirit of Virgil, which has fascinated centuries, was peculiarly sensitive to the enormity of human guilt ; he was painfully conscious of the world's need. Those who read carefully the *Georgics* and more especially the *Aeneid*, will detect many a passage in which this prophet dares to take a view of the status of man and the sinfulness of his actions different from that of the majority. The greatness of the Empire and its evident blessings did not blind him to the sin in which it was founded. Conway

---

[1] 'The complaint raised by Hebrew conscience in the dawn of history becomes the evening invocation of Hellenic philosophy.'—Hausrath, *Apostles*, i. 42.

[2] 'Throughout the world of St. Paul we see a mighty wandering of pilgrims desirous to wash away their sins at the great shrines and to be delivered of their need.'—Deissmann, *St. Paul*, p. 44.

asks, 'What is the tremendous machinery of punishment after death which the Sixth Book describes in the most majestic passage of all epic poetry (*Aen.*, vi. 548-627), but the measure of Virgil's sense of human guilt?'[1] Seneca is painfully conscious of the weakness and sinfulness of human nature.[2] With Paul he exclaims, 'we have all sinned. As our fathers complained of the moral degeneration of their days, so must we lament our corruption, and posterity will point to us as a sinful age. The fashion in vices may change, its reign is as powerful as ever : we are wicked, have been wicked, and shall continue to be wicked. After the restoration of all things, men will abandon innocence and relapse into sin.' In spite of his faith in the kinship of man with the Divine, he is forced to recognise the presence of an irrational element in his nature connected chiefly with the body, the *flesh* as he calls it, and this wars against the higher life ; and in spite of his Stoicism he confesses that man cannot help himself, God must stretch forth his hand to him : *adscendentibus di manum porrigunt.*

Union of Morality and Religion

We note a gradual convergence of morality and religion,[3] the inseparable union of which was consummated under Christianity. Political religion had perished, and personal religion was of supreme importance : the question was how to please God best. The prophets of Israel and the dramatists and philosophers of Greece had not laboured in vain in calling men to serve God with pure hearts and upright lives. The oft-repeated precept to follow God or imitate God signified a moral life.[4] The dividing lines

[1] *Virgil's Messianic Ecl.*, p. 37.
[2] Cf. *De Benef.*, i. 10, *de Clem.*, i. 6, *Ep.* 29.
[3] L. Campbell says that after Plato's day 'religion amongst thoughtful men could not longer be divorced from an elevated morality' (p. 367). Cf. *Theaetetus*, 176 B., where the upright man is said to have the truest likeness to God.
[4] Cf. Seneca, *Ep.* xv. 3. 'Vis deos propitiare ? Bonus esto : satis illos coluit quisquis imitatus est.'

among humanity were no longer racial or national, but moral: men were either good or wicked; virtue and vice were the criteria. The wicked were thus deprived of the protection of tradition and custom. There was an ever-deepening sense of the worth of the soul and the value of character as the inalienable possession of man. The desire for moral guidance and the need of spiritual support went together. Men were willing to practise renunciation, to mortify the body for the health of the soul. Even the life beyond was bound to this in a moral nexus. Thus ethics succeeded to the large place vacated by politics. The lives of men were standardised by the noblest examples of incarnate virtue. Religion had turned inward, and after having prompted to self-examination reacted upon conduct.

Religion Popularised

As noted already (p. 11), the epoch of the advent of Christianity was a democratic era. Jewish worship had in the Synagogue grown more popular, and this character was emphasised in the Diaspora. In Greece philosophy had left the study to make an attempt to reach the masses. It was the masses—often with leaders from the aristocracy —that put an end to the most powerful oligarchy of history, and set up the Empire. The emperors were dependent for the stability of their power on the favour of the populace. The religions of the Orient gained their victory over the West primarily by the patronage of the masses and in the face of long-continued official opposition. Popular preachers and lecturers, and a kind of ancient Salvation-army workers, found abundant scope and encouragement. Philosophers, religious teachers, politicians and statesmen were looking with as much anxiety upon the masses then, as the Church and the State are now. Among the masses was the greatest religious activity, and more faith than among their leaders; the people went their own way, leaving their aristocratic and literary brethren to their intellectualism. If the inner history of the pagan masses of Greece and Rome were written we should find many phenomena analogous to those which meet us in early Christianity—immense religious activity, the people taking the initiative and inaugurating movements that conquered the upper classes. Constantine merely passed approval on what the masses had done. Deissmann [1] has shown how Christianity started with the masses, working from beneath upwards, like the sap of the tree in spring, until gradually the authorities were brought under the spiritual power accepted by the poor and needy. At first not many rich or noble were counted in the Christian ranks : Christianity made its most successful propaganda among the lower strata of society. It would seem as if in the victory attending the movements (especially Christianity) originating among, or accepted and furthered by, the masses of the Roman Empire, history has written for us a warning that whatever makes its appeal to the hearts of the lower orders of society in one century—however opposed to the authority of state or church, however contemned by the cultured— shall in a later century be crowned with success.

Demand for Religions of Redemption

The yearning for political and social rest and stability, for certainty and authority in philosophy and religion, was parallel to a universal demand for salvation—salvation from the confusion and isolation of the individual, from the almost universal sense of decay and degeneration,[2] from

---

[1] *Das Urchristentum u. d. unteren Schichten* (1908), and *Light from the Ancient East* (*passim*), but cf. Harnack, *Der proletarische Char. d. Urchrist.* (*Reden u. Aufsätze*, ii. 175), and Orr, *Neglected Factors*, ch. ii.

[2] The ancients—with the exception of the Jews—had almost no sense of evolution or an 'increasing purpose' in world-history. Their view was diametrically the opposite of ours. They regarded human history as a steady degeneration, a progress to decay ; their Golden Age lay in the past.

the oppression of fatalism and astral worship, from the evils of dualism, the inherent evil of matter and the body, the hindrances that prevent the soul from returning to its 'dear fatherland,' the sense of estrangement from the Deity, from the darkness of death, and emphatically from the power of the demons. The term *Saviour* [1] was applied to several gods, to Zeus, Apollo, and Asclepius [2]; it was lent as a surname to other deities—Hermes, Poseidon, Serapis, the Dioscuri. Finally, as the partition between divine and human was broken down, the term *Saviour* was applied to men, even in their lifetime, as by the Athenians to Antigonus and Demetrius Poliorcetes. Antiochus the Great was also a Saviour. The Athenians addressed Julius as their 'Saviour and Benefactor'; the Ephesians addressed him as 'God manifest, the common Saviour of human life.' In the Halicarnassus inscription Augustus is 'the Saviour of the whole human race.' These examples of emperors addressed as Saviour, Deliverer, Benefactor might be greatly multiplied. Much of this was flattery; but it reflects therein the universal demand for someone to interfere when the times were out of joint, and restore security and bestow rest upon the world. Men were everywhere longing for a reign of peace. The salvation they sighed for was sometimes rather political and physical than moral and spiritual. But with the restoration of outward peace the demand for inner peace grew more imperious. Men wished to see a God incarnate. 'No one could be a god any longer unless he was also a saviour.' The Septuagint had doubtless accustomed the Greeks, and through them the Romans, to the conception of God as a Saviour. Men would tolerate no religion that

---

This is one cause of the despair of this age when the props of ancient systems were removed. Cf. Ramsay, *Expositor*, June 1907.

[1] Cf. art. Σωτήρ by Wendland in *Zeitsch f. neutest. Wiss.*, v. 335-53; Weiss, *Heiland* in *Relig. in Gesch. u. Gegenwart*, and Kaerst, II. i. 378 ff.

[2] The extension of the cult of this Healing-God is very characteristic of the period.

did not undertake to raise them above the weight of the finite, to remove the sense of estrangement, to bring them in the ecstasy of the Vision Beatific into mystic communion with the Divine, to bestow charismatic grace in the vicissitudes of life, to hold out a revelation and the hope of bliss beyond. Wendland remarks : ' Redemption is concerned not so much with guilt and sin as with corporeity and matter, finiteness and transitoriness. Guilt and sin themselves appear as physical defilement, since they are grounded in man's material nature. Therefore redemption is conceived of as essentially ' physical ' (naturhaft), and is determined by the dualism both of man's nature and of the two worlds. These conceptions and motives, first recognisable in Posidonius, dominate subsequent philosophical and religious development. In the time of Augustus the feeling of guilt and longing for communion and renewal emerge prominently.' [1] Only redemptive religions were in demand. This accounts for the popularity of the Oriental cults, for the success of Jewish propaganda, and for the attraction which Christianity exercised upon the masses.

Expectancy

The ancient world was persuaded that it would not look in vain for salvation. There was an attitude of expectancy in East and West about the time of the appearance of Christianity. Messianic ideas were in the air. The story of the Magi is evidence of a belief in a Saviour-King to be born : this story may connect us with the Eastern (Babylonian) settlements of the Jews, or with the Persian religion which believed in the coming of a supernatural person to assure the victory of Ormudz over Ahriman. In Judaea and Galilee such expectancy was most intense.

[1] 'Hellenistic Ideas of Salvation,' Amer. Journal of Theol., July 1913, p. 346.

The first two chapters in Luke portray with local colouring some types of those who were waiting for the Consolation of Israel. The Deliverer was expected soon. Any one who proclaimed himself Messiah found an enthusiastic following. The salvation expected from this coming Messiah was often, like that looked for by Greek and Roman, more political and social than spiritual. The prophetic and highly-strung spirit of the Baptist was sensitive to this hope of the age, which drove him out into the wilderness to preach repentance before the judgment of the Coming One.

The West was not a stranger to some vague Messianic expectation. With the establishment of the Empire, it seemed as if the great cycle had run its course and the golden age was about to return, when kindly Saturn was to reign once more and Justice return to earth to inaugurate a reign of peace and harmony. The Julian comet in 44 B.C. marked the last month but one of the *magnus annus*, after which the world would begin its course anew. Horace in his *Carmen Saeculare* hails a new epoch of peace and justice. The religious spirit of Virgil was most sensitive to such a hope. His Messianic *Eclogue* (*Ecl.* iv.) [1] prophesies the birth of a wonderful child destined to usher in a new and happy epoch. In its sublimity and form of expression this Eclogue so resembles the Messianic portions of Isaiah that for many centuries it passed as an inspired prophecy of the Christ. One of the latest writers on the Messianic idea in Virgil, Professor Conway, says, ' it can hardly, I think, be denied, that in both the *Georgics* and the *Aeneid* we continually meet with a conception which in many ways is parallel to the Jewish expectation of a Messiah ; that is to say, the conception of a national hero and ruler, divinely inspired, and sent to deliver not his own nation only, but

---

[1] Probably in reply to Horace, *Epode* xvi., in which for *Suis et ipsa Roma viribus ruit* Horace has no hope except the fantastic *Arva, beata Petamus arva, divites et insulas.* Cf. Ramsay, *Expositor*, June 1907.

mankind, raising them to a new and ethically higher existence.' [1]

He finds in Virgil the ' conscious possession ' of these ideas : (1) ' That the guilt of mankind had grown to be unendurable, so that the world was pitiably in need of regeneration. (2) That the establishment of the Empire was an epoch strangely favourable to some such ethical movement, and intended by Providence to introduce it. (3) That it was part of the duty of Rome to attempt the task. (4) That one special deliverer would be sent by Providence (or, in the *Aeneid*, that a deliverer had already been sent) to begin the work. (5) That the work would involve suffering and disappointment ; and that its essence lay in a new spirit, a new and more humane ideal' (pp. 31-2).

Mayor [2] and Ramsay [3] show that there was no difficulty for Virgil to have derived these beliefs from an Eastern (Jewish) source, either a Greek version of Isaiah (Ramsay), or the Jewish Sibylline books (Mayor). The Romans could hardly have so much to do with Syria from the second century B.C., without learning Messianic ideas. In the first century B.C. in Egypt the Romans might easily come to know the LXX or other Greek versions of Hebrew writings. Surely through the heathen adherents of the Synagogue, this ' finest optimism in the ancient world ' must have spread among the heathen to a large extent. It was certain to attract attention as the grand exception to the prevalent hopelessness of the age. Philo, whose works were so largely intended for Greek readers, refers to this coming age (cf. *On Rewards and Punishments*, 16). At the time of the Jewish war the Romans knew of this hope of the Jew. Tacitus [4] says that ' the majority (of the Jews) were persuaded that according to their ancient sacred scriptures at that very time the Orient should get the upper hand, and that from Judaea should come the rulers

[1] *Op. cit.*, p. 31.
[3] *Expositor*, June and August 1907.
[2] *Virgil's Mess. Ecl.*, iii.
[4] *Hist.*, v. 13.

of the world.' Suetonius[1] reports that 'an ancient and persistent idea was circulated throughout the whole East, that
it was fated that at that time the rulers of the world should
arise from Judaea.' Schürer[2] thinks that these two authors
drew from Josephus,[3] but this is not necessary; the
Synagogue with its 'God-fearers,' the LXX and the
Sibylline Oracles had made the idea of a Messianic age
familiar enough.[4]

The ancient world had turned its eyes to the East for
help: it was expecting Him who is 'the Desire of all
Nations.'

[1] *Vesp.*, 4.   [2] ii. 604, where other references are given.
[3] Jos. *B. J.*, 6. 5. 4, politically refers it to Vespasian.
[4] 'Das jüdische Messiasthum ist im ganzen Orient und auch im Occident
. . . ein geläufiger Begriff.'—Keim, *Rom u. d. Christentum*, p. 109.

CHAPTER V

THE JEW

Thus the sharp contrasts of the Sculptor's plan
  Showed the two primal paths our race has trod :—
Hellas, the nurse of man complete as man,
  Judaea, pregnant with the living God.—S. H. BUTCHER.[1]

And as long as the world lasts all who want to make progress in righteousness will come to Israel for inspiration, as to the people who have had the sense for righteousness most glowing and strongest, and in hearing and reading the words Israel has uttered for us, carers for conduct will find a glow and a force they could find nowhere else.—M. ARNOLD.

Victi victoribus leges dederunt.—SENECA (in Augustine).

WE come now to consider briefly the character, genius, and merits of the three great peoples who prepared the way of the Lord and to whom Christianity was first preached, and in whose languages was written the superscription on the Cross.

Character

Hebrew character[2] is more simple and monotonous than the Greek. The Hebrew was a man of few interests, his one absorbing interest being his relation to his God. Though oppressed by a sense of their inherent weakness and sinfulness, no people ever had a grander conception of their high calling and purpose in history ; they were possessed of a proud self-consciousness which raised them above all their

[1] *Harvard Lectures on Greek Subjects*, p. 42.
[2] This section and the next are condensed from the writer's articles, Hebrew, Greek, and Roman,' in *Review and Expositor*, April and July 1913.

conquerors. They believed that in them all the nations
of the earth should be blessed. There was a puzzling
dualism or strange contradiction in their character; in
spite of his deep yearnings after God the Jew manifested
a strange hankering after the baser and more material; his
spiritual history is one of ebb and flow—sin, repentance,
joy He had a conscience more sensitive than that of any
other ancient people. He was a stranger to some of the
worst perplexities and contradictions of life; he was content, like a child, not to pry too much into the secrets of
the Almighty; he left a large margin for the mysterious.
Jewish character is marked by its impressive solitariness.
The Jew dwelt apart. 'The two living realities, God and
the Soul, are face to face engaged in everlasting colloquy';[1]
there is much room for the thought of God and the contemplation of the Infinite. This solitariness of character
is all the more striking in a people that developed the most
tenacious social consciousness of antiquity. Akin to this
loneliness is the Hebrew sadness (not pessimism, which
was the form so usual to Greek sadness); his religion was
of a sombre cast though his ideal was joy. In his literature we find the *rerum lacrymae*, but 'we have not the
laughter as well as the tears of humanity'[2] from 'this
grimly earnest people.' We note also the Hebrew way
of looking at things *sub specie aeternitatis*—the everlasting and infinite in his character: 'He hath set Eternity
in their hearts.' Hope was the keynote of Hebrew character; no people ever hoped so long and so patiently.
They had firm faith that the Judge of all the earth
would do right, and they were willing to wait for Him.
They believed that Jahweh heard prayer and that He
would not forsake His inheritance. However distress-
ing the vicissitudes of their national life, however dark
the present, the future was theirs. 'The Best is yet to

---

[1] Butcher, *Harvard Lectures*, p. 15.
[2] *Ibid.*, p. 16.

be.' Their Golden Age lay always in front. Its most characteristic expression was the Messianic hope—the sublimest optimism in the old world—which, as a Jewish rabbi says, ' has become the driving-wheel of all civilised humanity.'[1] ' Though He slay me, yet will I trust in Him,' was faith which allowed God plenty of scope to work out His purposes while His servants waited in patience. They were the only ancient people that grasped firmly the thought of a purpose in history. No race was ever so patient with its God. One of the most striking traits in Jewish character was its attitude to suffering. The Jew was a man of sorrows, and the world owes him the highest and most spiritual interpretation of human suffering. The Suffering Servant of the Deutero-Isaiah has appealed to the hearts of all ages as a prophecy of the Man of Sorrows. The Jew has shown us how to bear the heaviest burden of sorrow : he has convinced mankind that sorrow has not a negative but a positive value in human character and destiny. The steadfastness of Jewish character and the loftiness of his ideals have made him a lasting force in the world. A fitting symbol of this unconquerable people is the burning bush— burning but not consumed.

Mind and Genius

The Jewish mind and genius were also one-sided. The Jews had no genius for art, politics, or speculation. They did not dwell upon nature to idealise it but soared immediately to God. The only form of art cultivated among them was religious lyrical poetry, in which they have never been surpassed. Their thoughts were constantly projected beyond into the infinite which eludes all art (except, perhaps, music). Their mind was dominated by one idea—the religious ; it was calm and contemplative, unquestioning, unmetaphysical ; concrete, or at least realistic, it dealt in

[1] Kohler, *Grundriss einer system. Theologie d. Judentums*, p. 283.

symbols rather than ideas : the power of grasping a com-
plex subject with due subordination of the parts to the
whole was not theirs. They had no sense of organic unity.
The Jew had not the restless inquisitive intellect of the
Greek, but he had a hungry heart that yearned after
righteousness and communion with God. Not artists themselves, ' they have left that new creative life of the soul
which makes art possible ; they produced that which
produced art.' [1] The unique, if one-sided, genius of the
Jew made for spirituality. He specialised in religion ;
we expect the merits and defects of a specialist. Romanes
says, ' if it had not been for the Jews the human race
would not have had any religion worth our serious attention as such.' It is where we feel noblest and most divine
that the Hebrew speaks to us—in our spiritual and religious
being, where sweet memories, purest motives, and deepest,
most imperious needs have their arena. He has bequeathed
to us priceless religious classics. In our prayers we can
often, like the ancient Hebrew, find no language but a cry,
or if we translate the cry into language we often cannot
do better than use the words which rose to Jahweh from
Israelitish hearts many centuries since.

The Diaspora

Like other ancient peoples the Jew at first lived and
worked behind closed doors, forming his character and
maturing his peculiar aptitudes. The dispersion (Diaspora)
of the Jews among the nations was probably the largest
single factor in the preparation for Christianity, and one
main reason for its remarkable success. The dispersion
of Israel was as necessary for her own world-mission and
for Christianity as was previously her seclusion. Several
causes contributed to drive this people forth on their
world-mission : forcible deportations, voluntary emigration,

[1] Forsyth, *Christ on Parnassus*, p. 72.

the inducements held out by friendly governments, the promise of special privileges, the allurements of trade, the disintegrating power of Hellenism. The Eastern Diaspora to Assyria, Media, Babylonia commenced some centuries before the Western, and was mostly due to compulsion; the Western was chiefly voluntary. Tiglath-Pileser of Assyria, who inaugurated 'the first experiment in political central-isation,' deported in 739 B.C. the northern portion of the northern kingdom; in 722 B.C. Sargon captured Samaria (which had been invested by Shalmaneser IV. in 725) and carried into Assyria 27,200 persons, which was apparently the greatest of these early deportations (2 Kings xvii. 6). A portion of these northern exiles may have drifted into heathenism; at any rate, the Ten Tribes never returned, and have been variously conjectured to be the ancestors of the Nestorians, western Chinese, Afghans, and even of the Anglo-Saxons. But a great number, if not the majority, retained their nationality: Josephus says, 'the ten tribes remain to this day beyond the Euphrates, countless myriads whose numbers cannot be told.' Sennacherib began the deportation of the southern kingdom, carry-ing away 200,150 people from Judaea. Esar-haddon and Assur-banipal probably continued the policy of deporta-tions. Israel was so depopulated that, from the time of Esar-haddon, the Assyrian kings sent colonies of heathen to occupy the empty territory. The Chaldean Nebuchad-rezzar finally uprooted Judah. When he defeated Egypt at Carchemish, 605 B.C., he carried away hostages from Judah, among whom were Daniel and his companions. Again, in the reign of Jehoiachin, he deported 10,000 of the principal inhabitants who might cause unrest. Finally, in 586 B.C., he captured Jerusalem and deported the remainder of the leading citizens, leaving only the poorest sort. These exiles were the founders of the powerful Babylonian colony which was a centre of Jewish life and thought for over 1000 years. Zealous of their traditions

and law, they boasted that only the chaff returned to
Judah under the Persian, and the finest of the wheat
remained at Babylon.   There was another eastern deportation (to Hyrcania), under Artaxerxes Ochus (*cir.* 350 B.C.).
Egypt was from an early period a place of refuge for those
in disgrace or trouble in Israel, as in the emigration after
the murder of Gedaliah (Jer. xli. 16 ff.).   The Tel-el-
Amarna tablets mention *Habiri* (supposedly Hebrews),
but not as residents.   The Assouan (Aramaic) papyri
testify to the existence of Jewish colonies under Persian
domination.   Pseudo-Aristeas refers to a deportation
under Psammetichus.

In the Greek period the Diaspora spread apace both in
East and West owing to the blending of nations, the
enormous intermixture of diverse populations, the recast-
ing of political constitutions, voluntary migrations, the
opportunities for adventure and the favour of rulers.
Alexander and the most of the Diadochi were well-disposed
toward the Jews, and offered them special privileges.   In
new foundations like Alexandria and Antioch Jews were
admitted as citizens.

Ubiquity and Power of Diaspora

For the spread of Christianity, the ubiquity and numbers
of the Diaspora are of importance.   We have evidence of
their presence East and West, in Mesopotamia and other
inner regions of Asia Minor, on the shores of the Black
Sea, in the Crimea, Syria, Egypt, Greece and the islands
of the Aegean, Macedonia, Crete, Cyprus, the Cyrenaica,
Numidia, the Province of Africa, Mauretania, Rome, Italy,
and, in the later Empire, in Spain, Gaul, and Germany
Especially from the second century B.C., the Diaspora
assumed tremendous proportions.   Josephus speaks of
the ' countless myriads ' of the descendants of the Ten
Tribes in Mesopotamia, and Philo refers to all this region

K

including Babylon, as having a Jewish population. The Sibylline Oracles declare ' every land and every sea is full of them ' (second century B.C.). Josephus says, ' there is no people on the earth that has not a portion of us,' and he cites Strabo as declaring that they had ' entered every city, and no place in the world can be found that has not received this race and been possessed by it.' Philo cites from the letter of Agrippa to Caligula that ' Jerusalem is the capital not of Judaea only, but of most countries,' and then follows a list of the widely scattered Jewish colonies. According to Philo, two-fifths of the populous city of Alexandria were Jewish in his day, and Philo reckons the Jews in Egypt alone as about 1,000,000. They were present in sufficient numbers in Alexandria, Antioch, Sardis, and elsewhere to be thoroughly hated, and to make reprisals in bloody frays. Josephus speaks of 2,700,000 as present at a festival in Jerusalem. Strabo says that one-fourth of Cyrene was Jewish. Their numbers in the Roman Empire are variously estimated from 8,000,000 and upwards, which with their social tenacity and splendid organisation rendered them formidable even to Rome. Their power in the Empire is attested by the fact that Rome, so intolerant of any *imperium in imperio*, endeavoured to pacify them and hesitated to provoke them. Rome curtailed none of the privileges they had secured under the Diadochi, but even protected and extended them. The Roman Emperors, with few exceptions, were favourable to the Jews. In the Roman civil wars both sides courted them. Caesar became their patron, and they lamented his assassination for days. Augustus continued the philo-Judaic policy, securing to the Jews free and undisturbed exercise of their worship throughout the Empire. Josephus mentions long lists of special legislation on behalf of the Jews. The law against private associations was relaxed in their favour ; Roman governors were required to secure Jewish subjects the unrestricted freedom of their rights; their religion was acknowledged as a *religio licita*; they were excused from participation in the imperial cult, for refusing to comply with which Christians suffered so cruelly, and from military service. Augustus enacted that they could not be summoned before a court on the Sabbath; if a distribution of money or corn fell on a Sabbath the Jews were to receive their portion next day, and for the distribution of oil they received a commutation in money. Their existence as a church in the state was recognised by Rome. For civil processes between Jews they were allowed to use their own law and hold their own courts; even Jews possessing Roman citizenship preferred their own courts. A measure of independence was also accorded them in criminal cases among themselves. They were allowed to collect and administer their own funds. Even after the fall of Jerusalem the Roman authorities scarcely curtailed their privileges, except by the diversion of the tax of two drachmae to the Capitoline temple. When some Greek cities, taking advantage of the Jewish disasters, requested the rescinding of Jewish privileges, the government peremptorily refused. Students of Roman history know that Rome would not have granted such an exceptional place to a hated people except on grounds of necessity. The hostility of the Jew was the greatest menace to the peace of the Empire.

Organisation

Their power was not due to their formidable numbers only, but to their splendid organisation. Though without any political genius they reared an organisation that defied Rome. The Jew never amalgamated with other races so as to lose his religion or racial consciousness. He met the scorn and hate of the world with the pride of a superior people. Wherever the Jew emigrated he sought out his brethren and formed a community. They had one law, one holy book, one God of covenant promises; they looked to one spiritual centre while it stood, they had one hope for the future. In every town where ten adults were found was a synagogue, or house of prayer. The synagogue supported Israel spiritually and strengthened her socially. These synagogues, like the Christian churches, were united by an indissoluble bond maintained by constant intercourse, frequent letters, and travelling members. The Jew, like the Celt, was one everywhere; if one Jew, like one Irishman, was injured, all were injured. The terrible uprisings under Vespasian, Trajan, and Hadrian bear ample testimony to their power to shake the Empire.

Wealth

Jewish wealth was considerable if we are to judge from the immense treasures which accumulated in the temple. The contributions were so large that sometimes as many as a thousand Jews were deputed to bring them to Jerusalem. We have a collection of Jewish bank-books from Babylonia from about the time of Xerxes. It would seem as if they had become bankers to their conquerors. Mithridates appropriated an immense sum, 800 talents, from the Jewish treasury in Cos. Cicero tells us of the enormous contributions for the temple from Asia confiscated by Flaccus, 62 B.C. It would seem as if the effect of these contributions on the exchange became one cause of anti-Semitism. Josephus tells of 2,700,000 people as present in Jerusalem at a festival; if we make a liberal deduction for the residents and for exaggeration, we have an enormous number of travellers from every quarter who had money and leisure to travel. Many other examples of Jewish wealth might be cited, as the presence in the principal synagogue in Alexandria of seventy-one golden seats. The finest buildings in Alexandria and Antioch were the leading synagogues. The corn-export business of

Egypt was largely in Jewish hands, as was also the rich traffic of Mesopotamia.

Jews in high position

Many Jews rose to positions of eminence and influence. Inscriptions show that the ' chief physicians ' of the cities of Ephesus and Venosa were Jews. At the time of the Jewish war some Jews were Roman knights. Alityrus, a Jewish actor, was in favour at Nero's court. In Egypt the Jews rose to the highest positions : the position of *alabarch* was frequently held by a Jew, as by Alexander, Philo's brother. Several Jewish names are found among the tax-collectors of the Thebaid. Apparently under the Ptolemies and the Romans the Jews were entrusted with the gathering of the Nile customs. Ptolemy Philometor is said to have entrusted the administration of the whole kingdom to Jews, and appointed two Jewish generals, Onias and Dositheus, over the army : his daughter, Cleopatra III., also put two Jews, Chelkias and Annanias, at the head of her army. The Jews were moreover successful in securing powerful patrons, especially among the Ptolemaic and the Roman rulers.

Anti-Semitism

The Jews first drank the cup of *odium generis humani*. The outbursts of anti-Semitism in Greek communities and in Greek and Roman writers are an index of the power, success, and wealth of the Jews. The Ionian cities complained before Agrippa that, while citizens, the Jews did not worship the city gods. Bloody anti-Jewish feuds were often carried on in Alexandria, Antioch, and other Greek cities. The petition of the Antiochians and Alexandrians after the war of 70 A.D. to the Roman authorities to deprive the Jews of citizenship and other privileges was refused. The fact that the wealthy island of Rhodes

produced two anti-Semitic writers, Apollonius Molon and
Posidonius, speaks for their wealth and power, as does anti-
Semitism in Germany at the present time. A papyrus
letter-writer warns his correspondent, 'look out for the
Jews.'[1] Many Roman writers speak disparagingly of the
Jews. Horace writes in mockery of their circumcision
and Sabbaths; Seneca calls them 'a most accursed race';
Tacitus accuses them of hatred to all men, of immorality,
of worshipping an ass; if the 4000 sent by Claudius to
Sardinia perished it would be a *vile damnum*. Petronius
represents them as worshipping a pig. Cicero, Quintilian, Juvenal, and Martial pour scorn upon them. The
fact that Roman writers are so much more anti-Jewish
than the Greek bears testimony to the increased prominence
of the Jew. He is only hated where he is present in force
and where successful. Finally, anti-Semitism found a fruitful soil in the Christian Church.

SERVICES TO THE ANCIENT WORLD, AND CONTRIBUTION TO THE PREPARATION FOR CHRISTIANITY

We come now to chronicle briefly what the Jews contributed to the uplifting of the ancient world and to the
preparation for Christianity.

Synagogue

The synagogue was the focus of Judaism, and has remained such ; it made Israel a spiritual power in the world.
Tradition assigned its origin to the earliest times, even to
the days of Moses. Its origin is wrapped in obscurity ;
it seems to have arisen in the needs of the Babylonian
exile. Though there is no mention of it in the Old Testament or the Apocrypha, we find the institution of the

---

[1] καὶ σὺ βλέπε σατὸν ἀπὸ τῶν Ἰουδαίων ; *Griech. Urkunden* (Berlin), iv.
No. 1079.

synagogue everywhere in New Testament times. The
exile was a critical period in the history of Judah and of
the world. The question at issue was : Can the God of
a Semitic people benefit his people in a foreign land and
away from the sacrificial cultus of the temple ? Israel
answered in the affirmative. If the Exile tore them away
from their homes it brought them nearer to their God.
The loss of their ancestral sanctuary, the cessation of
sacrifice, the need of a bond of union to maintain their
solidarity amid powerful disintegrating influences, the
possibility of a spiritual worship, resulted in the rise of
the synagogue. The returning exiles established the institution in Palestine alongside the temple cultus. The
synagogue was at once the source of Israel's spiritual
strength, the expression of her corporate life, the guardian
of her traditions and revelation, and the *point d'appui* for
her eminently successful propaganda. The synagogue became to each town what Judaea was to the world. It was
to the heathen a school of morals and religion ; it became
the cradle of Christianity. As the temple service passed
more definitely under control of the aristocracy, the synagogue grew in influence with the masses ; it was the
meeting-place of the people with their religious teachers.
There they heard the Law and the 1rophets ; there the
Hope of Israel was kept green. When the temple was
finally destroyed, the synagogue became all in all to
Israel. Wherever ten adult males were found in a town
a synagogue was formed. In the time of Augustus there
were many synagogues in Rome. In Antioch and Alexandria the two leading synagogues were among the grandest buildings in the city, and in each of these cities there
were many others. At the time of the Jewish war the
number of synagogues in Jerusalem is estimated at 394
or 480. In the New Testament we read of synagogues
in Galilee, Judaea, Asia Minor, Macedonia and Greece.
Inscriptions and ruins testify further to this widespread

institution. In Acts xv. 21 James speaks of synagogues 'in every city.' The Jew, like the modern Roman Catholic, tried where possible to rear his religious edifice on the most conspicuous piece of ground in the city. A Midrash declares that in early times the synagogue was built on 'the height of the city,' and a third-century teacher declares the city whose roofs overtop the synagogue to be given over to destruction. Sometimes the synagogue was situated outside the city, by a river or by the sea. The services were simple but impressive; they consisted regularly of the Shema, congregational prayer, and the reading of the Law and the Prophets, usually followed by a sermon and the benediction. They were held every Sabbath and on fast days : wherever ten men of leisure were found there was a daily service. Women were regular attendants at the services. The constant reading of the moral law and the spirituality of the prophets could not be in vain ; not only Jews but many earnest heathen were influenced. The importance attached to prayer was a great attraction for an age seeking support.

Schools

Inseparably connected with the synagogue were the school and library.[1] As in Roman Catholicism church and school are united, and the latter is a support and means of feeding the former, so it was in Judaism. The synagogue was primarily a teaching institution : school and synagogue are thus often mentioned together. The Jews were foremost in recognising the importance of early education. Philo says that in every city were διδασκαλεῖα, schools to teach religion and virtue. Thus the Jews were the first Sabbath-school teachers. We may reasonably conjecture that these schools proved to many children the gate to

[1] In Safed and Tiberias—and probably elsewhere—at the present day the synagogue is the Jews' reading-room.

the synagogue, attracting more than Jewish children.
The analogy of the school system in modern missions
as a feeder to the Christian Church strengthens the
probability.

Successful Propaganda

It was around the synagogue that the Jews carried on
their proselytising work. They were the first missionaries
and preachers. Believing that in Abraham and his seed
all the nations of the earth should be blessed, that the
God of Israel should be called the God of the whole earth,
that Israel should have a premier place as the medium of
better things for the race, Israel was more or less con-
scientious in the fulfilment of her mission. The influence
of the synagogue was not in vain. The enormous numbers
of Jews in the Empire cannot be accounted for by natural
increase ; conversions to Judaism were frequent till about
the time of the edict of Pius forbidding the circumcision
of proselytes. Apart from conversions, the influence
upon heathen who refused to take the decisive step was
very great. Who may venture to estimate the effect of the
Sabbath sermons and the reading of a holy book upon
earnest hearers ? In the synagogue was proclaimed a
lofty spiritual monotheism to which Greek thought was
tending. God was not only One, but He was just to mark
and punish iniquity, yet He was a Father with whom there
was mercy for the penitent. Israel made the largest
contribution toward that union of morality and religion
which was consummated in Christianity. However hated
and despised the Jew was, no serious heathen could be
indifferent to the attraction of a moral life. We can
scarcely imagine how refreshing these services of prayer
and exhortation must have been to heathen who lived in
a world that felt the burden of age and on whom were set-
tling an ennui and a weariness, whose golden age lay behind

them. They came into contact with a people who were continually renewing their youth, and whose golden age and brightest hope lay in the future. In an age when Oriental and Western religions were trying to purify themselves from the remnants of naturalism and making gross and vulgar things symbols of higher truth, a people was to be found whose symbols were of the simplest kind and yet more pregnant with spiritual truth than those of any rivals. In an age when ' man's unconquerable mind ' had in Greece been overtaken with lassitude and began to demand a criterion for truth, a sure guide in morals and an authority for man's spirit, this was a people who offered the authority of a holy book containing what was then the fullest revelation. Amid the isolation of individualism the synagogue offered the communion of saints. Merivale asserts that the Jew taught the ancient world to pray, and in this way hastened the conversion of the Empire. The Jew through the synagogue taught the heathen to pray both by example and precept : the persistent heroic example in prayer of a people conspicuous in so many ways proved an untold blessing. In the synagogue of Nazareth, and in the God-fearing home fostered by the ideals of the synagogue, He who taught us to pray learned to pray. The synagogue taught the Christian Church the power and example of prayer. In our religion we are almost wholly Jews, but at no time are we more Jews than when we approach the Mercy Seat.

It is universally acknowledged that Judaism owes part of its numbers to conversions from heathenism. It may be asked how a people so despised and hated, and so exclusive, could have carried on a successful propaganda and become the first great missionary people. There were, and still are, in Judaism two opposite tendencies— an expansive and an exclusive. The latter is largely Palestinian, the former of the Diaspora. The influence of Deutero-Isaiah and the great prophets, together with the

experiences of the Exile and the Diaspora, gave the upper
hand to universalism. As Israel recognised only one God
He must also be the God of the whole world, and she
recognised her mission as 'leaders of life to all.' The
legislation of Ezra and Nehemiah opened the way for the
incorporation of men of other races.

We have abundant evidence that this exclusive people
were most successful missionaries. Schürer [1] attributes
the success of their propaganda to three causes : (1)
Judaism presented its best aspect to the pagan world.
They dropped all that might be offensive, or threw into the
background what was unimportant or exclusive ; they
laid the emphasis on what was calculated to receive a
sympathetic hearing, such as their lofty idea of God and
the authority of a religion of revelation. (2) Their practical
aim after a moral and happy life. (3) The trend of the age
was toward Oriental religions which offered three attractions : (a) a monotheistic tendency, (b) a practical purpose
in offering remission of sin and moral cleansing (often formal
and external), (c) the promise of a happy life beyond. In
all these points Judaism far excelled all its Oriental com-
petitors. All were *missionary religions* and seized of an
enthusiasm to produce converts. The Judaism of the
Diaspora regarded it as its bounden duty to be a light to
the heathen. They not only laboured among the masses,
but established a literature, especially in Alexandria, to
commend their faith to the cultured. They manipulated
the Sibylline Oracles to acquaint the Greek world with
the hopes of Israel.

They laboured with extraordinary success. Josephus
boasts, 'Many of the heathen have come over to our law ;
some have remained, others unable to tolerate its strict-
ness have fallen off,' and 'among the masses there has long
been a great zeal for our mode of worship ; there is no
Greek nor barbarian city nor any nation in which our

[1] iii. p. 155 ff.

custom of keeping the Sabbath, fasting, the lighting of lamps, and many regulations in regard to food, are not observed.' Horace and Juvenal testify to the prevalence of Jewish customs among the Romans. Dio Cassius speaks of the zeal of people of other races for Jewish customs. Josephus says that a great multitude of Greeks had been received, and made as it were part of the Jews in the Syrian Antioch. Seneca declares that this accursed race, ' though conquered, have given laws to their conquerors.' Paul, on his preaching tours, found the synagogue attendance composed of Jews and God-fearing heathen. Women were particularly attracted by Judaism; it was easier for them to become converts, and women are more sensitive to the emotional element in religion. Sometimes influential converts were secured, like the prime minister of Queen Candace, or a lady of rank like Fulvia, or Poppaea, the mistress of Nero, or Izates and the royal house of Adiabene. Sometimes the Jews forcibly proselytised, as when Hyrcanus compelled the Idumaeans, and Aristobulus the Ituraeans (or people of Galilee), to become Jews.

Proselytes

There were many degrees among those influenced by Judaism, from the proselyte who became a full Jew, to all the different grades of the ' God-fearers' attached to the synagogue.

There was only one class of regular proselytes, those who broke entirely with their heathen past, accepted circumcision and a purificatory bath, and made an offering to the temple. Such were counted as full members of the Jewish community, and were debtors to do the whole law (Gal. v. 3). These converts were more zealous Jews than the Jews by race,[1] and were comparatively few in number.

---

[1] 'Proselytism was a sort of conquest or subjugation, for the benefit of the conquerors, not of the conquered, and it is fair to say that the Jewish

'God-fearers'

The most direct way in which the synagogue prepared a people for the Lord was as teacher of the numerous God-fearing [1] heathen. Vast numbers of interested inquirers came to Judaism. Many heathen, in accordance with the prevalent syncretism, were willing to make experiments among the competing religions, and when Judaism was once tried it retained those who were in earnest. They found a fellowship of kindred spirits, and were strengthened by prayer, by regular divine services with their aesthetic power, and by stimulating sermons urging men to live a moral life, promising a better social era under a Messiah, and holding out the hope of immortality. No serious heathen could be indifferent to a religion the lives of whose adherents commended their creed as much (or as little) as Christian lives commend our faith. Besides, no rival faith could so fully satisfy the general demand for redemptive or salvation religions. The Jew occupied a unique position as regards that which all men were seeking. Many inquirers were not persuaded of the necessity of giving up other cults, or were deterred from becoming Jews by the odium attaching to the race, by social or political considerations, or perhaps because they disliked the unique racial privileges claimed by the Jew. The Jews in their missionary zeal, and from a desire to strengthen their position, encouraged the approach of all serious heathen. If these heathen

proselyte did not form a link between the Jews and the Gentiles, but emphasised and widened the difference. Nor did the proselyte prepare the way for Christianity.'—Art. 'Proselyte' in Hastings' D.B.

[1] Some identify the 'God-fearing' with the proselytes, but with less justification. When Paul decided to turn to the Gentiles he went to the house of Titius Justus, one of the σεβόμενοι who was not a Jew, as he would have been if he had been circumcised. As there was a time when the term 'God-fearing' was applied to the pious Israelite, it was in all probability later applied to proselytes, and finally in the Greek period the term was used to designate the pious heathen who found consolation in the ministrations of the synagogue. Their vastly increasing numbers called for a designation.

were unwilling to submit to circumcision and keep the whole law they accepted the Jewish method of worshipping God as One, and without images; they observed the Sabbath and festivals, accepted baptism, and observed certain regulations about food. Some even went to Jerusalem to worship (John xii. 20). Paul found these God-fearing heathen in all the synagogues. These, of whom Israel was tutor, were the first to accept a gospel in which there was no racial privilege. When a Christian ecclesia was formed beside the synagogue, these heathen flocked to it, not only because it was the latest religious association, but because it proclaimed a larger message than could be heard in the synagogue.

The Greek Bible

The Septuagint version of the Old Testament is, next to the New Testament, the most world-historic book. We are not here concerned with its scientific value for philology and its importance for the study of the Hebrew Old Testament and the Greek New Testament, nor with the legends of its origin. Three theories are put forward to account for its origin : (1) the command of the bibliophile and philo-Judaic Ptolemy Philadelphus, who sent to Jerusalem for a Hebrew version (of the Law) and scholars to translate it, wishing perhaps to have the Law, by which the Jews were judged, in a Greek version ; (2) the needs of the Diaspora Jewish communities, the language of whose synagogue was Greek ; (3) the desire to have Greek scriptures for purposes of proselytising and for theological discussion. All three reasons doubtless contributed. The Law was first translated before the middle of the third century B.C., and the whole Bible was finished, at the latest, in the second half of the second century B.C.

For our purpose it is enough to notice three important services rendered by this version : (1) It was an inestimable

boon to the Greek-speaking Diaspora to have a version
of their Bible in a language 'understanded of the people.'
The LXX did for the religious life of the Diaspora what
the Authorised Version did for Britain and America,
and what that of Luther did for Germany. It became
the Bible of Hellenistic Judaism in Asia and in Europe,
and a unique bond of cohesion.[1] The LXX nourished the
democratic spirit of piety of the synagogue, and prevented
religion from becoming wholly dependent on a priesthood
having the monopoly of a dead holy tongue. This version
was also the necessary counterpoise to the disintegrating
forces of Hellenism. (2) The LXX became to the Jew a
powerful missionary organ, and to Hellenistic heathenism
a religious authority at a time when Greek thought was
veering toward the necessity of a Revelation. Such
translations were not in vogue in antiquity, particularly
in the rich Greek language: the appearance of the LXX
in the meeting-place of East and West, in the language
of the mediating Judaeo-Hellenistic philosophy, could
not fail to attract wide attention. The hosts of 'God-
fearing' heathen heard in Greek a message of salvation,
and many heathen making trial of different mysteries and
looking for some 'strong boat,' or 'sure word of God,' in
oracles or in Oriental religions, discovered in the LXX
what claimed to be an authoritative God-inspired guide.
Philo tells us that the translators before commencing work
prayed to God for help, and 'He heard their prayers that
the majority, or rather the *whole human race*, might be
benefited by giving heed for reformation of life to wise
and noble ordinances.' History has given the verdict
that their prayer was answered. (3) The LXX became the
first, and for a considerable time the only, Bible of early
Christianity, and a potent ally of the Gospel.[2] It was the

---

[1] The LXX 'kept millions in the old faith, to win fresh millions for whom
the Hebrew text would have remained a buried treasure.'—Hausrath.

[2] 'Greek Judaism with the Septuagint had ploughed the furrows for the
gospel seed in the western world.'—Deissmann, *New Light on N T.*, p. 95.

Bible of Paul and Luke and the early missionaries who carried Christ's evangel to 'all the world.' It was, next to the words of Jesus, their only recognised authority. Before Christian writings were made, preachers had already a Bible to hand. From it they culled their Messianic texts, and by it proved Jesus to be the promised Messiah. The LXX furnished them with a ready-made vocabulary and terminology, with forms of prayer and praise, with many terms which were as yet like empty vessels waiting to be filled with the new meaning of a fuller Revelation.[1] This LXX proved so useful to the Christians, that the Jews by the time of Jerome repudiated it as inferior to the 'Hebrew verity,' thus vindicating the Rabbinic description of the day on which the Law was translated as a 'feast of darkness,' a calamity 'like the day on which the golden calf was made.' Finally, the LXX helped to suggest to the Christian Church the formation of a Christian canon to be used alongside the LXX. As we study our New Testament we may gratefully remember the earnest effort of the Jew to procure a lamp for his feet and a light for his path.

Message of Israel

Thus Israel prepared the way for, and contributed to the establishment and organisation of, Christianity.[2] Her message, like her own character, may have been one-sided

---

[1] 'It created a language of religion which lent itself easily to the service of Christianity, and became one of the most important allies of the gospel.' Hastings' *D.B.*, iv. 437b.

[2] 'To the Jewish mission which preceded it the Christian mission was indebted, in the first place, for a field tilled all over the Empire; in the second place, for religious communities already formed everywhere in the towns; thirdly, for what Axenfeld calls 'the help of materials' furnished by the preliminary knowledge of the Old Testament, in addition to catechetical and liturgical materials which could be employed without much alteration; fourthly, for the habit of regular worship and the control of private life; fifthly, for an impressive apologetic on behalf of monotheism, historical teleology, and ethics; and finally, for the feeling that self-diffusion was a duty. The amount of this debt is so large that one might venture to claim the Christian mission as a continuation of the Jewish propaganda.'—Harnack, *Mission*, i. 15.

and partial, but it was the necessary complement to the labours of the other peoples. Israel held a premier place in all that pertained to the higher spiritual life of man. She herself cared little for culture, but she produced that which has produced the best modern culture. Before the appearance of Christianity, Israel carried on a preaching activity which elevated her own life and leavened heathenism. She brought earnest heathen to the very threshold of the kingdom of Christ. She heralded the most perfect salvation offered to the old world. Her conception of God, though far short of the Christian, was a worthy and attractive one : He was a personal self-revealing God, even a Father, a God of strict justice, yet willing to receive and pardon the penitent. Israel declared that God's righteousness demands moral living on the part of man : religion must go hand in hand with morality. She taught men to pray. She gave new youth to a weary world : having suffered herself, she taught men the meaning of suffering. She spoke of hope, looking for a kingdom of righteousness upon earth and a Messiah from Heaven to reign among men. In an age seeking consolations, no religion could compete with Israel's : even we ourselves in adversity become Jews that we may share in Jewish consolations.

Pathfinder for Christianity

In many respects Israel was the pathfinder for the senior of her daughter religions. She put into the hands of Christianity a holy book with the dogma of inspiration, the receptacle of an authoritative Revelation. She taught Christians the practice and much of the forms of prayer. She imparted to them her own steadfastness of character and her zeal to please God with an upright life. She bequeathed to the Church her missionary zeal and enthusiasm, her expectancy of a brighter future, her passion for monotheism. Many of the weapons employed

L

by Christianity against Jew and heathen were appropriated from the armory of Judaism. The Jewish canon was the forerunner of a Christian canon. The Christian Church took over not only the entire Jewish Bible and doctrine of inspiration, but also Jewish methods of handling scripture such as the citing of proof-texts, the use of allegory in one place and the strictest literalism in another. From Judaism Christianity borrowed that intolerance which was at first necessary to preserve her integrity. It was from Judaism that Christianity caught the idea of writing apologies and pseudonymous books in the interests of faith. Heathenism was never until its dying years laid hold of by the missionary idea. It was the Jew who discovered the plan of voicing his protests and dissatisfaction with the present under assumed names from heathen or Jewish history. Christianity found Jewish apocalypses in such a shape, that by changing the wording slightly, or interpolating a paragraph here and there, she had ready-made Christian apocalypses.

Judaism furnished the Christian Church with many useful hints toward the establishment of that compact ecclesiastical organisation which defied Rome. She taught the Church the necessity of a spirit of universal brotherhood and co-operation, whereby the strong were to help the weak, and the communities were kept in close contact with each other.

Early Christianity benefited by the most staggering calamity that ever befell the Jews—the destruction of Jerusalem. This put an end to Jerusalem with its temple cult as the religious centre of Judaism ; it subverted the hopes of Jews who were looking for a restoration and hurried them over into Christianity. Jerusalem could not now become the centre of Christianity, a fact which, if realised, would have given the predominance to a narrow Palestinian Christianity ; the fall of Jerusalem weakened the hands of the Judaisers as it strengthened the Gentile Christian section.

Lastly, the Jew of the Diaspora served as mediator between East and West : he was Oriental in his religion and Western in his culture, philosophy, language and enter-prise. Through him an Oriental religion conquered the West.

Such are some of the leading characteristics and services of a race in whom all the nations of the earth have been blest, ' whose is the Sonship and the Glory and the Covenants and the giving of the Law and the Service of God and the Promises, whose are the Fathers, from whom, in respect of his human descent, comes the Christ who is exalted above all, God blessed throughout the ages.'

CHAPTER VI

THE GREEK

Ἦσαν δὲ Ἑλληνές τινες ἐκ τῶν ἀναβαινόντων ἵνα προσκυνήσωσιν ἐν τῇ ἑορτῇ· οὗτοι . . . ἠρώτων . . . κύριε, θέλομεν τὸν Ἰησοῦν ἰδεῖν.

As the Hebrews in alliance with the Orientals exercised the religious hegemony, and the Romans the political, so the Greeks were unchallenged in their intellectual supremacy. The world that most eagerly accepted the Gospel had a Greek education. It is important to know the character and genius of the people in whose language Christianity has been transmitted to us, who were its first metaphysicians and philosophers, who later waked Christian Europe from barbarism, and who have not yet come to their own among us.

The Greeks are the most interesting and human of ancient peoples. Their environment was quite different from that of the Hebrew. Their fatherland was beautiful and varied as their own matchless genius. Bright sky, pellucid air, mountain ranges and passes, innumerable bays and fiords, island-studded seas—everything the Greek looked upon was beautiful. Yet the Greek was never as susceptible to the beauty of a landscape as the Roman; his beauty was that of form, harmony, and proportion. Aristotle characteristically finds the truest beauty in mathematics.

Greek Character

Greek character is more variegated and many-sided than either Hebrew or Roman: there are more numerous elements

in its composition.   No nation had such a passion for the
beautiful, which was the form in which they worshipped
goodness.   Their word καλόν means both *beautiful* and *good*.
The Greek was enamoured of material beauty.   He loved
this world and all its rational activities, and looked naturally
on the brighter side of things ; death, that called him
away from the joyousness of life, was a dread evil.[1]   The
Greek was keenly sensitive to the joys of life.   They
represent more than any other people the youth of the
world, hence succeeding ages of *aegri mortales* have gone
back to Greece to re-live their youth.   Plato makes an
Egyptian say, ' No Hellene is ever old ; in mind you are all
young.'   The spirit of Greece was ' youth, I do adore
thee,' and no literature contains sadder laments over
vanished youth.   They were an active folk, loving athletics,
lively and excitable, energetic and restless, early seized
by the *Wanderlust*.   Their history is full of revolutions.
They were liable to fits of popular emotion :   they could
sentence the male population of an island to death, and
immediately, overcome with remorse, rescind the decision ;
they could condemn a Socrates and repent too late.   Herein
they were unlike the Romans, who never repented of an
unrighteous national act.   In proportion to his keen
sensitiveness to joy the Greek was readily overtaken by
melancholy, which later deepened into pessimism.   No
other literature contains such eloquent laments over the
misery of our mortal lot, the brevity of life, the caprice
of fortune, the ruthlessness of death.   Over all Greek
happiness hangs a Damocles' sword.   The Greek was
actuated by unbounded aspirations, he was conscious of
the possession of powers for the full fruition of which life
refused sufficient scope.   As the element of trouble

---

[1] Cf. Matthew Arnold on the death of Sohrab :

> ' and from his limbs
> Unwillingly the spirit fled away,
> Regretting the warm mansion which it left,
> And youth and bloom and this delightful world.'

increased in his chequered history his melancholy grows more oppressive, until in the *Anthology* death is better than life. Here we must note a peculiar trait of Greek character : his abiding sense of the frailty of man, and the presence of death, snatching away love and joy and ambition, never unmanned him or impaired his energy ; these things rather stimulated him to high endeavour, to turn life to most account as his only portion, to do something to be remembered. For the Greek loved praise, 'that last infirmity of noble minds.' For him

> 'Fame is the spur that the clear spirit doth raise
> To scorn delights and live laborious days.'

To win the crown of parsley and have his name inscribed in marble was to the Greek what a consulship was to the Roman. The Greek aimed at self-culture as the Hebrew at self-repression ; his character is more rounded and complete than that of any of his contemporaries. He believed in the development of the whole man, the pursuit of everything that is ' proper to man ' :

> 'Hellas the nurse of man complete as man.'

Moderation is a prominent trait of the Greeks ; they are distinguished by a serenity and urbanity, the acme of culture. The Greeks were intensely social. Perhaps friendship was more prominent among the Romans, but comradeship and *esprit de corps* were more prevalent with the Greeks. They liked the company of their fellow-citizens, gossiping in the theatre and the market, and using their homes only for shelter at night. What's the news ? was their regular expression : they were always seeking some new thing. They were city-dwellers, not farmers nor shepherds. A Greek would pine in a lonely life; his wits were sharpened in lively intercourse with his fellows. Greece was the cradle of liberty and autonomy ; they were the first people who believed in home rule. They strove

to erect a political system based on rational freedom.[1]
The Orientals bowed low before an authority the wisdom,
origin, or reason of which they did not question : the
Greeks could do nothing without questioning. Authority
must justify itself to reason ; law is only written reason.
The bickerings of Greek history were the price the Greeks
had to pay for their wholly new experiment of self-govern-
ment with its conflicting theories, for liberty regulated
by law.

Greek Genius

The first trait of Greek genius is its striking originality.[2]
They were fearless mariners on the hitherto uncharted
ocean of thought : ' they were the first that ever burst
into that silent sea.' They had no bibliography. If they
borrowed anything from Oriental neighbours they so
thoroughly assimilated it that it became genuinely Greek.
A patchwork system such as might please the mosaic
genius of Rome would have been an abomination to them.
The Greeks invented instruments of precise thinking, and
set themselves the task of reducing chaotic thought to
a system. They discovered terms to use in the investigation of truth, and then formulae to hold the truths attained.
They were original in their way of thinking, in the results
they secured, and in the way in which they stated them.
They were the first to trust themselves implicitly to
thought, to ask the *Why* of things, and to dare to doubt.
The Greek mind was rationalistic. They not only dared to
ask questions and doubt, but believed they ought to find
an explanation. They were not endowed with unquestioning faith and meek submission to authority : they
were not reverential. There was no holy of holies
into which man endowed with reason was forbidden to

---

[1] Avoiding the rudeness of the tribal system on one hand, and despotism
on the other.
[2] Cf. *Odys.*, xxii. 847, αὐτοδίδακτος δ' εἰμί, θεὸς δέ μοι ἐν φρεσὶν οἴμας
παντοίας ἐνέφυσεν.

penetrate. Knowledge was laic and not the monopoly of a priesthood. Neither was theirs the Supreme Creator who simply appointed things as they are for man, but not for man to ask questions about or explain. They could not, like the Hebrews or the modern Arabs, roll over all difficulties to God with ' God has willed it.' They built theory after theory as steps to climb to truth : they were convinced of the connection of cause and effect. Like children they were always asking questions, and one question led on to another until they came to a barrier they could not surmount.

The Greek mind was essentially speculative : the exercise of reason upon every department was man's prerogative. Oriental knowledge was given by revelation or intuition ; nothing interested the Greek so much as the pursuit of knowledge. Leibnitz had the Greek spirit when he said that if an angel offered him knowledge in the one hand, and the pursuit of knowledge in the other, he would choose the latter. The Greek alone pursued and loved truth for itself ; he sought knowledge not for any ulterior motive but to satisfy a rational curiosity.

Greek genius was nothing if not systematic. The Greek could not carry two thoughts without systematising, correlating, or subordinating. No half-knowledge, no confused piling of ideas, no chaotic learning, but ordered mastered learning. He arranged, scheduled, labelled. Epistemology was born with the Greek. He laid down the canons to which thought must conform to be valid, discovered the categories with a view to precise thinking. He put his intellectual house in order. He felt the need of harmony, and sought unity in diversity and diversity in unity. The Greeks were the first real philosophers. They took great pains in reclaiming the domain of knowledge and mapping it out. They converted everything into an art. They found the confusion of Oriental warfare, and *they* evolved tactics ; they found the Egyptians measuring fields, and *they* built up geometry and mathematics; they learned writing from the Phoenicians, but *they* wrote; they found men piling chronicles, and *they* made it history; out of conflicting methods of social cohesion, *they* made politics; from theories of conduct and undefined right and wrong, *they* made ethics; they found men arriving at conclusions, and *they* invented logic; lastly, *they* turned the content of the Gospel into a theology.[1]

Another feature of the Greek mind was what we may call conceit. They had confidence in their own abilities; they were clever and they knew it. Their vice was intellectualism and a tendency to over-subtlety. Equally characteristic was an infinite capacity for taking pains. Outspoken criticism of public opinion and a splendid lay education demanded work which could defy criticism in every detail. They were like the Germans in their systematic methods and attention to details. Their architecture shows the acutest observation of lines and the elaboration of slight details which have made it inimitable. They moulded their language into the most perfect vehicle of human thought. If Demosthenes is the prince of orators he took the greatest pains in preparation. Isocrates is said to have spent ten years on his *Panegyric*. After Plato's death a tablet was found on which the eight opening

---

[1] 'The Greek mind is essentially discursive, analytical, and systematic, governing itself even in its highest flights by the ideas of measure and symmetry, of logical sequence and connexion. . . . The Muse of Greece, to use an expression of Goethe, is the companion of the poet and not his guide. The same mental characteristics are shown in the political life of the Greeks, in their historical literature, and, above all, in their philosophy. They are never satisfied to leave anything obscure or undefined, or to let any element stand by itself without being carefully distinguished from and related to the rest. The Homeric hero who cried for light, even if it were but light to die in, was a genuine representative of the Greek spirit. Hence, in spite of their great aesthetic capacity, their love of the beautiful and their power of creating it, there never was a nation less disposed to rest in the contemplation of a beautiful symbol, without trying to analyse it into its elements and discover its exact meaning. The Greek, again, was essentially reflective; he was never content to wield the weapons of thought without examining them; rather he sought to realise the precise value of every category or general term which he found himself using.'—Caird, *Evolution*, ii. 188-9.

words of the *Republic* were copied out in every possible order. It is only after years of sympathetic study of Greek work that one can detect the thousand little touches that contribute to the perfection of, say, the *Agamemnon* or the *Oedipus Coloneus*. The Greek never accomplished anything by happy chance as schoolboys imagine, but always with strenuous effort, though he understood that *ars est artem celare*. Thucydides was a true Greek when he tells us that he wrote his history to be 'a possession for all time.' A Greek proverb runs: 'The gods sell all things at the price of toil (or effort),' and the Greeks were willing to pay the price.

The moderation so striking in their character is even more striking in their genius. 'Nothing too much,' was their motto. They understood the secret of 'the half is greater than the whole': they always knew where to stop. They believed with Aristotle that a thing ought to have beginning, middle, and end in due proportion. Another feature is the self-forgetfulness of Greek genius compared with the Roman self-consciousness. The Greek concentrated all his attention on the work and not on the worker. In Roman work the personality and character of the author are revealed so that we know more about Roman writers from their own works than we know of any other ancient writers. The Greek always stands so far in the background as not to attract attention away from his work. He will give no hints of his own idiosyncrasies : if you wish to know him better, put the amount of careful study into his masterpieces which he did. When a schoolboy reads Thucydides for the first time, especially the seventh book, he is provoked at the self-restraint and silence of the author amid the tragedy of his country. Again, the Greek genius was idealistic as compared with the symbolism of the Orient and the realism of Rome. All our idealism takes its rise in Greece, chiefly in the works of Plato. They had a happy faculty of seeing things not as they are,

but as they ought to be : they brought the alchemy of
mind to bear upon matter and upon the common things
of life.

Greek thought and genius were essentially anthropocentric as opposed to the theocentric nature of Oriental
genius.   The Greeks began with man ; they could regard
God as only an enlarged edition of man.   Man is of supreme
interest to the Greeks, first in his harmony with, and then
in his opposition to, nature ; in his dualism and the contradictions of his being, in his unconquerable mind, his
kinship with the Divine.   Hamlet was a Greek when he
said : ' What a piece of work is man !   How noble in
reason ! how infinite in faculties ! in form and moving,
how express and admirable ! in action how like an angel !
in apprehension how like a god ! the beauty of the world !
the paragon of animals ! ' [1]   Here we must stop, for at
this point he drifts into Oriental mysticism.

Place of the Greeks in History

The Greeks have been of enormous significance in history.
They were the first Westerners who definitely left the ruts
of the past and cast aside convention.   They ushered in
a new era.

We are indebted to them for political and social experiments in which they anticipated all our modern theories.
The efforts they made to escape despotism on the one hand,
and anarchy on the other, remain of permanent value.
They brought to perfection the city-state which can never
be recreated.   They are our schoolmasters in art, science,
architecture, sculpture, music, literature, mathematics, and
medicine.   To them was committed the secular education
of the ancient world for Christianity, in the preparation
for which their language and philosophy were mighty
factors.   They introduced a new type of man, ' totus, teres

[1] Act II. sc. 2.   Noted also by Jebb, *Attic Orators*, I. xcv-vi.

atque rotundus,' complete as man, to correct and supplement the one-sidedness of Hebrew and Roman. In respect of perfect manhood they have still a message for all the ages. They strove after the perfection and harmony of our whole being, ' all that is proper to man.'

They were the most successful colonisers of antiquity, and in this respect played an important rôle. At least two Greek colonies decided the course of world-history—Syracuse and Byzantium. Another Greek (Macedonian) colony, Alexandria, became the first and chief centre for welding the nations for Christianity ; in it the philosophy of the West and the Revelation of the East united to bless humanity. During the eighth and fifth centuries B.C. the Greeks planted colonies on all the shores of the Mediterranean and adjacent seas, as far west as Marseilles and as far east as the Black Sea. From the last quarter of the fourth century B.C., Greek colonies were founded inland in Asia and Egypt. Greek colonies played a prominent part in early Christianity.

Greece rendered signal service to both the ancient and the modern world in educating the two conquering peoples—the Macedonians and the Romans. Had it not been for the influence of Greece, these peoples would have brought wholesale devastation with their conquests. When Macedon became her apt pupil and with her aid conquered the East, there was opened a boundless future for Greek culture, enterprise, language and philosophy. The Greeks went forth to civilise and educate. Had it not been for the spell of Greek culture, the Roman would have proved the Tamerlane of antiquity : he would have ruthlessly wiped out the East with the thoroughness with which he wiped out Carthage, Etruria, and Corinth. Rome came to Greece a barbaric conquering people, but went home with an endowment of culture, refinement, and humanity, though she often better reproduced Greek vices than Greek virtues.

Greece gave to early Christianity a world unified in language and culture. It is a striking fact which speaks volumes for Hellenism that the Hellenised world most eagerly accepted Christianity, and that our Oriental Gospel has never taken root in its own soil as it did first in the Greek, and through the Greek, in the Roman world. There was plainly some strong affinity between Hellenism and Christianity. The dispersion of Greek scholars and Greek books after the fall of a Greek colony, Byzantium, helped to arouse Christian Europe from the darkness of mediaevalism and usher in the Renaissance which made the Reformation possible. Men cannot sleep where the spirit of Greece enters. And 'to the modern world, too, Greece has been the great civiliser, the ecumenical teacher, the disturber and regenerator of slumbering societies. She is the source of most of the quickening ideas which re-make nations and renovate literature and art. If we reckon up our secular possessions, the wealth and heritage of the past, the larger share may be traced back to Greece. One-half of life she has made her domain— all, or well-nigh all, that belongs to the present order of things and to the visible world.' [1]

Greece not only introduced the Western spirit but she defended it against the encroachments of the East (Persia), until the Macedonian and the Roman undertook the task. For this alone she has deserved well of history. Superior as the East was to the West in religion, if Marathon and Salamis had gone against Greece it would have been more disastrous for the world than if Hannibal had conquered at Zama. 'In those earlier ages, the victory of the East over Greece would have been the triumph of nature over man, of necessity over moral freedom, of a caste system or of despotism over free organisation and intelligence, of stagnation over progress, of symbolism over beauty, of the arid plain over the mountain and the sea. The

[1] Butcher, *Aspects of Greek Genius*, p. 43.

actual victory of East and West, which took place at the
triumph of Christianity, had in it no such sinister meaning.
Greece had already won freedom in all its branches—
freedom for society, freedom for the individual, freedom for
thought. She had written her spirit in books and on
tables of stone . . . which record the supremacy of mind
over sense, of spirit over matter. She had shown how the
love of beauty might be united with the love of truth, art
with science, how reason might be made imaginative. . . .
Henceforth it is in the confluence of the Hellenic stream
of thought with the waters that flow from Hebrew sources
that the main direction of the world's progress is to be
sought.' [1]

GREEK THOUGHT

The most perennial contribution of Greece to all time
is Greek thought. Greek philosophy is the most profound
and comprehensive ever produced by one people, the
rich result of 1200 years' indefatigable endeavour after
reality. Her philosophy, directed to every point of the
compass of thought, is of fascinating interest. We have
its whole history before us : we can trace the steps by which
men sought to reduce chaos to cosmos, how they offered
one solution of the problem of man and the universe after
another, and finally how philosophy raised questions
which only religion could answer, how its last voice was
a call to men to seek the synthesis of life in revelation and
religion. They followed the natural order of man's
progress, taking first the outward look, then the inner,
and then the upward ; [2] or, nature, man, God. Their first
philosophy was that of the object and the impersonal until
the time of Socrates; their next concern was with the subjective or personal; their last was the search for a synthesis

---

[1] Butcher, *ib.*, p. 45.
  Cf. Caird, *Evolution of Religion* (3rd ed.), vol. i. p. 77.

which Greek philosophy did *not* find because *no* philosophy can.

The atmosphere of free civic Greece provided many incentives to thought. There was boundless publicity and outspoken criticism intolerant of anything but the best. Each Greek was a member of the body politic and required to think. The right to vote led him to acquaint himself with the issues of public life, and to seek the best method of obtaining a hearing. Their thinking was not chained to the past nor hampered by tradition, nor under the censorship of a priesthood : no silencing authority forbade *rerum cognoscere causas*. All knowledge was lay. They had no text-books either to guide or hamper. With naïve self-confidence, 'like little wanton boys that swim on bladders,' they launched forth, dreaming not of the abysmal deeps, the shallows, and the starless nights.

Early Schools

The four earliest schools were (1) the Ionic, which inquired into the origin of the world, of what it is composed, which discovered the ἀρχή or substantial cause of things in some one material principle. (2) The Pythagoreans, who, viewing the world as a cosmos, sought the essence of things in number and proportion. They saw unity in multiplicity. This was the first practical school of morality in Greece, the first which united religion and morality. They introduced mysticism into Greek thought, and were the precursors of Platonic spiritualism ; they proclaimed the unity of God, the idea of future retribution and reward, the transmigration of souls, the duty of a pure life and the need of self-examination. (3) The Eleatics, who denied the possibility of absolute genesis and decay and so the plurality of things. Only essences are real and all essences are one : the best can only be one. The universe is a unity, plurality and variety being only appearance to senses that are not to be trusted. The Eleatics rose to God by the *à priori* or metaphysical method, as Anaxagoras by the teleological. They 'externalised the conclusions of the pure reason itself,' and 'formally created the metaphysical system of the universe.'[1] They presented a monism, which could lead either to monotheism or pantheism.[2] Their motto might have been, ' the One remains, the Many change and pass.' (4) The Physicists. Heraclitus formed the transition stage from matter to mind. He was so impressed with the reign of change that he saw no law except that of ceaseless change—'all things are in a state of flux, nothing continues,' or, in the words of Tennyson, 'Nothing was born, nothing will die; all things will change.' So he demanded an explanation of genesis and decay, and thus stated the problem which the Atomists answered by the combination and separation of atoms. Anaxagoras who closes this period definitely separates spirit from sense : he made the epoch-making declaration that nature is intelligible only as the work of an Ordering Mind. He saw order in nature and became the first of Greek theists. As contrasted with the materialistic monism of his predecessors he bequeathed to Greek thought that dualism which it never surmounted.

In this early period we note a steady growth from concrete to abstract, from a natural to a spiritual principle, from chance and chaos to intelligence. Greek philosophy was in this period ' in respect to its *object* a philosophy of nature ; . . . in respect to its *procedure*, a dogmatism ; *i.e.* it seeks to obtain a theory of the objective world before it has given account to itself of the problem and conditions of scientific knowledge . . . in its results it is *realistic*, and even materialistic ; not till the end of this period was the difference between spiritual and corporeal brought to consciousness by Anaxagoras.'[3]

[1] Butler, i. 346.
[2] Zeller, *Outlines*, p. 23.
[3] Pfleiderer, *Vorbereitung*, p. 7.

The most important truth propounded in this period, that of Anaxagoras, must wait for a Socrates and Plato to take it up. A new spirit passed over the Greek world about the middle of the fifth century B.C. Scepticism had been introduced. How was the truth of the many theories to be tested ? Suspicion fell upon scientific theorising as idle and aimless : the interest was already shifting from the outer world of nature to the inner of spirit. Already some of the Physicists and Eleatics had challenged the cognisability of objects by sensible perception. Where and what was the criterion ? Greek love of praise conspired to corrupt philosophy. Knowledge fetched applause, and philosophy had a market value. In the absence of printing the philosopher must be an orator or even a demagogue to reach the public ear. Add to this ' the tendency of Greek genius to dwell upon form rather than inner reality.' With the march of triumphant democracy and the awakening after the Persian wars each wanted an education to fit him for practical life. Here set in the demand for the practical that asserted itself prominently in the post-Aristotelian period.

Sophists

The Sophists appeared for good or evil in Greek history. Indifferent to city patriotism, their object was to train men for practical life in a manner remunerative to themselves. They were thoroughgoing sceptics, maintaining that knowledge is impossible, and cannot lead to reality, and, if attained, could not be communicated. They doubted everything : they neither formed a school nor do their theories form a system. They were subjectivists : truth is relative to each man in each of his moods ; there is no absolute, objective, universal truth ; no standard to which to appeal. Laws are mere convention entailing no moral obligation. What is lawful in Megara may be

M

unlawful in Athens. They were individualists : each may do what is right in his own eyes. Protagoras laid down the principle of the movement : ' Man is the measure of all things ; of those that are how they are ; of those that are not how they are not.' Their method, eristic, was calculated not to reach conviction but ' to make the worse appear the better reason.' They are blamed by Socrates, Plato, and many moderns for corrupting Greek society. They were rather the keen observers and spokesmen of their day : they merely put into words what Greek states practised, ' might is right.'

The Sophists were the educators of the Greek spirit and harbingers of the Greek Enlightenment. The net result of Sophisticism was to raise the question, What is truth ? and where is the criterion ? They broke down convention by setting natural right against it ; they weakened popular superstition ; they made thought supreme over external authority ; they demonstrated that science is as helpless to give a moral basis for man's life as to give an explanation of the universe ; they gave voice to the failure of the guesses of earlier schools and made scepticism henceforth a power in Greek thought. Sweeping away the morality of tradition, civic and legal, they compelled thoughtful men to inquire if man has a moral nature and on what it rests. Bringing science and morality equally into confusion, they ushered in an era of moral (Socrates and Plato) and scientific (Aristotle) investigation. They made philosophy anthropological.[1]

Socrates

Socrates, ' almost the ideal of humanity itself,' inaugurated a new era in the higher life. He called philosophy

[1] ' Their *merit* is that they claimed on behalf of man that the principle which is to explain experience must be in harmony with his self-consciousness. Their *defect* is that they have construed man too poorly, and have regarded self-consciousness as little more than individual opinion or feeling.' —Kilpatrick, *Philosophy*, in Hastings' *D. B.*

from physics and sophistry to logic and morality, from nature to man. He completed the work of Sophisticism in making thought anthropological. His position was 'the proper study of mankind is man.' He sought knowledge for the practical purposes of moral reformation. To the dogmatism of the early schools and the scepticism of Sophisticism he opposed 'humble inquiry.' In answer to the attack of the Sophists upon the possibility of knowledge he maintained that knowledge is attainable through the fixing of concepts by the dialectic method: this gives the ultimate reality, things in themselves. He asserted the existence of objective, universal truth: the criterion is the harmony of our notions and conceptions with the thing in itself. That universal True and Right is the standard for our notions and conduct. He thus vindicated the validity of thought. Correct thinking meant correct action, for he identified virtue with knowledge; hence salvation is by wisdom, for no man who knows right will do wrong. Socrates was oblivious of man's perverted will. He has been well termed the 'father of moral science': he established morality upon a new and firm basis, finding its sanction not in custom, tradition, law, or even the authority of state, but in man's innate moral consciousness. 'Conscious morality in the ancient classical world begins with him, because he is the first to substitute the authority of the individual for that of the state.'[1] He advocated the freedom of man's will and the right of private judgment: 'I must obey God rather than you,' he said to his judges. He made the first Greek appeal to man's conscience, 'the wife from which one can never be divorced.' He believed that he possessed a *daemon*, or divine voice restraining him from evil, and that all have an intuitive sense of right and wrong. When the organism of the state was threatening to break up, he came forward to rescue and guide the individual, calling upon him to

[1] Wealey, *Preparation for Christianity*, p. 35.

reflect upon the inestimable worth of his soul. He elevated
Anaxagoras' ordering Mind into a supreme God to be
worshipped in purity of heart. About the immortality
of the soul he was uncertain. His emphasis upon *Know
Thyself* proved epoch-making : 'a life without self-
examination is not worthy of man.' He became the
herald of man's personality, the prophet of self-consciousness, opening up a vast unexplored continent wherein so
many followers from Augustine to our day have experienced
the pain and immensity of personality. His mission was
that of a soul-curer and reformer; but he was conscious of
the inability of abstract truth to elevate man. He unconsciously felt the need for an Incarnation and a Revelation.
He longed for illumination from heaven, some supernatural guide, god or demon. If the Heavenly Love were
only to take bodily form. ' Oh, if virtue had only a body
and men could see her with their eyes, how they should
run to embrace her.' Add to this the wealth of his personality,[1] and the unfading impressiveness of his dying
moments.

Minor Socratics

Of the Minor Socratics the Megarians took up the
speculative side of Socrates' teaching, the Cynics and
Cyrenaics its subjective, individual, negative and practical
aspects. The Megarians held that the senses give but the
changing appearances, and only thought the reality. They
identified the Good with the unchanging One of Parmenides.
All Being is a Unity whether termed Deity, Intelligence, or
Reason. Only the actual is possible, and only the unchange-
able is actual. The world of multiplicity is illusory, reality
belonging to the Universal.

---

[1] ' Eine Persönlichkeit, die in ihrer inneren Selbstgewissheit und religiös
begründeten Überzeugungstreue als eine eigentümlich neue Erscheinung in
der antiken Welt, als ein Vorläufer und Prophet des Christentums zu
betrachten ist.'—Pfleiderer, p. 16.

The Cynics and Cyrenaics—the precursors of the Stoics and Epicureans—derived their doctrines each from a distortion of Socrates' teaching. Socrates had inseparably connected virtue and happiness, which Antisthenes (founder of the Cynic school) distorted into ' virtue is happiness,' identifying virtue with pain, and Aristippus (founder of the Cyrenaic) into ' happiness is virtue,' which led to licence. The aim of both was to render man independent—the one by training the will to suppress the desires, the other by compelling nature to gratify them.

Plato

Plato continued the work of Socrates in the search after ultimate reality and a deeper spiritual unity. Commencing with the Socratic form of the Anaxagorean *Nous* and the concept philosophy of his master, he examined the eternal One of Parmenides and the Being of Heraclitus, to find both unsatisfactory. We must by induction rise from the individual to the universal, for only the Universal is real and self-existent, not existing merely in our or God's thought of it. The purpose of knowledge is practical—to make men better citizens and to elevate them above sense. The central point of Plato's philosophy is his theory of Ideas, which was his solution of the problem of reality. The things we see here are not real ; they are mere shadows, faint copies of the archetype in the spiritual world. This *eidos* or *idea* is the essence of things. Ideas and things are related as the pattern and the copy. Plato's system is monistic in so far as the copies or things are immanent in the idea; it is monism by means of pure idealism. But as Plato gave a metaphysical existence to ideas, separating things from ideas and ideas from things, there resulted a dualism. He sets in irreconcilable antithesis sense and spirit, body and soul, transient and permanent.

At the apex of the ideas stands that of the Good towards which all is striving. He solved the problem of knowledge by saying that all learning is only remembering what we have known in a previous existence. The only use of things is that they suggest to us their eternal ideas or archetypes, as a photograph reminds us of an absent friend. To Plato the soul is of tremendous value. It is akin to the Divine, and in a previous existence has consorted with the highest ideas of Beauty and Goodness, of which it is enamoured. Salvation consists in education and knowledge, for 'we needs must love the highest when we see it'; Plato could not imagine the will of man deliberately choosing evil to its own hurt. The soul yearns to return to its true fatherland to contemplate the Good. Man's chief end is to rise above the perishing, soar to God by Love, 'the wing of the soul,' and imitate God so as to become as like Him as possible. Virtue is the only path to happiness, which is found in the pursuit of the highest until we see God.

Plato was keenly alive to the dualism of our nature; its complexity tortured him. How could such a spiritual being hanker after the transient? How grow forgetful of its true home? Plato's answer was, Because of the flesh, which we must put off to see God; it is the answer of Paul, 'The carnal mind is enmity against God, is not subject to the law of God, neither indeed can be.' The soul is like a charioteer driving two spirited horses, a white one which strives upward, and a black one which pulls in the contrary direction. The body is a burden which cannot come into the scheme of salvation. But the soul is infinitely precious: Plato seems often to anticipate 'What shall it profit a man if he gain the whole world and lose his own soul?' The grandest day in Greek thought was the day on which Plato approached the subject of the immortality of the soul. Every student is familiar with his references to this doctrine in the *Apology*, the *Timaeus*, and *Republic*,

more especially in the *Symposium* and *Phaedrus*, and with
its treatment in the *Phaedo*. We unconsciously associate
ourselves with the listeners in reading the *Phaedo*, feel
the force of the objections, share in the alarm at the
exquisite dramatic crises as Socrates unfolds the five
arguments for immortality which to us are antiquated.
But Plato also anticipated our chief reasons—apart from
the Resurrection of Christ—for this faith, the kinship of
the soul with the Divine, the moral argument, and the
longing for continued life. Plato had entered the kingdom
of the spirit.

It was no small boon to humanity to have his lofty
spirituality diffusing its influence 400 years B.C. One of
the world's greatest religious teachers, he taught in inimitable prose-poetry that man doth not live by bread alone,
that only the things of the spirit are of absolute and
eternal worth. His Love was a passion for the Eternal,
the regret for a better world. No one understood more
profoundly the unutterable yearnings of the soul. The
words of Augustine are truly Platonic, 'Thou hast made
us for Thyself, and our hearts are restless till they rest in
Thee.' He felt

> 'Those first affections, those shadowy recollections
> Which, be they what they may,
> Are yet the fountain light of all our day,
> Are yet the master-light of all our seeing,
> Uphold us, cherish and have power to make
> Our noisy years seem moments in the being
> Of an eternal silence.'

He realised that if man knew himself, his craving is not
to satisfy one part of his nature, or one passion, but to find
satisfaction for an infinite spirit. Any student can point
out flaws in Plato. With all his flaws he stands, and shall
stand, one of the great uplifters of man. No wonder he
was the schoolmaster of so many Christian Fathers.

Aristotle

Aristotle, 'the master of them that know,' was the subtlest thinker of Greece.[1] Plato had denaturalised man into pure spirit. To Aristotle this was repugnant: he would not call men away from earth, but to duty and activity. Happiness is the end of life, but does not consist in the satisfaction of momentary caprices but in the poise of all the faculties, pleasure being not the aim but the concomitant of right action. Conduct is not to be judged by general laws but by the interpretation each has made to himself of those laws. Plato held appetites to be evil in themselves; Aristotle as neither good nor bad in themselves; they become good by subserving good, evil by subserving evil ends. All depends on the purpose or end. The things of earth are not to be rejected for other-worldliness; all things are materials of conduct, instruments to work out ends, the raw material of virtue or vice. Plato had led men up the mount to be entranced by the loveliness of Goodness, to see the littleness of the transient; Aristotle led men down to the plain to develop what is ' proper to man.' Plato's doctrine would lead to asceticism and other-worldliness; Aristotle insisted on workaday goodness and a rounded life. Man must observe the golden mean by which to choose the amount of pleasure or pain good for our moral constitution. Man's chief end is the activity of his multifold nature toward a rational purpose. For Plato the love of God was the cause of the world's creation In Aristotle there is an unbridged chasm between his Absolute of Pure Thought and inert Matter. His God is so self-sufficient that he has no need of man or the universe. The prime Mover, activity cannot proceed from him except

[1] He is the father of the analytic method, as Plato of the synthetic, also the creator of zoology and botany. He assigned its place to empiricism, rescued the individual from Plato's universal, rejected the entity of ideas apart from things, substituted for the Platonic dualism of ideas and things that of Form and Matter.

in so far as he is the object of the world's striving. 'God does not love the world, but the world loves God.'

Aristotle supplied the wholesome corrective to Platonism. Plato made philosophy a religion ; Aristotle a science. He set scientific knowledge to balance transcendentalism and mysticism ; enthroned the head beside the heart. He set Greek thought on its course of another six hundred years which Plato would have overleapt. Aristotle's philosophy is that of sweet moderation ; he is no extremist like Plato, but the sanest thinker of Greece ; he is the enemy of the ascetic ideal as against the social and energetic. The individual is of too great worth to be swamped in the Universal, but the individual can function wholesomely only in society. If his works are cold, scientific, prosaic compared with the religious glow and imagination of Plato, they are none the less essential to the world's education. It is easy to see how the spirituality and idealism of Plato appealed to the Christian Fathers who were not untouched by *Weltschmerz* ; but the essence of Aristotelianism is as necessary to bring in the kingdom of God *upon earth*. Platonism has affinities with the temperament of the dreamer and futurist, but only the sober earnest Christian worker can practise Aristotelianism, which places happiness not in dreaming but in activity. If Plato is the interpreter of religion, Aristotle is the world's moralist.

Post-Aristotelian Philosophy

A new stage in Greek thought commences after Aristotle. A great change has set in. The world is growing one commonwealth as the *polis* falls ; as public and civic life are crushed out, ethics displaces politics. The old moral restraints and bases of conduct are undermined. Individualism is rampant. Speculation must give place to practice, as the bewildered individual imperiously demands moral guidance. The search is now not so much for knowledge, as how to use that already acquired. Only practical questions can secure a hearing. In the desire to find a moral guide men are willing to try any and every system ; hence there is a strong tendency to syncretism. Philosophy becomes less Greek and more cosmopolitan, less philosophy and more religion.

The chief phases of post-Aristotelian thought are Stoicism, Epicureanism, Scepticism, Eclecticism, Neo-Pythagoreanism, Graeco-Judaic philosophy, and Neo-Platonism.

Stoicism

Stoicism was a splendid discipline and preparation of the Empire for Christianity : it has remained the ally of Christianity and an inspiration to our best poets, like Browning. Stoicism was not a pure Greek product, much of its spirit and many of its teachers coming from the East. Its message was that not things but our thought of things matters :

> 'The mind is its own place, and in itself
> Can make a heaven of hell, a hell of heaven.'

Health, disease, pain, poverty, wealth are in themselves neither goods nor ills: only when we take them up into our inner life do they have any meaning. The Stoics proclaimed the supremacy of virtue as man's chief end, and the duty of self-control. Reason was appointed guardian or exterminator of the affections, and duty took the place of interest, for the Stoics were the first pagan preachers who enthroned duty in its high place ; they put a supreme value on character. They were pantheists, believing in a Spirit diffused throughout all, and operative in a universal law. Salvation is anthropocentric, man being potentially his own saviour. It consists in the eradication of the passions, the suppression of the emotions, and the cultivation of the will. While they held to the reign of a universal

law, they equally maintained the freedom of the will, in
the exercise of which, according to reason, consists the
dignity of man. No sympathy or help is demanded from
God or men. Inward peace arises from resignation to the
will of God. Virtue is self-sufficing: we ought to do good
though neither Gods nor men behold our action. The
Stoics took up the Platonic idea—to imitate or follow
God. Seneca says, 'I do not obey God: I consent with
Him.' The reward of self-denial is an approving conscience
and self-complacency. The hope of immortality is not
necessary. Thus man's reason and will are the instruments
of salvation, self-control and duty the law of life, and
imperturbability the crown:

> 'Si fractus illabatur orbis
> Impavidum ferient ruinae.'

In knowledge the Stoics were empirics. Their system was
a blend of materialism and pantheism. The soul is
material and immortal only to the end of the aeon. Stoicism
advanced personality by putting a new emphasis on will
and duty. It proclaimed the brotherhood of man, the
Providence of God, the reign of moral law, and an interpretation of suffering.

Other Greek schools were uttering their voices. The
Peripatetics took practically no part in religious affairs:
they were occupied with commenting on their master's
works and with natural science. They had no spiritual
gospel to offer to a weary world.

Epicureanism

Epicureanism, the first reasoned system of happiness,
was atheistic or deistic in religion and utilitarian in morals.
'Follow nature,' but nature prompts to eschew pain and
pursue pleasure; therefore pleasure is the *summum bonum*.
The criterion in knowledge and conduct is sensuous per-

ception. The world is the result of the fortuitous concourse of atoms ; the deity leads a life of tranquillity undisturbed by the travail of humanity. Even this system was a gospel for its day; it freed men from the tyranny of fatalism, from the fear of the gods, of death and future punishment, and all the burdens of superstition. Salvation was negative and individualistic ; no rewards were proposed, no terrors threatened ; there was no God suffering with and for man. Salvation is confined to this life ; there is no place of repentance, no room for hope. The soul is a composite of the rarer and finer atoms which are dissipated at death. Beyond the *flammantia moenia mundi* there awaits us only *leti secura quies*. Such is the gospel whose motto is *dux vitae dia voluptas*. This very philosophy which claimed to liberate man is guilty of what it charged against superstition, *Omnia suffundens mortis nigrore*. Natural hesitancy in leaving ' the warm precincts of the cheerful day ' is overcome by such consolations as that the longing for immortality arises from man's pride ; with life are extinguished all bitter regrets, all yearning after happiness ; ' when we are death is not, when death is we are not ' ; greater than we have died, and we should be resigned to a universal law. Epicureanism did not inculcate sensualism, though it easily conduced to it. Epicurus distinguished higher and lower pleasures ; sometimes pain should be endured in order to lasting pleasure. He tried to regulate the abounding passion of his age for pleasure by applying Aristotelian moderation to crude Hedonism. Epicureanism furthered personality (1) by asserting man's freedom ; (2) man does not really want the gratification of isolated desires but peace and pleasure for his *whole* being.

Sceptics

The Sceptics likewise invited men to retire to the impregnable fortress of their inner being and rest in self.

They negatived the possibility of knowledge; conviction is unattainable. Every proposition may be equally well supported or refuted. They cast aside all dogma except that of the impossibility of certainty. Man must rest in suspense of judgment about objective reality, and content himself with his subjective consciousness. Objective consciousness is illusory. They forgot that the ' consciousness of self is realised only with, and in relation to, the consciousness of the not-self to which it is opposed, and that if we could altogether cancel the latter, the former would disappear with it.' [1] The Sceptics, like Bishop Butler, made Probability the guide of life, as ancillaries to which they offered the practical wisdom of ancestors, or the verdict of the majority embodied in custom and law. As the schools mitigated their extreme positions, Scepticism toned down its dogma of the impossibility of knowledge, admitting degrees of probability, and interposing a kind of knowledge half-way between probability and certainty, as did Philo of Larissa. Antiochus, the teacher of Cicero, saw that probability implies truth as a standard, and that certainty is necessary to conduct. He found truth in the tenets common to the different schools, and thus conducted Scepticism over to Eclecticism. The school was revived under Aenesidemus and his pupils, who offered two additional guides of conduct, feelings and experience.

Eclecticism

Eclecticism, ' the creed of weary minds,' was not a school but a mode of thought running through all the later schools. It was due to the cosmopolitanism of the age, the lack of any original system, the penetrating criticism of Carneades and the Sceptics, the practical demand for a guide of conduct, the religious tendency of all serious schools, and lastly, the supremacy of the

[1] Caird, *Evolution of Theology in the Greek Philosophers*, ii. 125.

practical Romans. We find this syncretism first among the Greek schools, and then in the blending of Greek thought with Oriental mysticism. Its motto was the Horatian *nullius addictus jurare in verba magistri*. The result of Eclecticism was a general acknowledgment of man's innate moral consciousness as confirmed by the *consensus gentium*. This is the basis of conduct and responsibility : man is born for virtue, with ideas of right and wrong, apart from education and beyond demonstration. Eclecticism diffused a craving for religious truth and certainty which Christianity was to meet. Men were hesitating on the brink of knowledge before plunging into mysticism : the weary spirit was inclined to ask for a revelation.[1] 'The era of subjective and individual philosophy was brought to an end, and the era of religious philosophy inaugurated.'

Neo-Pythagoreanism

The Neo-Pythagoreans were the precursors of Neo-Platonism. They disseminated higher ideas of God, the immortality of the soul, and mysticism ; they held that sense and reason are not the only fountains of knowledge. They made philosophy a life, and inculcated ascetic morality. Their object was to supply a religious need. They looked to Revelation for truth and to sacramental grace for help.

Judaeo-Greek Philosophy

The chief representative of Judaeo-Greek thought is Philo, in whom more than in any other East and West

---

[1] 'Only a slight impulse was needed in order to lead the spirit in its search for truth beyond the limits of natural knowledge to a supposed higher fountain. This impulse Greek thought appears to have received through that contact with Oriental views of which Alexandria was the centre. The main part on the Oriental side was played by Judaism. . . . The last motive in this speculation was the yearning after a higher revelation of truth ; its metaphysical supposition was an opposition of God and the world, of spirit and matter, as intermediaries between which men took refuge in demons and divine powers. Its practical consequence was a combination of ethics and religion which led partly to asceticism and partly to the demand for a direct intuition of the Deity.'—Zeller, *Outlines*, p. 305.

are blended. His God is transcendent, including all reality and perfection, self-sufficient, the source of Good only. We know He exists, but not what He is : no definite predicate can be used of Him ; He is simply the I AM. Philo, as a Jew, adhered to the personality and moral attributes of God, even if the metaphysical attributes landed him in self-contradiction. Over against God in sharpest contrast stands a second principle—matter, the work of a subordinate deity. To bridge the chasm Philo posits a galaxy of intermediaries—powers, servants, angels, ideas, the highest of which is the *Logos*, who gives God certainty as to His universe and man hope as to God's goodness. He is the ambassador, the image of God, the first-born son of God, a second God. It is doubtful whether Philo endowed the Logos with personality. Man, as in Plato and the Old Testament, is a fallen creature ; the body is evil and the affections are to be eradicated. Reason must be set over against sense. Evil consists in escaping from God to self ; good is the escape from self to God to whom man is akin. Faith and Love are the helps of the soul. Salvation is the rising above sense and intelligence, even above the Logos, in self-unconscious ecstasy to behold the pure reality of God. ' The attempt to go beyond conscious thought had as yet been unknown in Greek philosophy. Even after Philo two centuries elapsed before it was an accepted dogma.' [1] ' Reason,' says Philo, ' departs when the spirit of God enters the soul, and returns when the spirit departs.' Man's chief end is not the realisation of man as man, but absorption in the Divine. Philo stated the problem [2] which Plotinus professed to solve.

[1] Zeller, *Outlines*, p. 325.

[2] 'If he has not solved the great problem of his time, we may fairly say that he first *stated it in all its fulness*. . . . He first gave utterance to both of the two great requirements of the religious consciousness, the need for rising from the finite and relative to the Absolute, and the need of seeing the Absolute as manifested in the finite and relative ; although he could find no other reconciliation of these two needs except externally to subordinate the latter to the former.'—Caird, ii. 208.

Neo-Platonism

The founder of Neo-Platonism was the Egyptian Plotinus. This system is Greek thought tinged with Oriental mysticism; it draws from Aristotle, Stoicism, Philo, but its largest element is Platonism. The whole system centres round the idea of God. God is to Plotinus even more transcendent than to Philo. He has no need of the world or man, is endowed with no external motion or love. He is apparently not endowed with personality; He is abstract Thought, pure Subject, the negation of all that is finite, unknowable. The world of the phenomenal is the shadow of a shadow; it is not the work of God, and indeed God takes no notice of it. How then account for the world at all? Plotinus could surmount this difficulty only by metaphors: the world is the overflow of the plenitude of the One or the effluence of the infinite, as heat is of a fire; it exists because of the 'necessity of nature,' that 'Being should produce an image of itself.' Plotinus closes his eyes to the unbridged dualism, though he too posits intermediaries such as Pure Intelligence, the Soul of man, or the Soul of the world. Man is, as to Plato and Philo, a fallen creature who remembers his native land in a supersensuous world, and is tortured by his finiteness. Escape consists in rising above self-consciousness to complete absorption in the Infinite. The light of reason is extinguished, says Plotinus, when the soul sees God, and returns when the vision is lost; in the Vision Beatific the 'soul forgets its life in the flesh and forgets even itself.' Personality, which dawned with Socrates, surrenders its pain and flees from its perplexity to a Nirvana. Its cry is 'Oh, that this too too solid flesh would melt.' If the soul is not lost in the senses, it is absorbed in the Infinite. There is no room for any thought except the thought of God: the soul empties itself to go to God empty, but never to be filled; it is ' the flight of

the Alone to the Alone.' Plato and Philo had set finite
and infinite in irreconcilable antithesis : ' Plotinus throws
down the bar between finite and infinite.' He never
dreams of the reconciliation of subject and object in a
higher ideal unity. Man is nothing because God is
everything.

Summary

Neo-Platonism is the necessary outcome of Greek
thought : it is the result (and the failure) of Greek (and
Oriental) dualism, for which it finds no solution except
the absorption of the lower in the higher. The problem of
knowledge had for over a thousand years agitated the Greek
mind ; here is the despair of knowledge and self-despair.
The trend of Greek philosophy was from concrete to
abstract, from phenomenal to reality, from form to essence ;
here all things are deprived of essence except the Absolute.

Philosophy had raised problems which only religious
experience could solve ; Greek thought recognises that
there is a world beyond knowledge and reason. Knowledge must give place to Revelation ; the heart requires
satisfaction as well as the head. Greek thought had not
laboured in vain ; it had victoriously finished its course.
Its failure was its success by assuring men that there must
be a principle of harmony, a synthesis of life, which has to
be sought in spiritual experience. Neo-Platonism was
the last determined effort of Greek thought to overcome
dualism by making a leap toward unity. It demanded
the religious solution.

CHAPTER VII

THE ROMAN

Ut inenarrabilis gratiae per totum mundum diffunderetur effectus Romanum regnum divina providentia praeparavit.—POPE LEO THE GREAT.

The Roman world forms the supremely important point of transition to the Christian religion, the indispensable middle term.—HEGEL (*Philosophy of Religion*).

EARLY Christian writers were much impressed with the fact that the establishment of the Roman Empire and the advent of Christianity were synchronous. Christianity came in the heyday of 'the grandeur that was Rome.' We must note briefly the character and genius of those who finished the preparation of the world for Christ and who made possible the spread of a universal religion.

Roman Character

The Romans have often been compared with the modern English, as the Greeks with the French, but this comparison goes only a short way. There was a fierce directness and intensity in the Romans, which made their character, like the Hebrew, one-sided. A large element in it was what we may call 'common sense,' a calculating worldly wisdom without any tinge of idealism or mysticism. They were distinguished for *gravitas*—a combination of dignity and self-confidence—and by *constantia*—a doggedness and steadfastness of character which made them more akin to the Hebrew than to the Greek.

Not original in genius but prosaic,[1] they were essentially conservatives in their outlook upon the world. They were an official people, and surely the originators of all 'red-tape' systems. Nothing strikes a reader of their constitutional history so much as their immense respect, not only for law, but for forms and formulae : the masses were often checked in revolutionary schemes by being reminded of prescribed forms. The Greeks marked their chronology by the Olympiads ; the Romans, an official people, by consulates. They prided themselves on being a religious people—*religiosissimi mortales*, says Sallust ; many Roman and Greek writers attributed the greatness of Rome to her scrupulous piety. The *pius Aeneas* was supposed to be a type of the Latin race. Their religion was political : Hegel treats it as the historic example of a religion of utility. They were born soldiers, more patriotic than any ancient people, and zealous of military honour : *dulce est pro patria mori* is a constant sentiment in their literature. The individual Roman was but a link with a glorious past ; hence the worship of the *Manes* is genuinely Roman. On a thousand battlefields, and for a longer period than any other people, the Romans poured out ungrudgingly treasures of blood for the *Senatus Populusque Romanus* or the *Imperium Romanum*. The Roman had no fear of death. The Hebrew could die because he lived in his race, and later because of faith in a resurrection. The Greek, brave in battle, regretted death as taking him away from this delightful world. The Roman with innate Stoicism of character could die without emotion for the good of Rome : ' the martyr's ecstasy had no place in his dying hour.' He had a keen sense of duty. The Roman sentinels whose remains were found at the gates of Pompeii were types of their race. Like most peoples who have made the world debtors, the Romans were self-conscious and

---

[1] 'Among the Romans the *prose* of life makes its appearance—the self consciousness of finiteness.'—Hegel. *Phil. of Relig.*, p. 299.

self-assertive. Indomitable pride was a large ingredient in their character. Closely connected with this was their aggressiveness : the Roman was the John Bull of antiquity. Many of their wars were pure aggression, but the Roman never repented. The circumstances of his early history taught him self-control and self-reliance : he prized discipline ; one of the stones found in the Roman wall between England and Scotland reads 'To the Discipline of Augustus.' The habits that the Roman formed as an agriculturist never entirely left him. In the city he longed for his country villa or seaside residence to enjoy his well-earned *otium*. The Roman was a domestic man, attached to home and wife and children. The Penates guarded the sanctity of marriage, while the Vestals stood for the purity of virginity : no ancient history supplies as with so many noble matrons. There are other elements less worthy in Roman character. They were materialists ; they set their heart on power, and to gain the world they lost their soul. They cared less for the things of the spirit than did Hebrews and Greeks. Rapacity and greed in the acquisition of wealth and vulgar ostentation in the use of it was a common feature of Roman society. Ill-gotten gain undermined character ; power engendered overweening pride and insolence. There was also an ingrained coarseness in their nature which the culture of Hellas could not eradicate. They were indifferent to culture until they came to Greece, and never assimilated its essence : the Roman soldier who killed Archimedes was a type of Rome. The most repulsive feature of the Romans was their cold-blooded callousness to suffering ; hence their delight in the amphitheatre where the groans of dying men were music to their ears. The ruins of amphitheatres rise up against them in judgment. In the Colosseum, the most majestic material monument of Rome, thousands of men died to make a Roman holiday. They were indifferent even to their own lives, so that—especially in the closing Republic and early Empire—suicide was frightfully common. The Roman always reserved the right of giving his own quietus—*patet exitus*.

Genius

The genius [1] of the Romans was not original but of high mediocrity (though Rome produced perhaps the most wonderful man in history—Caesar) ; it was massive, consequently its most characteristic expression was architecture, which combines art and size. The Roman mind was not subtle, speculative,[2] and metaphysical like the Greek, nor intuitive like the Oriental, but docile and concrete. They were essentially imitative, and good paymasters, always willing to borrow or steal anything they could find better from other peoples, be it gods, art, or philosophy. They proved themselves excellent organisers. Order was their first law. And this made them unequalled in legislation. As the Greeks turned everything into an art, the Romans turned what interested them into an institution ; they made their religion institutional as the Roman Church has done with Christianity. They were intensely practical, *rebus natus agendis*; they were master utilitarians especially in their religion. They were thorough in their work. Cato was a true Roman when he closed every debate with *censeo delendam esse Carthaginem*, and it was destroyed. In their devastations they were very drastic; they blotted out almost without a trace the civilisations of Etruria and Carthage, annihilated the Samnites, burned Corinth and Jerusalem to the ground. Their buildings were built for all time. Some of the streets of London are old Roman roads, many of their bridges are still stand-

---

[1]   'Tu regere imperio populos, Romane, memento,
      Hae tibi erunt artes, pacisque imponere morem,
      Parcere subjectis et debellare superbos.'—Virg., *Aen.*, vi. 851 ff.
[2] Cic. (*Tusc.*, ii. 1. 1), cites Ennius as saying, ' philosophari sibi necesse esse, sed paucis : nam omnino haud placere '—a genuine Roman sentiment.

ing, the sewage system of Timgad is in wonderful preservation. The *Cloaca Maxima* (sewer) in Rome is still
working after 2500 years.

Rise of the Empire

The people of the toga extended **their sway until the**
boundary of their dominion was the Euphrates on the East,
the African sands on the South, the Rhine, Danube, and
Scottish Highlands on the North, the Atlantic on the West.
The Republic conquered almost all that was permanent
Roman territory. The task of the Republic was to conquer;
that of the Empire to civilise, conciliate, and unify. The
Mediterranean was converted into one great inland Roman
lake, and for the first time all the progressive peoples of
the world lived for a considerable period under one flag.
Of course, the extent of Roman dominion varied from time
to time, especially on the Southern Rhine and in North
Britain, on the Danube (Dacia was not permanently
Roman) and the Euphrates. But it will help the reader
more clearly to realise its extent around the beginning of
the Christian era to say that it covered the territory of
modern Spain, Portugal, France, south of England, Hol-
land, Belgium, Switzerland, Italy, South-western Austria,
Southern Germany, Montenegro, Servia, Bulgaria, part of
Roumania, Greece, Turkey in Europe, and nearly all
Turkey in Asia, Egypt, Tripoli, Tunisia, Algeria, Morocco,
or a territory, roughly speaking, of 3000 miles long by
2000 broad. The population in the early Empire is usually
estimated at about 100,000,000, and under the Antonines
probably rose to 150,000,000.

The establishment of the Roman Empire was the
grandest political achievement of any era; [1] it was the
work of Rome's greatest man, Caesar, and his worthy

[1] This section is condensed from the writer's article, 'Roman Empire and
Christianity,' in *International Standard Bible Encyclopaedia* (Chicago, 1914).

successor, Augustus. The Empire was the slow result
of a long process. The social conflicts of Rome could
find no solution except in supreme power raised above
all classes. The yoke of a narrow, selfish oligarchy, who
endeavoured to control politics, religion, social interests,
and justice itself, grew intolerable to the commons.
Internal dissensions were settled by compromise while
external dangers threatened the Republic. The inevitable
collision came in the days of the Gracchi over the division
of the spoils of Attalus, King of Pergamus (133 B.C.).
Henceforth, the nobles and the people, oligarchy and
democracy, are engaged in bloody conflict until, with the
election of the first *princeps*, democracy secured the
upper hand, and in the hour of victory surrendered its
rights to despotic rule. The ancient traditions and
institutions had been undermined; the nobility were too
effete and selfish to administer, the people too corrupt
to elect and control administration. In the prevalent
corruption resulting from Roman conquests and idleness,
the rich had become richer and the poor poorer; a sober
middle class was wanting to mediate between the extremes
of society. The whole social equilibrium was upset.
Justice was impossible before tribunals in the hands of a
privileged class accessible to bribes and jealous to protect
their own order. Elections were impossible because of
bribery and faction; nomination by a supreme power was
needed. The political machinery of the free state refused
to work because each authority checkmated the other. Empire or one-man rule was the triumph of the individualism
which set in during the second Punic war; the struggle
of individuals could only result in the survival of the fittest.
Political parties degenerated into factions led by ambitious
leaders whose aim was self-aggrandisement: they nomi-
nated their lieutenants and dictated policy. The whole
trend was toward monarchy. In the *Republic* Cicero
makes Scipio declare for monarchy. There was a universal

thirst for power. The Senate sought a succession of extraordinary commissions for its members : the tribunate of C. Gracchus was autocratic enough. When Pompey received a command in Spain he, in regal fashion, remained in Italy and operated through legates. There was a general reluctance to lay down commands ; office was extended to long periods or repeatedly conferred ; Marius was consul seven times, Sulla five, and Cinna three. Prolonged military commands accustomed armies to their generals, to whom they transferred the allegiance due to the state. The secret of empire had already been discovered in the adherence of strong armies. Too often civil power was surrendered into the hands of a dictator, as to Sulla and Caesar. When one man could not have his own way he combined with colleagues, as in the triumvirates, which each manipulated for his own interest. The most hopeless feature of this period was that military authority secured the ascendency over civil. All classes and parties were exhausted and prepared to welcome supreme power. True patriots acclaimed a solution that promised peace and stability to society : the large numbers of traders and small merchants and freedmen desired peace at any cost. The oppressed provincials were more accustomed to despotic power, and, besides, they could not be worse harassed under any other form of government ; they sought a master to whom they could appeal against injustice. Add to this the influence of the Oriental idea of power over the minds of Roman rulers ; the emperors gradually extended their autocracy until Diocletian converted the monarchy into an Oriental despotism. The conquests of the Republic had rendered imperial power a necessity. An oligarchy engaged in perpetual class conflict at home was not fitted to rule a widely scattered and diverse dominion. The variety of people and nations under the Roman eagle could be better governed under monarchical rule, just as the Austro-Hungarian and the

British Empires are perhaps better held together under monarchy than under any other form of government.

Mission of Rome

If the Empire was founded in aggression and bloodshed, it can hardly be disputed that it proved the greatest blessing to its subjects; its establishment was hailed with an outburst of universal applause. Many of the Caesars were vicious men, but they were unconsciously the instruments of God's purpose in history. Rome, especially the Empire, executed a large mission for the ancient world. Its rulers are an illustration of the saying of Cromwell that we never rise so high as when we are unconscious of what we do. The mission of Rome may be thus summarised :—

1. Rome first protected the West against the East, and then kept guard in both West and East while Western culture and Eastern religions, especially Christianity, conquered her Empire. The student of Greek and Roman history is familiar with the constant Oriental peril. Greece in her day stayed it; with a political or military predominance of the East the centuries would have passed noiselessly over us, as over the East, without setting up any great landmarks of progress. Carthage was the first Oriental power with which Rome came in conflict. Every schoolboy is distressed that his hero did not conquer Scipio at Zama, until he later comes to realise what the spread of Carthaginian civilisation over the Mediterranean shores would have meant: Zama settled the future of the Mediterranean and of Western Europe. The Orient found again no mean champion in Mithridates of Pontus, who was finally driven back by Pompey. The question decided in the Roman civil wars at Actium was whether the Eastern or Western half of the Empire should hold the sword; Actium was a second Zama. Another strong

Eastern power Rome held in check for long, Parthia, until it revived as a Persian power under the Sassanides.

The East had always exercised a curious fascination over Roman minds. From the days of Hadrian it was quite evident that the centre of gravity was shifting eastwards. With the removal of the capital to Constantinople, that became an accomplished fact. Roman emperors had previously become Eastern monarchs. When East did secure the ascendency over West, Rome was able to surrender her educating and civilising mission to an Eastern religion.

2. Rome protected and extended Greek culture. Hellenism was so closely allied to Christianity that what Rome did for Hellenism she did for Christianity. It was from the Greeks that the Romans acquired a taste for the things of the spirit. It gave new vigour to exhausted Greece to find the mighty Romans sitting at her feet as pupils and imitators. The respect with which Rome treated Greek culture raised its value over the Empire, and Rome opened the whole world to the intellectual conquests of Greece.

3. Rome continued and forwarded most of the social and political work of Greece. The Greek ideal was equal liberty under law for all. Roman statesmen acquainted themselves with the political speculations and institutions of Greece. Rome showed how men could live in large national unities and in one Empire under justly administered laws. They learned to follow the logic of facts better than the Greeks could ever have done. They contributed toward the solution of many social problems which agitated Greece : they slowly extended the franchise and made conquered people and even slaves Romans. They fought out to the bitter end the strife of classes versus masses until an overlord led the latter to victory. But the Romans were not so democratic as the Greeks, because they were not so well educated and were more content

with formulae. The Roman constitution was theoretically democratic but practically oligarchical. Oligarchy maintained a tyranny through Republican history, and in the Empire gave place to despotism. These political considerations are of importance for the democratic organisation of early Christianity.

4. The more immediate mission of the Empire was to consolidate and civilise, to call order out of social chaos, to restore peace and security to society. Rome had a genius for order and organisation. Had the civil strife been protracted much longer, the whole fabric of ancient society must have fallen hopelessly to pieces and the newly conquered provinces lapsed into anarchy. For centuries Rome had been engaged in ruthless conquests. She had pulled down ; now she must build up. The Empire gave a weary world a period of rest and recuperation from untold suffering and social upheavals. She first removed the causes of quarrelling by wiping out old prejudices, by preventing class from making reprisal upon class ; she forbade nations to go to war, and removed diversity of governments ; she put an end to the bitterness of city rivalry and extended means of communication.

The justly celebrated Roman peace—*pacis Romanae majestas*—was the first world-peace, lasting for more than two hundred years. The whole civilised world was practically at rest when Christianity appeared. After centuries of commotion, life could resume its normal course and men could devote themselves to the works of peace and to the demands of their inner life. The Romans were the harbingers of the ' peace on earth, good will to men,' of the Evangel. The temple of Janus was closed three times during the reign of the first emperor, and an *Ara Pacis* was erected in Rome 13 B.C. This peace was ' settled peace, too, such as never came again till after Waterloo,' and an inestimable boon to that exhausted world. Had a lasting peace not been restored, ancient society would

have been engulfed before it had fulfilled its historic
function.[1] All who represented the traditions of the past
would have been wiped out, and thus a steadying principle
lost. But for this peace, that bankruptcy which overtook
the later Empire would have come three centuries too
early. The provinces were exhausted by the armies
billeted on them, by compulsory contributions, huge im-
posts for revenue, by the decimating and shifting of the
population; their lands were untilled, their implements
removed, their buildings in ruins, their sons drafted into
the Auxiliaries or killed in Roman quarrels. Roman
peace at least postponed threatening calamity. Agriculture
revived; the wilderness was reclaimed, for the Roman
could turn the desert into a garden. The second century
A.D. was probably the happiest era of the old world. In
peace enormous cash came again into circulation; bullion
and coin concealed in civil commotion now furnished
employment. This money was sent back to the provinces
to pay Roman troops or to meet vast orders of luxuries.
All, except those needed for garrison duty, returned to
the productive labours of peace: the Romans, like the
British, governed by prestige and authority and not by
large garrisons: an army of about 300,000 men guarded
a territory now guarded by millions. Commerce revived
under the aegis of peace. The Mediterranean, cleared of
pirates, was a safer highway of trade and travel than at

---

[1] Virgil could well say, 'Deus nobis haec otia fecit.' The Halicarnassus
inscription hails Augustus as 'Saviour of the whole human race whose
providence fulfilled and surpassed the prayers of all' (σωτῆρα τοῦ
κοινοῦ τῶν ἀνθρώπων γένους οὗ ἡ πρόνοια τὰς πάντων εὐχὰς οὐκ ἐπλήρωσε
ἀλλὰ καὶ ὑπερῆρεν). Another inscription says of the same emperor, 'he
gave a new aspect to the world that would gladly have perished' (ἐτέραν τε
ἔδωκεν παντὶ τῷ κόσμῳ ἥδιστα ἂν δεξαμένῳ φθοράν). Cf. Origen citing
Melito (c. Celsum, ii. 30). 'In the days of Jesus righteousness arose and
fulness of peace; it began with his birth. God prepared the nations for his
teaching by causing the Roman emperor to rule over all the world; there
was no longer to be a plurality of kingdoms, else would the nations have
been strangers to one another, and so the Apostles would have found it
harder to carry out the task laid on them by Jesus when he said, "Go and
teach all nations"' (cited in Harnack, Mission, i. 20).

any time up to the middle of last century. Peace gave an impetus to intellectual and moral life. Men exchanged not only material but spiritual wares. In the period of turmoil man's interest centred upon his very existence, illicit paths to self-aggrandisement were many, and every man's hand was against his brother; but now that the laws of society were again vindicated, men had leisure to direct attention to the needs of the inner life. Under Augustus there was a religious revival.

5. Rome not only restored order but she unified the world and blended the nations in preparation for the Gospel:[1] all lived together under her roof. It was a discovery to find that men of every race and nation, of every degree of culture, and of social distinction, could live together in peace. All civilised peoples practically lived under one rule. Augustus erected a golden milestone in the Forum as the world's centre. Never had the happiness or misery of humanity so depended on the decisions of a single will in one centre. Cosmopolitanism reached its acme in the Empire: the world was one commonwealth. The Romans, though they refused home rule to the provinces, were tolerant of their traditions, customs, religion, and a certain degree of local autonomy. With few exceptions, and those in the interest of good government, Rome left every man to his gods and maintained the tolerant policy inaugurated by Alexander. The Republican policy conceded no rights to the conquered. Caesar inaugurated a conciliatory policy toward the conquered, and was the first Roman to dream of extending Roman rights and citizenship to all. Under the Empire the more liberal policy was carried out. The gulf between Romans and provincials was gradually bridged until Caracalla granted citizenship to all the free inhabitants. The Empire and the Church were simul-

---

[1] W. T. Arnold notes that the two centrifugal forces in the Empire were (1) the essential difference between East and West, and (2) the new religion—Christianity.

taneously aiming at universalism. The place of Rome as
the centre of the world to which all roads led, the presence
of the ubiquitous Roman authorities, the living symbol
of power in the emperor, the imperial cult, the elevation
of provincial and non-Roman emperors, the increasing
numbers of Romanised freedmen, Roman law and language,
the extension of Roman citizenship—all worked for the
unification of mankind.

The Roman did not—could not—complete the work
of unification which is still a dream. It behoves us,
trammelled by the traditions of feudalism, to criticise
leniently Roman efforts to make the world a good place
to live in. After Rome's work of pacification there still
remained the antithesis of bond and free. The poor and
hungry masses are with us as they were with the Romans.

6. Rome protected what is now modern civilisation
against the irruptions of the Northern barbarians, until
they, educated by her law and language and impressed
with her greatness, became docile pupils of the Christian
Church, and with their unspent energies took up the inheritance of Rome to pass it on to later generations. But for
Rome, the Parthians, Saracens, and Ottomans on the East,
and the barbarians on the North might have blotted out
modern civilisation. Rome thus proved the link between
the old and the new, and passed on to us ' the long results
of time.' Augustine says of the Roman Empire *sua se
magnitudine fregit*, but from its ruins arose modern
civilisation.

7. Rome not only rescued the West, but she civilised
and prepared it for Christianity as Greece had done
the East. Though Rome conquered the East she was
Hellenised there. In the West she came in contact with
inferior civilisations which she Romanised by impressing
upon them her language, laws, and institutions. What
Greece had done for her she in turn did for the West.
Her language lives in the Romance tongues, her laws in

all Western codes. While Christianity was spreading in
the riper Eastern section, Rome was preparing the West
for the Gospel, teaching barbarians respect for authority,
imparting a taste for intellectual and spiritual things,
building bridges and roads, and supplying Christianity
with a uniform language. It should not be forgotten that
Christianity came to the West—to Rome and South Gaul
—in Greek and to Greek communities, but after this initial
stage the Christian preachers were able to penetrate the
West on the tracks of Roman civilisation.

8. To catalogue the material benefits conferred on the
world by Rome is beyond the purpose of this book. Rome's
spiritual weapon was her law : she kept order and acted
as policeman while the emissaries of the Cross preached.
Rome did much in commonplace and material things.
She kept untiring watch on the Nile, Euphrates, Danube,
and Rhine. She built roads and erected bridges for the
heralds of the Cross ; she spared no toil in building aqueducts to carry an abundant supply of fresh water to cities ;
she introduced sanitary arrangements which—as Timgad
shows—are thoroughly modern. If Rome could ruthlessly
destroy she could also turn the desert into a garden.
Travelling through North Africa, one finds abundant proof
that Rome was a blessing to those provinces which have,
until recently, lain waste. Remains of Roman villas
and baths with mosaics are found in regions where for
miles there are now only nomad tents. The same is true
of Syria and Asia Minor.

9. The Roman Empire formed the political framework
for Christianity. Here was a universal Empire crying out
for a universal religion. The Judaic section of the early
Church would have rendered Christianity merely a reformed
Judaism. It was a Roman citizen, who appreciated the
Empire, that enthusiastically supported in a Greek city the
mission to the nations. The Empire was a standing
challenge to Christianity : it enlarged the horizon of

Christian missionaries. Surely Christ must reign over a dominion as wide as that of Caesar. If the Empire embraced all men, why should Christianity aim at less ? With but few faint and uncertain traditions (as that of Thomas and Bartholomew in India, and of Thomas in Parthia), the activity of Christian preachers lay wholly within the Empire, because the Empire was practically synonymous with *humanitas*—the *genus humanum*. There were three determining factors in the spread of early Christianity : (a) the Jewish settlements of the Diaspora ; (b) the area in which Greek was spoken, and (c) the centres of population and Roman administration on the great Roman roads ; these three usually coincided. Christianity gained its first foothold in Europe in two Roman colonies—Philippi, which was so Roman that it had no Jewish synagogue, and Corinth, refounded by Caesar.

CHAPTER VIII

THE LANGUAGE OF CHRISTIANITY

Die Bibel, deren Gott *Jahveh* heisst, ist die Bibel eines **Volkes**; die Bibel deren Gott κύριος heisst, ist die Weltbibel.—DEISSMANN.

First International Tongues

A UNIVERSAL Empire and a universal religion demanded a universal language. Nationalities were so mixed and blended that a common linguistic medium was a necessity. The question of a universal language, natural or artificial, did not at first concern the ancients. Yet we know of early international languages. Egypt and Assyria seem to have been the first to need such a medium. In the Tel-el-Amarna tablets (about 1400 B.C.), we have the diplomatic correspondence in old Babylonian of the Pharaohs Amenophis III. and IV. with the kings of Assyria, Babylonia, Mitani (Mesopotamia), and Cyprus, and the Egyptian officials and vassals in Canaan.

The Persian Empire stretching from the Indus to the Nile was without a uniform language for its dominions : the old Babylonian still maintained a place in the centre of the former Babylonian Empire. Old Persian was made the court language—the language in which the Behistun rock memorials are carved. But westwards from the Euphrates Aramaic was adopted as the official language, and became the first international tongue. It dislodged the sacred language in Palestine, was spoken by the Eastern Diaspora, was used by Egyptian officials, and is found in

O

the Jewish papyri of Elephantine. Aramaic, however, never spread beyond the Orient, and never took root in Indo-Germanic soil. It is to the Greeks we owe the language that was not only the international bond of the Orient but the first medium for East and West.

But the tongue spoken by the people calling themselves Hellenes was for long by no means a unity. It was broken up into dialects as distinct from one another as are the present Romance tongues. How did a world-speech arise out of these dialects ?

The Koiné

Several causes contributed toward a common Greek language. The increasing cosmopolitanism defied dialects; the breaking up of Greek autonomy and exclusiveness rendered men more interested in other Greek clans. The Greek genius for commerce, the hosts of mercenaries, the standardising of Attic, all pointed to a common tongue. But the mightiest factor was the campaigns of Alexander. He united Greece, then amalgamated Greek and Macedonian, with them conquered the East and opened it up to Greek language and culture. In his army Greeks from all parts met : they no longer regarded themselves as Athenians, Spartans, or Boeotians, but Hellenes. And Greek was the only linguistic medium which Alexander found available to govern his vast territory. He planted Greek colonies everywhere, in which Greek clans and Macedonians side by side with Orientals needed a common language. As unity was thus impressed on Greece from without, and the world opened to her culture and enterprise, the dialects which represented her exclusiveness gave way to a *Koiné* from the fourth century B.C. onwards. Thus arose that Greek language known as the *Koiné*, *i.e.* ' common language,' or Hellenistic Greek—the language in which the New Testament is written and in which the Gospel was first carried to the nations. This *Koiné* is built on the basis of Attic with contributions from the various other dialects.[1] The language of the New Testament [2] and of early Christianity is predominantly the vernacular spoken language as distinguished from the literary *Koiné* of writers like Josephus and Polybius.

Greek was the *lingua franca* of the eastern part of the Roman Empire, the language of culture, commerce, diplomacy and administration. The spread of the Greek language was a very favourable circumstance for the preaching of the Gospel. Under Alexander and the Diadochi, Greek not only strengthened its position on the sea-coast, but penetrated inland in Egypt and in Asia Minor. Every new Greek foundation was a centre of Hellenism. The Greeks, like the modern English-speaking peoples, did not take the trouble to learn foreign languages: they obliged foreigners to learn Greek. When the Roman appeared in the East, Greek was too firmly rooted to be dislodged : though Roman pride could recognise only Latin as the official speech, they found in Greek a useful bond and ally of their administration. A Greek translation appeared along with Latin official documents : the Latin was always the original, as Roman officials would not deign to issue Greek documents and then make translations from them.

Importance of Greek

It was not by accident that Christianity appeared at the one time in history when Greek was the sole international medium for all the civilised peoples of the Empire. It was the first moment in history when all men could easily exchange thought. The spread of Greek neutralised the

---

[1] Cf. Thumb, *D. griech. Sprache*, ch. iii.
[2] Cf. the writer's article, 'The Koiné, the Language of the New Testament,' in *Princeton Theological Review*, Jan. 1910.

confusion of Babel. And Greek was the language in which an Aramaic Gospel became a world-evangel : all the missionary activity of early Christianity was practically confined to Greek-speaking people. The early missionaries did not learn the enchoric vernaculars, and apparently attempted no peasant mission : they probably regarded the Parousia as too imminent, or recognised that if the Greek-speaking peoples were Christianised the Kingdom would soon come among the rest. Further, it was in Greek soil that Christianity took at first its firmest root, and on Greek territory it carried on its most active propaganda, and by means of Greek secured its first footing in the West. Such considerations show us how important and indeed necessary for the success of Christianity was the spread of Greek. It would hardly be fair to attribute the rapid spread of Christianity merely to the fact that all *spoke* Greek. As Mahaffy remarks, wherever Greek was spoken or known it was accompanied by a certain amount of Greek culture and Greek thought, the needs and the ideals of the Greek spirit. That the Gospel was so successful on Greek territory proves therefore that not only the Greek tongue but the indefatigable efforts of the Greek spirit prepared the way for Christ—if in no other way than by raising problems which only Christianity could solve, and by giving clear expression to needs that only Christianity could satisfy. It is worth while to dwell briefly on the expansion of Greek and the influence which it exercised.

Spread of Greek

It is significant that the most Hellenistic book in the New Testament—the Fourth Gospel—tells us that when Jesus learned that some Greeks had expressed the wish ' we would see Jesus,' He answered, ' the hour is come that the Son of Man should be glorified.' This was tantamount to a confession that if the Greek world accepted Him the whole world would follow. Cicero in 62 B.C. says, 'if anyone thinks he will reap less fruit of glory from Greek verses than from Latin he is totally mistaken ; for Greek is read by practically the whole world, while Latin is confined to its own territory, which is narrow indeed.' Throughout the East Greek was so well known that the Romans were obliged and even glad to accept it as a means of administration. An encyclical letter (1 Peter), addressed to Jewish Christians of the Diaspora ' in Pontus, Galatia, Cappadocia, Asia and Bithynia,' was written in Greek. Paul addressed Roman Christians in Greek, and the author of the Epistle to the Hebrews uses the world-language. The Jerusalem mob expected Paul to address them in Greek (Acts xxi.). Justin Martyr of Shechem knew no Hebrew or Aramaic, and uses only the Septuagint. An Ethiopian eunuch read a Hebrew prophet in a language that Philip, a Hellenist, easily recognised ; he was reading the fifty-third chapter of Isaiah. In the grammar-schools of the West Greek was taught beside Latin, while in the East apparently Latin was not taught beside Greek.

In Rome and Italy Greek was well-known. Horace complains that ' captive Greece led captive babarous Rome.' From the second century B.C. Rome fell more and more under the spell of Greece. Romans sent their sons to Greek universities, or retained Greek tutors for their children, and private Greek chaplains as moral directors in their homes. Greek literary slaves fetched large prices. Greek artists, architects, and less honourable professions found abundant employment in Rome. The medical profession was almost entirely Greek. Roman libraries consisted largely of Greek books. The Roman theatre imitated Greek models in its best days. Latin was forged into a literary language on Greek models. The earliest historians of Rome, Fabius Pictor and Alimentus, wrote in Greek. Cicero testifies that about the beginning of the first century B.C. Italy was full of Greek arts and learning

The grandest characters of Rome were moulded and consoled by a Greek religious philosophy, Stoicism ; the less
spiritual had recourse to the licence and negations of
another Greek philosophy, Epicureanism. Cato Uticensis
died by his own hand after reading the *Phaedo*. The elder
Cato, an opponent of everything un-Roman, learned Greek
in his old age lest the god of the lower world should not
understand Latin. Marius's ignorance of Greek is noted
as exceptional by Plutarch. A Roman emperor penned his
self-analysis in Greek. Juvenal speaks of the Greeks as
a *gens acceptissima* to the wealthy Romans, and com-
plains ' non possum ferre, Quirites, | Graecam Urbem.'
He vents his spleen on the *Graecula* wife who does not
care to know Latin, but expresses her fears, wrath, joys,
cares, and all the secrets of the heart in Greek (*Sat*. vi.,
184 ff.).   Greek love-terms were in vogue among the
Romans, and Roman lovers often employed Greek to
set forth their lady's charms. Roman statesmen and
generals often carried to the field a Greek philosopher as
a war correspondent. Foreign lecturers like the Egyptian
Plotinus would lecture in Greek at Rome. The Greek
towns throughout southern Italy created a Greek atmosphere. It was not Italy but Africa or Syria [1] that first
demanded a Latin Bible.

Greek in the Diaspora

The attitude of the Jews toward Greek culture and
language is important for the history of Christianity.
Here we must distinguish those of the Diaspora from those
of Palestine. Those of the extreme eastern Dispersion
in Babylonia and the Euphrates region spoke an eastern
Aramaic, and there up to late times rabbinic schools
flourished. In the countries of Asia Minor as far as

[1] A good case for Syria (Antioch) is made by H. A. A. Kennedy in *The Old
Latin Versions*, Hastings' *D. B.*, iii. 54 ff.

Mesopotamia, inscriptions prove that the Jews spoke Greek: we have similar evidence for the Crimea. In Egypt where the LXX was called for, and where Jewish writers used Greek, the common language of the Jews was Greek, as also in Cyrene and Crete. In the Aegean islands their language was also Greek, as we infer from the Rheneia and other inscriptions. Their tombstones in Rome prove that there they spoke Greek. Hebrew is not found on Jewish tombstones, and we may be sure that if the sacred language had been at all familiar we should find it there. The language of the Jewish Dispersion was the universal language. All the relics of Diaspora writing from the last centuries B.C. are in Greek. Greek was the language of their commerce, tombstones, propaganda, Scriptures, even of their prayers and synagogue worship. That Greek was the language of their synagogue and worship is most striking, for men are most conservative in holy things. Yet this may be accepted as an established fact in opposition to Lightfoot and others. 'The language of the worship (in the synagogue) was, as a rule, without doubt Greek,' says Schürer. The very fact of the enormous success of the Jewish propaganda compels us to suppose that it was carried on in Greek. We find Paul addressing in the synagogues Israelites and God-fearing heathen whose common language was Greek. Besides, the Jews in their proselytising zeal would not be likely to use an unknown tongue in the synagogue, the fulcrum of their proselytising. That the LXX was the Diaspora Bible and used in the synagogue services is testified by several Church Fathers. The two inscriptions from Rheneia, the island burying-place of Delos, show that the LXX was the Bible of the Diaspora there as early as 100 B.C. If the Hebrew text was used in the synagogue it was paraphrased into Greek. It is also altogether unlikely that the scattered Jews surrounded by those speaking the universal language, and always ready to learn from the

Greeks in everything that did not touch upon religion,
should desire or be able to maintain their home language
in which they could not communicate with outsiders.
Paul, though educated at Jerusalem, is familiar with the
Old Testament only in the LXX. Zahn is surely mistaken in arguing from the word *Abba* that Aramaic was
the language of his prayers ; the word was used like *Pater
noster* among us, and Paul follows it up immediately with
the Greek equivalent. Cleomedes refers to the bad Greek
used in the synagogue. The translating of the Hebrew
text into Greek was universally allowed. One exclusive
authority forbids the *Torah* to be translated into any
language except that of the Javanim, *i.e.* Greeks.

Greek in Palestine

The home-keeping Palestinian Jew was more conservative. But Palestine forming, as it were, the pivot of East
and West, could not effectually exclude Greek influence.
Greek customs were known, Greek names for articles of
common use were employed, but the vernacular language
of Palestine and Syria was western Aramaic. The people
of the land were familiar only with Aramaic. In the
synagogues of Palestine as of Babylon the Hebrew text
was paraphrased into Aramaic. Josephus confesses he had
a poor mastery of Greek pronunciation : he also says that
the Jews (of Palestine) did not encourage the knowledge
of Greek (*Ant.*, xx. 11, 2). Even in Jerusalem the people
understood Aramaic better than Greek, as we infer from
Acts xxi. 40 ; xxii. 2. Titus summoned the people of
Jerusalem to surrender in Aramaic. In the Christian
church of Scythopolis, in the time of Diocletian, it was
necessary to have an official to translate Greek into
Aramaic, and in Jerusalem as late as the end of the fourth
century Greek was so little understood that the bishop
required somebody to translate his sermons into Syrian,

i.e. Aramaic : ' For the mass of the people the knowledge of Greek is not proved. In reality one must suppose that the lower classes in Palestine had either no acquaintance, or only a scant acquaintance, with Greek,'[1] but Schürer admits that this scanty knowledge was very widespread.

On the other hand, Palestine was not only surrounded by Hellenism, but Hellenism penetrated even into the Holy Land and spread in its capital. Palestine was hemmed in by Greek towns on the west coast, on the north and the east. It contained Greek centres like Samaria, Scythopolis, Tiberias, and Caesarea Philippi on the borders. Great commercial highways traversed the country. Palestine both before and after the Hasmoneans was governed by rulers of Greek culture. The Hellenising process under the Seleucids was carried on successfully, and was stayed only by the mad efforts of Antiochus Epiphanes to hasten it. Even then it was not arrested by the higher classes but by the common folk. The Herodians again took up the work of Hellenising, but the native opposition to them, and hostility to the Roman government, rendered the people by this time exclusive. The higher classes spoke Greek and were familiar with Greek culture. The Hasmoneans employed Greek and Aramaic on their coins, the Herodians and Romans only Greek on the Judaean coinage. In the capital Greek must have been more or less familiar owing to the sympathy of the leaders, and especially owing to the enormous numbers of Hellenistic Jews visiting the festivals, and thousands of them returned to spend their last days under the shadow of the temple. We read (Acts vi. 9) of the synagogue of ' the Libertines, and of the Cyrenians, and of the Alexandrians, and of them of Cilicia and Asia,' where a synagogue of each is probably implied. Also vast numbers of Greek proselytes and God-fearers visited the Holy City. These Hellenistic Jews and proselytes

[1] Schürer, ii. 84.

spoke Greek and must have been people of some substance, which in itself would encourage others to learn their language, and, as before remarked, Greek-speaking people obliged others to learn their language. In Galilee of the nations a portion of the city populations was undoubtedly Greek. When Jerome was looking for a copy of Aquila he could not find one except in a Galilean synagogue. At the trading centres like Capernaum we must suppose that Greek was familiar. When Philip went down into Samaria to preach Christ, he presumably did so in Greek. Zahn says that the inhabitants of the towns were familiar with Greek, and Palestine at the Christian era had numerous flourishing towns. In the war of Quietus (al. Titus) the religious authorities forbade parents to give their children a Greek education, from which we infer that such education had been common.

Language of Jesus

What language did our Lord speak? The question is rather not whether He could speak Aramaic or Greek, but which language did He habitually speak? While it is impossible to dogmatise, there can be little doubt that Jesus habitually used Aramaic in daily intercourse with His disciples and in His public teaching and prayers. Jesus was counted 'unlearned': He was one of the people, and His message was primarily to the peasant class and to the poor and the little ones. He was trained in the seclusion of Nazareth, where there is no reason to suppose any appreciable foreign influence. A few of His original expressions are preserved to us: His cry on the Cross was in the language of His childhood. At such a crisis one uses the language that comes nearest the heart. Besides, the Synoptic differences are often explicable on an Aramaic original: this argument in recent years has gained considerably in cogency.

Jesus knew and could use Greek when occasion required. Some of His public utterances may have been made in Greek. When Jesus journeyed into a Greek region outside Galilee we read of no interpreter being necessary; the Syro-Phoenician woman, a Greek, understood Him, and He understood her. She seems also to have understood His conversation with His disciples which was probably in Greek. A great part of Jesus' public ministry was in Galilee, where a considerable proportion of the town populations must have been Greek, especially at a customs-centre like Capernaum. When certain Greeks desired to see Jesus He apparently required no intermediaries. One whose Gospel was intended for all nations could hardly be indifferent to what He must have known to be the universal language. His trial before Pilate must have been conducted in Greek. We shall not be far wrong in saying that Jesus habitually used His native Aramaic in His private devotions and public teaching, but could command Greek when it was necessary, or when He could secure a better hearing.

Greek was the language used at the earliest conversion of Gentiles (Ethiopian eunuch and Cornelius), in Greek the first mission was carried beyond Jerusalem to Samaria, in Greek the Gospel outgrew Palestinian Judaism and started on its world-mission in Syria and Asia, in Greek the Gospel was transferred from Asia to Europe (Philippi, Thessalonica, and Corinth), in Greek the Gospel was domiciled in Rome and the West; the correspondence, literature, and liturgy of the Roman Church for two centuries was Greek, its bishops bore Greek names until towards the end of the second century; the majority of the catacomb inscriptions until the middle of the third century are in Greek, not Latin; in Greek the Gospel first migrated westwards from Rome to South Gaul. The Greek language was in some way allied with the Gospel : it was a promise of the universalism of the Gospel that it adopted the universal language

—the language which all races and creeds spoke or understood, and in which the first outlines of universal history were recorded.

The Gospel went first where the greatest need was felt —to the eastern Greek-speaking half of the Empire. This soil was most fully prepared. The East had been educated by centuries of culture and had been offered the best that Orientalism, Judaism, and Hellenism could afford. Its moral and spiritual capacities were greater; it was waiting for deliverance in a way unknown to the barbaric West. It had been penetrating the secrets of its own nature; knowledge had brought disquietude; the heart was crying for sympathy and longing to find a harmony above all discord. The mysteries of the East had nourished longings they could never satisfy; the voice of philosophy was uncertain. Where was a Revelation to be found ?

The Latin West

While the Gospel was being preached in Greek in the East, the Romans were preparing the way for its extension to the West. The peoples of the Danube and the Rhine, Northwestern Spain and Britain, were not yet half civilised. It was the task of Rome to make these peoples ready for the Gospel, to furnish Christianity with another universal language, to unify, to civilise and educate by her law and discipline for the discipline of the Gospel. Hers it was, too, in her own senility to hand over the great tasks in which she had so signally succeeded, and that in which she had so egregiously failed, to the *sera atque ideo inexhausta juventas* of the North. She conserved what was best and most essential in the old to bequeath to her historic successors. She finally surrendered her sceptre to the Church to which she had given a language and a polity and a world-outlook. The Vulgate proved to the West what the LXX had been to the East; it was for hundreds of years the only universal Bible of Europe; it became directly or indirectly the parent of all the vernacular versions of Western Europe (except the Gothic).

Thus the Greeks and the Romans translated an Aramaic Gospel into universal languages for the peoples of the earth.

CHAPTER IX

IN THE FULNESS OF TIME

When the fulness of the time came God sent forth His son; . . . to sum up all things in Christ.

The 'fulness of the time' for the Gospel came when Greek conquered Jew and Jew conquered Greek, and the world inherited the legacy of their struggle through Roman hands.—MAHAFFY.

How were Pity understood,
Unless by Pain? BROWNING.

East and West converging

CHRIST appeared at the time when all the striving and hopes of all peoples were converging to a focus, when the vast majority of mankind were hungering for religious support,[1] when East and West had been wedded, when men were expecting a new era, when the philosophy of Greece and the religious consciousness of the Hebrew were pointing toward a new Revelation. Christ came at the one time in history when all civilised nations lived, as it were, under one roof, when the happiness of mankind depended on the will of one, when all were able to communicate in

[1] 'To raise religious need to such a level that the quickening impulse necessarily awakens in unsatisfied aspirations, and the mind becomes creative, was the task of those last two centuries B.C., which were granted such scant measure of earthly happiness.'— Hausrath (*N. T. Times—Apostles*, i. 34). 'It was into no unspiritual world that the Christian religion came, but a world rather of seething hopes and dreams and premonitory glimpses. These hopes the Gospel was to realise. But it realised them, we may believe, not by borrowing ideas, or decking itself out in ancient symbols, but by the exhibition of a fact within the field of history in which were more than fulfilled the inextinguishable yearnings of the world's desire.'— Mackintosh, *Person of Jesus Christ*, p. 533.

one language, when men were unanimous as to the perils
and needs of the world, when there was peace on earth,
when there was ' *one* empire, *one* universal language, *one*
civilisation, a *common* development toward monotheism,
and a *common yearning* for saviours.'

Greatest Crisis in History

The advent of Christ synchronised with what is admittedly
the greatest crisis in all history, ' the coming of age of the
human race,' [1] when all that men had struggled for during
long centuries seemed likely to disappear from earth,
when chaos threatened to reassert its primeval reign.
Never before or since has the world been so utterly
exhausted [2] as at this *Wendezeit*, after the internecine
Greek strife, the incessant conflicts of the Diadochi, the
rebellion of Oriental nationalism, the bloody riots of the
Hellenistic cities, the increase of mercenaries and outlaws
(almost as unprincipled as the Crusaders), the ruthless
conquests and yet more ruthless civil wars of Rome, the
reign of terror under the emperors who executed the
judgment of Heaven upon the oligarchy that had wrought
more havoc than any other single institution, the decima-
tion of populations, the fearful increase of slavery. The
cry of the whole world was

> εὑδέτω δ' ἄμετρον κακόν,
> μεταιβολία δέ τις φανείη, Ζεῦ πάτερ, ἐκ σέθεν.

Many other causes, political, economic, social, were sapping
public and private morality and undermining religion.

[1] **Deissmann,** *New Light*, p. 78.
[2] If we could imagine the exhaustion of Germany after the Thirty Years'
War extending over the rest of Europe we should have an analogy to the
state of affairs in the closing Republic. 'The general impression we receive
from the records of the New Testament is assuredly that they were written
under a prevailing sense of human misery.'—Merivale, *Conversion*, p. 88.

The Greek city-states and Greek kingdoms had pursued one policy—might is right. Violence had at length in Rome seated itself on the throne of the world. Thoughtful men must have been overwhelmed at first with the idea of world-empire passing into the hands of a military people without education, culture, or religion. It seemed a worse prospect than if modern Europe were to pass under Russian absolutism. The masses having secured the upper-hand over their oppressors surrendered their rights to absolute power in return for *panem et circenses*. The cessation of healthy public and political life which had engrossed the time and inspired the best efforts of men created a perilous vacuum. Undisciplined individualism asserted itself. Forced labour, considered cheaper than free, created less demand for free labour; there was an abnormal influx of free paupers into the cities to live by casual labour and on the doles of imperial paternalism. All nations had failed to bear the test of prosperity; the subjects of Rome observed that to gain the world she had lost her soul. The middle classes—the last strong-hold of a nation's virtue — had disappeared. In the social upheavals wealth passed from those long used to it into new spendthrift hands. There was a mass of paupers and a few plutocrats. *Latifundia perdidere Italiam*, says Pliny, and the statement holds good for most of the Empire. Property was insecure because of the discontent of the masses and confiscation. Bankruptcy arising from stupid finance early threatened the Empire. The provincials were oppressed under the Republic by the iniquitous exactions of the Roman oligarchy and its creatures, and under the Empire by grinding taxation. Terrible visitations of earthquake in Asia, as in Antioch, Philadelphia, Rhodes, caused much suffering and financial insecurity. The quiet and prosperity of the Flavian and Antonine eras—the happiest period for the old world—were the lull before the final disastrous storm.

Opportunity for Oriental Worships

National faiths had collapsed. The West was looking to the East for gospels. This was the opportunity for the Oriental cults, for the Great Mother and Attis, for Isis and Serapis, for the Syrian Goddess, for Mithras, for Judaism, and finally for Christianity. In the isolation and suffering of the age personal and religious concerns were of supreme moment. Men were earnestly seeking a guide for their moral life and an authority for the spirit. Logic was not the only path to knowledge ; there is a region to be entered only by faith, and rationalism was yielding to faith. The elements of man's personality were becoming more prominent ; the search inaugurated by *Know Thyself* had issued in pain. Precepts were too lifeless : ' It requires a new dogma, a great revelation, a startling reform, to carry with it the weak and wavering masses of humanity, who have not the strength or the patience to work out their own salvation.' [1] Examples of flesh and blood were demanded as incentives to teach men to live and die. There was in Greek philosophy, especially the post-Aristotelian, ' an ever-growing tendency to personify the ethical ideal.'

Christianity offered a Synthesis in the Incarnation

Christianity brought a harmony for the burdensome antinomies of that age. Revelation confirmed the truth of natural religion and reason, and added something indispensable. Christianity was the synthesis of and the authority for the truths proclaimed by all systems. It elevated the abstract monotheism of Greece, the henotheistic monotheism of Oriental cults, the deistic monotheism of Judaism into a universal spiritual Fatherhood ; it corrected abstract monotheism by the truth of polytheism that the Godhead is not simple and jejune but

[1] Mahaffy, *Silver Age*, p. 399.

P

has in itself a rich and manifold life; it blended the immanence of pantheism with the transcendence of scepticism, mysticism, and Hebrew thought; it glorified the human sympathy of Oriental cults through the historic life and death of a Man of sorrows.

Christianity gave what the world most needed—the driving power of personality. The Incarnation of the ' Desire of all nations ' answered the universal question of Seneca : *Ubi enim istum invenies quem tot saeculis quaerimus ?* ' Where shall He be found whom we have been seeking for so many centuries ? '

BIBLIOGRAPHY

(Restricted to a selection of the works consulted)

I. ANCIENT AUTHORS

The chief ancient authors of importance for the period here covered are—Plato, Aristotle (esp. *Nic. Ethics* and *Politics*), Plutarch, Polybius, Dio Chrysostom (Dindorf in Teubner, 2 vols., Leipzig, 1857), Maximus of Tyre (Didot, Paris, 1840), Epictetus, Aristides Rhetor (Dindorf in Teubner, 2 vols., Leipzig, 1829), Musonius Rufus (Teubner, 1905), Josephus, Philo, Sibylline Oracles, Justin Martyr, Origen (*con. Celsum*), Clement of Alexandria, Menander, Philostratus, Lucian, Athenaeus, Eusebius, Diogenes Laertius, Cicero, Horace, Virgil, Persius, Lucan, Seneca the Younger, Petronius, Tacitus, Suetonius, Martial, Lucretius, Caesar (*B. Civ.*), Apuleius, Plautus, Terence, Sallust, Pliny the Younger, Minucius Felix, Marcus Aurelius, Juvenal.

CHARLES, R. H. *Apocrypha and Pseudepigrapha of the Old Testament* (Eng. tr., 2 vols., Oxford, 1913).

KAUTZSCH, E. *Die Apokryphen u. Pseudepigraphen des A.T.* (German tr., 2 vols., Tüb., 1900).

HENNECKE, E. *Neutest. Apokryphen* (German tr., Tüb. and Leipzig, 1904).

PREUSCHEN, E. *Antilegomena* (2nd ed., Leipzig, 1905).

II. INSCRIPTIONS, PAPYRI, FRAGMENTS, ETC.

BOECKH, A. *Corpus Inscriptionum Graecarum*, 1828-77.

Inscriptiones Graecae, in course of publication by the Berlin Academy since 1873.

Corpus Inscriptionum Latinarum, by MOMMSEN and others since 1863.

ORELLI-HENZEN. *Inscriptionum Latinarum amplissima collectio* (3 vols., Zür., 1828-56).

BORMANN-HENZEN-ROSSI. *Inscr. urbis Romae Lat.* (vol. vi. pt. 1 and 2 of *C. I. L.*, 1876).

LE BAS-WADDINGTON. *Voyage archéologique en Grèce et Asie Mineure* (Paris, 1847-76).

HICKS-HILL. *Manual of Greek Hist. Inscriptions* (2nd ed., Oxford, 1901).

LINDSAY, W. M. *Handbook of Lat. Insc.* (London and Boston, 1897).

MICHEL, C. *Recueil d'inscriptions grecques* (Brussels, 1900).

DITTENBERGER, W. *Sylloge inscriptionum Graec.* (2nd ed., 3 vols., Leipzig, 1898-1901); *Orientis Graeci Inscr. selectae* (2 vols., Leipzig, 1903-5).

REINACH, TH. *Recueil des inscript. juridiques grecques* (Paris, 1895-8).

KAIBEL, G. *Epigrammata graeca ex lapidibus collecta* (Berlin, 1878).

BÜCHELER, FR. *Anthologia Latina* (metrical inscr.) (Leipzig, 1895-7).

ROSSI, G. B. DE. *Inscr. Christianae Urbis Romae* (2 vols., Rome, 1857-88).

LATYSCHEV. *Inscr. antiquae orae septentrionalis Ponti Euxini, gr. et Lat.*, i. and ii. (St. Petersburg, 1885).

MOMMSEN. *Res Gestae divi Augusti* (Berlin, 1883).

AUDOLLENT, A. *Defixionum Tabellae* (Paris, 1904).

PATON AND HICKS. *Inscr. of Cos* (Oxford, 1891).

KERN, O. *Inschr. von Magnesia am Maeander* (Berlin, 1900).

FRÄNKEL. *Inschr. v. Pergamon* (2 vols., Berlin, 1890-5).

CAGNAT, R. *Inscr. graecae ad res romanas pertinentes* (Paris, 1901-).

NEWTON, HICKS, HIRSCHFELD. *Anc. Gr. inscr. in the Brit. Mus.* (i-iv., Oxford, 1874-93).

LETRONNE, M. *Recueil des inscr. grecques et latines de l'Egypte* (2 vols., Paris, 1842-8).

DESSAU, H. *Inscr. Latinae selectae* (2 vols., Berlin, 1892-1906-).

ARNIM, H. v. *Stoicorum veterum fragmenta* (3 vols., Leipzig, 1903-5).

DIELS, H. *Doxographi Graeci* (Berlin, 1879).

HERCHER, R. *Epistolographi Graeci* (Paris, 1873).

MULLACH, F. G. A. *Fragmenta philosophorum graecorum* (3 vols., Paris, 1881-3).

PETER, H. *Scriptores Hist. Augustae* (2 vols., Leipzig, 1865).

RITTER, H.—PRELLER, L. *Hist. philosophiae Graeco-romanae* (9th ed., Gotha, 1913).

PREGER, TH. *Inscriptiones gr. metricae ex. script. praeter anthologiam collectae* (Leipzig, 1891).

USENER, H. *Epicurea* (Leipzig, 1887).

Griechische Urkunden from the Berlin Museum (4 vols., Berlin, 1895-1912).

Elephantine-Papyri (Rubensohn, Sonderheft of above, Berlin, 1907).

MILLIGAN, G. *Selections from the Greek Papyri* (Cambridge, 1910).

WITKOWSKI, S. *Epistulae privatae graecae quae in papyris Lagidarum servantur* (Leipzig, 1906).

SCOTT, W. *Fragmenta Herculanensia* (Oxford, 1885).

WILCKEN, U. *Griech. Ostraka* (Leipzig, 1900).

SAYCE, A. H. *Aramaic Papyri discovered at Assuan* (London, 1906. p. 35, Eng. tr.).

GARRUCCI, R. *Graffiti de Pompéi* (2nd ed., 1856).

GRENFELL AND HUNT. *Amherst Papyri* (2 vols., London, 1901); *Oxyrhynchus Papyri* (10 parts, London, 1898-1914); *Hibeh Papyri* (part 1, London, 1906); *New Classical Fragments, and other Greek and Latin Papyri* (Oxford, 1897).

GRENFELL, HUNT, SMYLY. *Tebtunis Papyri* (part 1, London, 1902).

GRENFELL, HUNT, HOGARTH. *Fayûm Towns and their Papyri* (London, 1900).

MITTEIS AND WILCKEN. *Grundzüge u. Chrestomathie d. Papyruskunde* (2 vols., Leipzig and Berlin, 1912).

CRÖNERT, W. *Memoria Graeca Herculanensis* (Leipzig, 1903).

MAHAFFY-SMYLY. *The Flinders Petrie Papyri* (3 vols., Dublin, 1891-1905).

III. MODERN AUTHORITIES

(a) HISTORY

ARNOLD, W. T. *Roman System of Provincial Administration* (new ed., rev., Oxford, 1906).

BAUR, F. C. *Church History of the first three Centuries* (Eng. tr., 2 vols., London, 1878-9).

BEVAN, E. R. *House of Seleucus* (2 vols., London, 1902).

BOUCHÉ-LECLERCQ, A. *Histoire des Lagides* (4 vols., Paris, 1903-7).

BURY, J. B. *History of the Roman Empire* (27 B.C.-180 A.D.) (London, 1893).

DROYSEN, J. G. *Gesch. d. Hellenismus* (2nd ed., Gotha, 1877).

EWALD, H. *History of Israel* (Eng. tr., 8 vols., 1-3rd ed., London, 1876-86).

FERRERO, G. *Greatness and Decline of Rome* (Eng. tr., 5 vols., London, 1907-9).

FINDLAY, G. *Greece under the Romans* (2nd ed., Edinburgh and London, 1857).

GROTE. *History of Greece* (12 vols., new ed., London, 1869).

HARDY, E. G. *Christianity and the Roman Government* (London, 1894).

HARNACK, A. *Mission and Expansion of Christianity in the first three Centuries* (Eng. tr., 2 vols., London and New York, 1908).

HAUSRATH, A. *New Testament Times (Times of Jesus*, 2 vols., Eng. tr., London, 1878-80; *Apostles*, 4 vols., London, 1895).

KAERST, J. *Gesch. d. hellenistischen Zeitalters* (2 vols., Leipzig, 1901-9).

LONG, G. *Decline of the Roman Republic* (5 vols., Lond., 1864-74).

MAHAFFY, J. P. *Empire of the Ptolemies* (London, 1895); *History of Egypt under the Ptolemaic Dynasty* (London, 1899).

MERIVALE, C. *Fall of the Roman Republic* (London, 1856); *History of the Romans under the Empire* (new ed., 8 vols., London, 1865-8).

MILNE, J. G. *History of Egypt under Roman Rule* (London, 1898).

MOMMSEN, TH. *The History of Rome* (Eng. tr., rev. ed., 5 vols., New York, 1894); *The Provinces of the Roman Empire from Caesar to Diocletian* (Eng. tr., 2nd ed., rev., 2 vols., New York, 1909).

ORR, J. *Neglected Factors in the Study of the Early Progress of Christianity* (London, 1899).

RAMSAY, W. M. *The Church in the Roman Empire* (New York and London, 1893).

SCHAFF, P. *History of Christian Church* (*Apostolic Christianity*, 2 vols., New York, 1883).

SCHÜRER, E. *Gesch. d. jüdischen Volkes* (4th ed., 3 vols., Leipzig, 1901-11).

(b) RELIGION AND MORALITY

ADAM, J. *Religious Teachers of Greece* (Aberdeen, 1908).

ANRICH, G. *Das antike Mysterienwesen in seinem Einfluss auf das Christentum* (Göt., 1894).

BAUER, B. *Christus u. d. Caesaren* (2nd ed., Berlin, 1879).

BEURLIER, E. *Le cult rendu aux empéreurs romains* (Paris, 1891).

BIGG, C. *The Church's Task under the Roman Empire* (Oxford, 1905).

BOISSIER, G. *La religion rom. d'Auguste aux Antonins* (2 vols., Paris, 1874).

BOUSSET, W. *Die Religion des Judentums im neutest. Zeitalter* (2nd ed., Berlin, 1906).

CAIRD, E. *The Evolution of Religion* (3rd ed., 2 vols., Glasgow, 1899).

CAMPBELL, L. *Religion in Greek Literature* (London, 1898).

CARTER, J. B. *Religious Life of Ancient Rome* (London, 1912).

CHARLES, R. H. *Eschatology, Hebrew, Jewish and Christian* (2nd ed., London, 1913).

CUMONT, F. *Religions orient. dans le paganisme romain* (Paris, 1906); *Mysteries of Mithra* (Eng. tr., Chicago, 1903) ; *Textes et Monuments figurés relatifs aux Mystères de Mithra* (2 vols., Brussels, 1896-9) ; *Astrology and Religion among the Greeks and Romans* (New York and London, 1912).

DENIS, J. *Hist. des Théories et des Idées morales dans l'antiquité* (2nd ed., Paris, n.d.).

DIETERICH, A. *Eine Mithrasliturgie* (2nd ed., Leipzig, 1910) ; *Nekyia* (Leipzig, 1893) ; *Abraxas* (Leipzig, 1891).

DÖLLINGER, J. J. I. *The Gentile and the Jew* (Eng. tr., 2 vols., London, 1906).

DRUMMOND, J. *The Jewish Messiah* (London, 1877).

FAIRWEATHER, W. *Background of the Gospels* (Edinburgh, 1908).

FARNELL, L. R. *Higher Aspects of Greek Religion* (London, 1912).

FARRER, J. A. *Paganism and Christianity* (London and Edinburgh, 1891).

FOWLER, W. W. *Religious Experience of the Roman People* (London, 1911); *Roman Ideas of Deity in the last Century before the Christian Era* (London, 1914).

FRIEDLÄNDER, L. *Roman Life and Manners* (Eng. tr., 4 vols., London and New York, 1908-13).

FRIEDLÄNDER, M. *D. relig. Bewegungen innerhalb d. Judentums im Zeitalter Jesu* (Berlin, 1905); *Synagoge u. Kirche* (Berlin, 1908).

GLOVER, T. R. *Conflict of Religions in early Roman Empire* (London, 1909).

HARRISON, J. E. *Proleg. to the Study of the Greek Religion* (Cambridge, 1903).

HATCH, E. *Influence of Greek Ideas and Usages upon the Christian Church* (New York, 1890).

HEGEL, C. W. F. *Philosophy of History* (Eng. tr., London, 1857).

JONG, DE, K. H. E. *Das antike Mysterienwesen* (Leiden, 1909).

KEIM, TH. *Rom u. d. Christentum* (Berlin, 1881).

KENNEDY, H. A. A. *St. Paul and the Mystery-Religions* (London, 1913).

KING, C. W. *Gnostics* (2nd ed., London, 1887).

LECKY, W. E. H. *History of European Morals* (2 vols. in 1, London, 1911).

LOBECK, C. A. *Aglaophamus* (2 vols., Königsberg, 1829).

MAASS, E. *Orpheus* (Munich, 1895).

MARTHA, C. *Moralistes sous l'empire rom.* (8th ed., Paris, 1907); *Études morales sur l'antiquité* (Paris, 1883).

MEAD, G. R. S. *Thrice-Greatest Hermes* (3 vols., London and Benares, 1906).

MERIVALE, C. *Conversion of the Roman Empire* (2nd ed., London, 1865).

NORDEN, E. *Agnostos Theos* (Leipzig and Berlin, 1913).

OTTO, W. *Priester u. Tempel im hellenist. Ägypten* (2 vols., Leipzig and Berlin, 1905-8).

PETRIE, W. M. F. *Personal Religion in Egypt before Christianity* (London and New York, 1909).

REITZENSTEIN, R. *Poimandres* (Leipzig, 1904); *D. hellenist. Mysterienreligionen* (Leipzig, 1910), *Hellenist. Wundererzählungen* (Leipzig, 1906).

RENAN, E. *Marc-Aurèle et la fin du monde antique* (Paris, 1882).

ROHDE, ER. *Relig. der Griechen* (in *Kl. Schriften*, ii. (1901), p. 314-39); *Psyche, Seelencult u. Unsterblichkeitsglaube der Griechen* (2nd ed., 2 vols., Freiburg-i.-B., 1898).

SCHMIDT, H. *Veteres philosophi quomodo iudicaverint de precibus* (Giessen, 1907).

UHLHORN. G. *Conflict of Christianity with Heathenism* (Eng. tr., New York, 1879).

WALTON, A. *Cult of Asklepios* (Ithaca, 1894).

WENLEY, R. M. *Preparation for Christianity* (Edinburgh and London, 1898).

WESTERMARCK, E. *Origin and Development of the Moral Ideas* (2 vols., London, 1906-8).

WISSOWA, G. *Die Religion u. Mythologie der Römer* (2nd ed., Munich, 1912).

(c) Philosophy

ARNOLD, E. V. *Roman Stoicism* (Cambridge, 1911).

BIGG, C. *Neoplatonism* (London, 1895).

BONHÖFFER, A. *Epictet u. d. Stoa* (Stuttgart, 1890).

BUSSELL, F. W. *School of Plato* (London, 1896).

BUTLER, W. A. *History of Ancient Philosophy* (2 vols., London, 1856).

CAIRD, E. *Evolution of Theology in the Greek Philosophers* (2 vols., Glasgow, 1904).

DRUMMOND, J. *Philo-Judaeus or Jewish-Alexandrian Philosophy* (2 vols., London and Edinburgh, 1888).

EUCKEN, R. *Lebensanschauungen d. grossen Denker* (Leipzig, 1890).

FERRIER, J. F. *Lectures on Greek Philosophy* (Edinburgh and London, 1888).

HEGEL, C. W. F. *Philosophy of Religion* (Eng. tr., 3 vols., London, 1895).

PFLEIDERER, O. *Vorbereitung d. Christentums in d. griech. Phil.* (Tüb., 1906).

WINDELBAND, W. *History of Ancient Philosophy* (Eng. tr., New York, 1900).

ZELLER, E. *Outlines of the History of Greek Philosophy* (Eng. tr., new ed., London, 1895); *Pre-Socratic Philosophy* (Eng. tr., 2 vols., London, 1881); *Plato and the Older Academy* (Eng. tr., London, 1876); *Aristotle and the Earlier Peripatetics* (Eng. tr., 2 vols., London, 1897); *Socrates and the Socratic Schools* (Eng. tr., 2nd ed., London, 1877); *Stoics, Epicureans, and Sceptics* (Eng. tr., new ed., London, 1880); *History of Eclecticism in Greek Philosophy* (Eng. tr., London, 1883); *Relig. u. Phil. bei den Römern* (in *Vorträge u. Abhandl.*, 2nd series, pp. 93-135).

(d) Culture, Society, Antiquities

ABBOTT, F. F. *Common People of Ancient Rome* (New York, 1912)

BALLU, A. *Timgad, une cité africaine* (Paris, 1904).

BULTMANN, R. *Der Stil der Paulinischen Predigt u. die Kynisch-stoische Diatribe* (Göt., 1910).

BUTCHER, S. H. *Some Aspects of Greek Genius* (3rd ed., London, 1904); *Harvard Lectures on Greek Subjects* (London, 1904).

COULANGES, F. DE. *La cité antique* (2nd ed., Paris, 1866).

DEISSMANN, A.   *Light from the Ancient East* (Eng. tr., London, 1910); *Das Urchristentum u. d. unteren Schichten* (2nd ed., Göttingen, 1908).

DILL, S.   *Roman Society from Nero to M. Aurelius* (London, 1904).

FOWLER, W. W.   *Social Life at Rome in the Age of Cicero* (London, 1908); *The City-State of the Greeks and Romans* (2nd ed., London, 1895).

GRAHAM, A.   *Roman Africa* (London, 1902).

HAHN, L.   *Rom u. Romanismus im griech.- röm. Osten*, etc. (Leipzig, 1906).

LIVINGSTONE, R. W.   *Greek Genius and its meaning to us* (Oxford, 1912).

MAHAFFY, J. P.   *Hellenism in Alexander's Empire* (Chicago, 1905); *Silver Age of the Greek World* (Chicago and London, 1906); *Survey of Greek Civilization* (Meadville, Pa., 1896); *What have the Greeks done for Modern Civilization ?* (New York and London, 1909).

MARQUARDT, J.   *Das Privatleben der Römer* (Leipzig, 1878); *Röm. Staatsverwaltung* (3 vols., Leipzig, 1873-8).

MARUCCHI, O.   *Roma sotterranea cristiana* (Rome, 1909); *Le Catacombe romane* (Rome, 1903).

MAU-KELSEY.   *Pompeii : Its Life and Art* (new ed., New York, 1902).

MOMMSEN, TH.   *Röm. Staatsrecht* (3 vols., Leipzig, 1871-88).

PUTNAM, G. H.   *Authors and their Public in Ancient Times* (2nd ed., New York, 1894).

RAMSAY, W. M.   *Cities of St. Paul* (London, 1907); *Cities and Bishoprics of Phrygia* (2 parts, Oxford, 1895-97).

STOBART, J. C.   *The Glory that was Greece* (London, 1911); *The Grandeur that was Rome* (London, 1912).

TUCKER, T. G.   *Life in the Roman World of Nero and St. Paul* (London, 1910).

WALLON, H.   *Hist. de l'Esclavage* (3 vols., Paris, 1847).

WENDLAND, P.   *Hellenistisch-röm. Kultur* (2-3rd ed., Tüb., 1912); *Philo u. die Kynisch-stoische Diatribe* (pp. 1-75 : Wendland-Kern, *Beitr. z. Gesch. der griech. Phil. u. Relig.*, Berlin, 1895).

(e) LITERATURE AND LANGUAGE

CHRIST, W.   *Gesch. d. griech. Lit.* (4th ed., Munich, 1905).

CROISET, A. AND M.   *Abridged History of Greek Literature* (Eng. tr., New York, 1904).

DEISSMANN, A.   *Bible Studies* (Eng. tr., Edinburgh, 1901); **art.** *Hellenistisches Griechisch*, in Herzog-Hauck [3].

HARNACK, A.   *Gesch. der altchrist. Lit.* (2 vols., Leipzig, 1893-1904).

JORDAN, H.   *Gesch. d. altchrist. Lit.* (Leipzig, 1911).

MACKAIL, J. W.   *Latin Literature* (New York, 1902).

MOULTON, J. H.   *Grammar of New Testament Greek* (3rd ed., i. Proleg., New York, 1908).

NORDEN, E.   *Antike Kunstprosa* (2 vols., Leipzig, 1898).

ROBERTSON, A. T.   *Grammar of the Greek New Testament* (New York and London, 1914).

SCHWYZER, E.   *Die Weltsprachen des Altertums* (Berlin, 1902).

SELLAR, W. Y.   *Roman Poets of the Republic* (3rd ed., Oxford, 1889); *Roman Poets of the Augustan Age* (Oxford, 1892).

SUSEMIHL, F.   *Gesch. d. griech. Lit. in d. Alexandrinerzeit* (2 vols., Leipzig, 1891-2).

TEUFFEL-SCHWABE.   *History of Roman Literature*: i. Republican Period; ii. Imperial Period (Eng. tr. by Warr, London, 1891-2).

THOMSON, J. E. H.   *Books which influenced our Lord* (Edinburgh, 1891).

THUMB, A   *Die Griech. Sprache im Zeitalter d. Hellenismus* (Strassburg, 1901).

ZAHN, TH.   *Greek Language among the Jews*, pp. 34-73, vol. i. of *Introduction to New Testament.*

The student need not be reminded of general works of reference: as ROSCHER, *Ausführ. Lexicon d. griech. u. röm. Mythologie* (Leipzig, 1884-1913); GRUPPE, *Griech. Mythologie* (Munich, 1906); *Jewish Encyclopaedia*; HASTINGS' *Dictionary of Bible*; *Encyclopaedia of Religion and Ethics*; DAREMBERG ET SAGLIO, *Dict. des Antiquités*; HERZOG-HAUCK, *Real-Encyc.* [3]; PAULY-WISSOWA, *Real-Encyc. d. klas. Altertumswiss.* (1892-   ); *Religion in Geschichte u. Gegenwart* (ed. by SCHIELE).

INDEX